The ELDERS HANDBOOK

Library of Congress Catalog Card No. 79-54143

ISBN 0-934874-00-X

Printed in the U.S.A.

The ELDERS HANDBOOK

A
PRACTICAL
GUIDE
FOR
CHURCH
LEADERS

By
Gerard Berghoef
Lester De Koster

Christian's Library Press
Grand Rapids, Michigan

THE AUTHORS

Mr. Gerard Berghoef is a native of the Netherlands, who emigrated to the United States early in the 1950s. He is presently a furniture manufacturing executive, and has served the Christian Reformed Church as an elder for twelve years.

Dr. Lester DeKoster is a native of Michigan, and has been professor of speech and director of the library for Calvin College and Seminary. Presently he is Editor of *The Banner*, official weekly publication of the Christian Reformed Church.

First printing—Fall, 1979
Second printing—Spring, 1980

The authors are grateful for
the close cooperation and constant encouragement
of our wives, Audrey Berghoef and Ruth DeKoster,
and the assistance of Wayne DeJonge
in layout and production.

THE ELDER'S PROFILE

This Handbook is structured by St. Paul's parting instructions to the Elders of the Church at Ephesus, as recorded in Acts 20:28-31:

Keep watch over yourselves,
Keep watch over the flock
Of which the Holy Spirit has made you Guardians;
To feed the Church of the Lord
Which He won for Himself by His own blood.
Savage wolves will come in among you,
Therefore be alert.

TABLE OF CONTENTS

PREFACE

The future of our strife-worn and violence-ridden world is dependent upon the Church. Progressive development of the full resources of the Church is dependent upon a vigorous lay membership, made functional and effective through the lay eldership, under stimulus of the Word of God preached by a forthright ministry.

Our secularized world is unaware of its dependence upon the Church. And the Church seems more than half-forgetful of its centrality to the health and welfare of mankind. This book comes, therefore, as a practical manifesto. It assumes the Church's fundamental role in civilized progress as ordained witness to revealed Truth — without which all men perish and our world falls into chaos.

Only the Church survives time and change. Only the Church transcends the rise and fall of states and popular trends. Tides of evangelical revival rise and crest, and then dissipate unless caught up into the Church for permanent impact upon man's world.

The free world owes its democratic institutions and scientific accomplishments to the liberating role taken by the Church through her pulpits and lay membership in and after the Reformation. Revealed Truth practically preached and courageously lived toppled autocracies and freed Western man. Out of this liberation emerged political democracy, universal education, diffusion of culture, respect for human rights, competitive enterprise, technological progress, and widespread prosperity.

Unhappily, the Christian roots of modern democratic culture have been permitted to wilt. Life has gone secular. The Church herself has frequently betrayed the Bible, source of her power, through scholars who have all but made of it an ordinary book. Education generally repudiates religion. Morality is divorced from divine law. Liberties once enjoyed under Church-inspired discipline threaten now to become license, eroding the family, the school, business and politics, and society at large.

The times urgently require an authoritative witness to divinely inspired Truth. Such witness in word is the appointed task of the Church's pulpits. Such witness in deed is the calling of all believers. The guidance of both is required of the ruling elder, to whom this book is dedicated.

We look to a reinvigorated priesthood of all believers, prophetically taught by God's ordained ministry, under the leadership of God's appointed elders for the creative witness in word and deed upon which the future of civilization depends.

This book is an effort to supply the ruling elder, by whatever other name his office is known in various Protestant communions, with the tools he needs to do well the service God requires of him.

The crises of our culture multiply.

The challenge of the eldership grows greater every day.

May this manual help you meet that challenge creatively, and suggest, too, what all believers may expect from those appointed by God to rule over them.

The Authors

PART I

KEEP WATCH OVER YOURSELVES

PART I

"KEEP WATCH OVER YOURSELVES"

How the elder can progressively qualify himself for keeping the better watch over God's household as he develops skills in keeping watch over himself — in the light of the inspired Word of God. The elders' watchfulness as both individual and collective, both in doctrine and in life. Practical suggestions for such watch-keeping are followed by hints for improving speaking in meetings and in public, with a concise guide to parliamentary procedures. This section concludes with specific recommendations for improving the foundations of successful leadership, namely the management of time and the coordination of efforts toward carefully planned goals.

Chapter 1.

THE CHALLENGE

The Church has no time for despair, no place to hide.

She is challenged to renewal of all her efforts by the confusion and aimlessness of our times.

We see the ruling eldership as especially called to leading such renewal.

We see the priesthood of all believers as calling upon the eldership to take hold for such renewal.

We offer this handbook to assist the elder in performing this service.

Power to lead renewal is not from within. Such power comes from God through the medium of His inspired Word. The Bible is the basis for all we say here.

The Church is the Body of Christ, His agent in history, made by the Spirit through the Word. Christ rules in His Body through offices instituted in the New Testament for that purpose.

We know that offices in the Protestant churches bear many names, like: teaching elder or minister, ruling elder, trustee, presbyter, bishop, priest, pastor, deacon. While the names thus differ, the responsibilities of leadership in Christ's Body are essentially the same, namely that the inspired Word shall be plainly preached, that the sacraments shall be faithfully administered, and that self-sacrificial priesthood among believers shall be encouraged and, when necessary, disciplined. All this under the responsible leadership of the ruling office we designate as eldership. To strengthening this office we offer this manual.

We recognize that other names are also employed to designate the collective ruling office, not only eldership but council, session, board of trustees, consistory and the like. Again, though terminology may differ, function is essentially the same: plurality of leadership for the welfare of the Church.

By whatever the name, the Church's governing leadership is challenged by opportunity to set the Church once more on the hilltop of witness to the world by the Word of God preached and the Word of God obeyed.

To this we challenge you.

FROM THE BEGINNING

Later chapters (especially Chapter 18) will develop the thoughts briefly sketched here, but it is clear that God willed from the origins of His Church that His people should be led by elders. It was thus in ancient Israel. It was so in New Testament times. It is recorded that, "they appointed elders for them in every Church" (Acts 14:23), with reference to Paul and Barnabas. St. James takes elders for granted: "Is any among you sick? Let him call the elders of the Church" (Jas. 5:14).

We note that the elders are always spoken of as several. They were selected or elected from among the unordained believers, the laity. And the Reformation re-established lay rule of the Church through the eldership.

The Church is theocratic, not democratic. She is ruled by a King. His scepter is the inspired Word. His agents are appointed according to that Word: preaching or teaching elder, ruling elder, and deacon.

The New Testament uses two terms to designate the office of ruling elder, namely "presbyter" and "bishop". These terms are used interchangeably for the ruling (and also teaching) office, as in the account of St. Paul's last meeting with the elders of the Church at Ephesus: "He sent to Ephesus and called to him the *presbyters* of the Church" (Acts 20:17). Later, when these were come to him, Paul says, "Take heed to yourselves and to all the flock, in which the Holy Spirit has made you *bishops*" (Acts 20:28).

This manual is written in the light of Paul's parting instructions to these presbyter-bishops, whose official heir the ruling elder of today is.

And to this ruling elder still comes Paul's challenge in his own inspired words. Some of them form the divisional headings which follow.

Are you an elder or elder-elect?

Accept the challenge of the times as put by the inspired Apostle to your predecessors in Ephesus.

Are you one of that priesthood of all believers who together constitute the Church, the Body of Jesus Christ?

Challenge *your* leaders to assume all of the responsibilities laid upon them by the Lord of the Church!

Are you among those early set aside in the Church as teaching elders, known today as the ordained ministry?

Challenge your elders to rule the Church well, that together with you they may inspire, guide, and govern the Body to serve her Lord in history.

Chapter 2.

THE ELDER IN THE CONGREGATION

The inspired Apostle begins his instructions to the eldership with this injunction: keep watch over yourselves. Top priority. One learns to keep good watch over the congregation as he grows in keeping ever better watch over himself. Watchful self-discipline is required of each elder individually, and of all the elders collectively: keep watch...over yourselves!

EACH HIS OWN CLASSROOM

As an alert elder go to school to your own experience.

In your daily life you learn firsthand what seeking to be Christian involves. Your life illumines the lives of those over whom you are chosen to keep watch. The pressures upon you enable you to understand the temptations of others, even though no two lives run in exactly the same course. Your troubles mirror others' problems; your joys their joys. Your progress in obedience can stimulate your encouragement of others; your failures will deepen your sympathies for others' shortcomings. Your growth in the Christian life gives a lilt to your step and an enthusiasm to share. Life for the alert elder is a God-given opportunity to grow into his office by, first of all, keeping watch of himself.

In the school of experience the elder learns, too, to avoid certain traps. He observes that one who is quickly satisfied with himself may be quickly dissatisfied with others. Something to be avoided. You notice, too, that one who sets few high goals for himself probably sets few high goals for the Church.

Be encouraged by the Lord's promise: "He who is faithful in a very little is faithful also in much." Be admonished by His warning: "He who is dishonest in a very little is dishonest also in much" (Luke

16:10). Keep careful watch over yourself.

HOW KEEP WATCH?

Watchfulness in the Church always comes to focus on belief and behavior, or, doctrine and life. This is true both of self-discipline and of watchfulness over the congregation: 1) what do you believe? 2) does such belief control how you act all the time and everywhere?

In fact, belief and behavior are commonly twins. They imply each other. We can hardly believe one way and act another. What we truly believe is usually what governs our actions. How we act tends to reflect what we really believe. Our days and how we spend them are as beads strung upon the threads of our beliefs.

Watchfulness, then, examines faith — as to what we believe; and life — as to how we act. Though in so doing he finds himself his own classroom, the elder does not become his own teacher. God is the elder's Teacher, as to faith and life, and God's inspired textbook is the Bible.

Through the words of the Bible, as through a glass fitted to his eyes, the elder is required to watch over himself and over others. He must "see" the world as God's *creation*, not man's possession. He must see others as *neighbors*, and the Church as Christ's holy *Body*. Such lenses are words of the Word, graciously revealed for us to keep watch by. Lay the Biblical words upon your outer and inner eye. Only through them will the elder see himself, others, and God's world aright: "The entrance of Thy words giveth light" (Ps. 119:130).

A. As To Doctrine...

The elder is watchful over himself as to doctrine, in these ways:

1. Through constant, systematic companionship with the Bible. We cannot read, study, meditate upon, and pray over God's Word too much: "Oh, how I love Thy law! It is my meditation all the day," cries the Psalmist. "How sweet are Thy words to my taste, sweeter than honey to my mouth!" (Ps. 119:97; 103). Only the elder who has this experience can share it. Seek it. Ask God for it. Cultivate it.

2. Through the symbols of the faith. The teaching of the inspired Word is summarized in the creeds, confessions, and catechisms of the Church. These are called the "symbols" of the Christian faith, for they reflect the content of faith to both Church and world. Familiarize yourself with the great creeds developed by the early Church, and listed in Appendix A to this chapter: the Apostles Creed, the Nicene, and the

Athanasian Creeds. Know and study the symbols which proclaim and teach the beliefs of your own denomination (many are listed in Appendix B at the end of this chapter). Discuss your symbols at elders' meetings. Invite your pastor and others to lead such discussions. Organize elders' conferences within your denomination to study your confessions. One can never know them too well. They are standards which measure the content of your own faith, standards created by the Church in obedience to the Apostle's command: "Always be prepared to make a defense to any one who calls you to account for the hope that is in you" (I Peter 3:15).

Knowledge of the creeds qualifies the elder to evaluate trends and fads in religion, to separate wheat from chaff in preaching and publication, to sit as layman in judgment upon the ordained and the learned. An important part of self-watch is growth in mastery of creed, confession, and catechism. Are you busy doing that?

3. Through self-examination. Hold your *own* beliefs up to the light of your denomination's symbols. Are they in harmony? If not, do you know how doubts and difficulties may be properly brought before the Church for consideration and judgment? Your Church Order will provide for that.

B. As to Life...

The elder is watchful over himself as to how he lives.

Doctrine is never an end in itself. The inspired Scriptures are given for specific purpose: "All scripture is inspired by God and profitable for teaching, for reproof, for correction, and for training in righteousness, that the man of God may be complete, equipped for every good work" (II Tim. 3:16-17). God has very definite intentions for those whom He redeems by the blood of His Son: "For we are His workmanship, created in Christ Jesus for good works, which God prepared beforehand, that we should walk in them" (Eph. 2:10). Therefore, the Church is herself obligated by her Lord to teach all her members to do good works as He defines them: "teaching them to observe all that I have commanded you" (Matt. 28:20). The elder must be watchful that he be first among the learners in order that he may be best among the teachers.

You can keep careful watch over your progress in God's school by mirrors like these:

1. The will of God as summarized in the Moral Law, expressed in the Ten Commandments of Exodus 20 and Deuteronomy 5.

2. The positive summary of the Commandments, as taught in both

the Old and New Testaments: "You shall love the Lord your God with all your heart, and with all your soul, and with all your mind" (Deut. 6:5; Matt. 22:37); "You shall love your neighbor as yourself" (Levit. 19:18; Matt. 22:39).

3. By the inspired commentary on the Commandments found in the Prophets of the Old Testament, including Deuteronomy, and in the Gospels.

4. By the detailed applications of the Law set before the Church by St. Paul in the practical conclusions of most of his letters, and by the other Apostles, especially St. James and St. John.

5. By the ideals set before the Church in the teachings of Jesus, especially those summarized in the Sermon on the Mount, Matthew 5-7.

6. By meditation daily on the abundant Biblical promise of blessing, here and for eternity, upon those who love — that is seek to obey (Jn. 14:21) — the Lord: "All things work together for good to them that love God" (Rom. 8:28).

7. By never forgetting that everyone, yourself included, shall one day give an accounting before the judgment-seat of the Most High for our use of His gifts of life, days, talents, and possessions — as taught in Christ's parable of the pounds (Luke 19:12-27) and elsewhere: "For He will render to every man according to his works" (Rom. 2:6); "And I saw the dead, great and small, standing before the throne, and books were opened. Also another book was opened, which is the book of life. And the dead were judged by what was written in the books, by what they had done" (Rev. 20:12). Reflect that each one writes in those books by his life every day.

C. As to Doctrine and Life Together...

The inspired Word of God conveys sound doctrine. Watch carefully how you master it. The inspired Word of God conveys power. See to it that this power masters you.

Even as we resolve to keep watch over ourselves in doctrine and life, we realize that success in such undertaking resides in God's hand. We can but turn to where His guidance is found, namely the Holy Scriptures. And we can but depend upon His Holy Spirit, whose presence we seek through obedience to the Word: "...the Holy Spirit whom God has given to those who obey Him" (Acts 5:32).

The watchful elder rests heavily upon the Bible, God's inspired Word. By the power of His Word God created all things (Gen. 1; Ps. 33:6). By the power of His Word God sustains all things (Is. 40:26).

24

Through His Word God re-creates fallen and sin-stricken man (Is. 55:10-11; Matt. 13:3-23). It is to the Word of God in the Scriptures that we turn for both the Truth, which we accept in faith, and doing the Truth, which is God's gift through the Spirit.

Keeping watch over himself leads the elder ever closer to the Word. Your Bible must be your constant companion throughout your eldership.

REWARDS OF WATCHFULNESS

A. Understanding

Do not confuse knowledge with understanding. One may know much, yet understand little. Knowing is the fruit of diligence in study, while understanding is the fruit of using knowledge in life. Understanding of God's Word is given through the Spirit to those who seek to obey that Word. We come to under-stand the Bible by in fact standing-under its commands. You may not notice such growth in understanding in yourself, but others will profit from it, and the Church will be blessed by it. You come through obedience to a natural authority in your important office. All by keeping watch over your own obedience.

B. Wisdom

Wisdom cannot be acquired directly. Wisdom cannot be taught by one to another. Understanding which is nourished by experience, deepened by persistent effort to better obedience, gradually matures into wisdom. Wisdom is understanding put to the service of love. Wisdom comes slowly, and with age, if it comes at all. This is why the elder is. . .elder.

Unlike some bodies, the eldership will be as strong as the strongest link — that is the wisest member — in its chain. Pray, strive, labor, learn, and trust that you may grow into such a link, for the good of the Church and blessing of the Lord.

A WORD OF CAUTION

The conscientious elder must never be overwhelmed by the magnitude of his responsibility in comparison with the extent of his weakness and failures. Your authority for ruling the household of God does not rest upon your success in self-discipline, nor even upon perfect headship in your own household. The elder's commission is from God. Your office

25

is ordained by Him, and your rule is in His name and power, not your own. Do not, then, let your failures in doctrine or life discourage you. Let them only spur you to greater effort.

Take courage from the example of St. Paul.

The great Apostle urges believers to be imitators of himself (I Cor. 4:16; 11:1; Phil. 3:17). But he bitterly deplores his inability to do the good which he wills to do (Rom. 7:18-19; Gal. 5:17). Yet, this same Paul can declare before his judges in the Sanhedrin that, "I have lived before God in all good conscience up to this day" (Acts 23:1), and in one of the last of his testimonies he can write, "I thank God whom I serve with a clear conscience..." (II Tim. 1:3).

How could the same inspired penman write such seemingly contrary things about himself? How could he describe himself as both "imitator...of Christ" (I Cor. 11:1) and "chief of sinners" (I Tim. 1:15)?

The explanation, in which the elder may find great comfort for himself, lies in Paul's distinction between striving and attaining, between willing the good and wholly doing it. Of himself the Apostle says, "Not that I have already obtained this (the resurrection) or am already perfect; but I press on to make it my own, because Christ Jesus has made me His own." He adds this admonition: "I press on toward the goal for the prize of the upward call of God in Christ Jesus. Let those of us who are mature be thus minded..." (Phil. 3:12; 14-15).

It is not the measure of Paul's accomplishment, but the set of his will to do the will of God that satisfies his conscience — and may satisfy ours despite our failures. It is our Lord's admonition to "seek" God's kingdom (Matt. 6:33). We are to "strive to enter in by the narrow door" (Luke 13:24). Our willing to do the will of God guides us into Truth, understanding, wisdom, despite our often coming short of perfection. Such is the Lord's own promise (Jn. 7:17), and the experience of the inspired Apostle.

Your good conscience, then, as you do the Lord's work in the eldership, can rest as did Paul's in striving to "fight the good fight". So doing, you can look forward with him to the victor's "crown of righteousness, which the Lord the righteous judge, will award to me on that Day, and not only to me but also to all who have loved His appearing" (II Tim. 4:7-8).

Confess to God, repent, resolve to correct, your failings, but never let these deter you from the work of the eldership, so long as your will is indeed to do the will of God.

BEWARE OF PRIDE

Yours is the calling to rule as one who serves, as did the Lord our Master. Enforce God's Word, not your own, with the courage of humility. Expect no acknowledgment, reward, recognition. Do all for the good of the Church. Let I Corinthians 13 be your constant guide and companion: "Love is patient and kind; love is not jealous or boastful; it is not arrogant or rude. Love does not insist on its own way; it is not irritable or resentful; it does not rejoice at wrong, but rejoices in the right. Love bears all things, believes all things, hopes all things, endures all things" (vv. 4-7). Thus led, you will be secure from high-handedness. You will not hinder the Lord's work in doing your own.

As slaves of Christ, heed Paul's admonition to slaves of men: "Slaves, be obedient...in singleness of heart, as to Christ; not in the way of eye service, as men-pleasers, but as servants of Christ, doing the will of God from the heart, rendering service with a good will as to the Lord and not to men, knowing that whatever good any one does, he will receive the same again from the Lord..." (Eph. 6:5-8).

COLLECTIVE WATCHFULNESS

Keep watch over yourselves, not only individually but also as an eldership, collectively.

Just as the elder can become his own classroom, the eldership as a body can become its own academy, its own training-center. By mutual encouragement, for example, the eldership practices its encouragement of others. By mutual admonition in love, the eldership develops its skills in admonition of the erring in the congregation. By mutual searching of the Scriptures to shed light upon your calling, the eldership creates good habits which can be passed on.

God has "breathed" (inspired) the Bible, Paul says, for these purposes: teaching, reproof, correction, and for training in righteousness (II Tim. 3:16). The Bible is thus, obviously, adapted by God to the elders' task of serving Him through governing the Church. Let time be given, in elders' meetings, for such application of the Word to yourselves.

Mutual watch-keeping, done in all the frankness of love (remember I Cor. 13!) will weld the eldership together in a body sinewed by the very Word of God. Where the Word is used as God intends, for mutual teaching, reproof, correction, and training, an eldership will grow in the power of the Master, and in the service of His Body. An eldership in which there is tension, dissension, and strife is a scandal before the Lord. This must not be permitted. Do not neglect keeping watch over yourselves in prayer and openness to the Scriptures.

The elder who is determined to keep good watch over himself in doctrine and in life will welcome all contributions which fellow-elders can make to such watchfulness. He will recognize that any inability to absorb criticism is evidence of spiritual immaturity in himself, and will struggle to overcome that handicap.

We suggest some guidelines to bear in mind:

1. **Unity:** The Church is described in Scripture in various ways: the Body of Christ, a city, a household, a building, a temple. Each of these metaphors suggests a whole, built up out of several parts, each part playing its own role. No part is complete in itself so that all parts will be drawn together in mutual need. No individual, on the other hand, has been given his own gifts for exclusive self-use. All gifts are given for the benefit of the whole. The challenge always facing the eldership, then, is creatively drawing the individual, with his gifts, into the service of the Body — and, putting the strength and resources of the Body into the service of the individual.

To perform this difficult and delicate task well, the elder must know the source, extent, and purpose of his authority in the Body. Remember that you are responsible to Jesus Christ, the Head of the Body, who has instituted your office and chooses to rule His Church through it, under the Word. The Church is a theocracy; she is not a democracy, even though she uses the means of popular election to fill the offices established by Christ in the Word.

As elder, you neither represent the membership of the congregation, nor are you beholden to them — tempting as this theory would be to citizens of a political democracy. The eldership makes judgments according to the Scriptures, as interpreted by the confessions, and with due recognition of your denominational Church Order. You do not govern the Body by popular opinion or referendum, though you should be sensitive to what the congregation thinks. To the people of God the inspired mandate is clear: "Obey your leaders and submit to them; for they are keeping watch over your souls, as men who will have to give account" (Heb. 13:17). Let this admonition impress both congregation and elder: there will one day be an accounting of this stewardship. Rule well (that is according to the Scriptures) in order that obedience may be unto the Lord, not as unto yourself.

So close is the relation between elder and congregation that the Body becomes accountable for the behavior of its eldership, and the eldership will be held accountable for the behavior of the membership.

All this is implied in the unity of the Body.

In practice, this mutual responsibility implies that the eldership shall give full and clear account of its stewardship through full reports to the congregation. This does not mean betrayal of confidences, exposure of personal matters, or dark hints of deep secrets. It does mean a free accounting of all that pertains to the Body as a whole. An occasional newsletter to the membership would be wise. Frank reports and openness to questions at congregational meetings is important. Knowledge can bind together those who share it.

Unity also implies strenuous efforts by the eldership to arrive at consensus upon matters before them. Better to postpone, if possible, close decisions than to impose them by narrow voting margins. There will always be differences of opinion, of course, and sometimes a vote will be the only resolution of a matter which has begun to waste time. But, especially on questions dealing with faith and life, the eldership should search the Word for a common light. Bear in mind that the Word itself speaks with one voice on all crucial matters of faith and behavior.

2. Plurality: This fundamental principle of Protestant church government is boldly written over the pages of the New Testament. The exercise of authority is not an exercise in superiority. Each to his calling, and the eldership is called collectively to administer, under the Word, the affairs pertaining to the whole Body.

The New Testament, like the Old, always speaks of the elders in the plural. And no hint is given that one among the equals is "more equal" than the others. One, probably the minister, will indeed preside over meetings — this is requisite to good order. But none lords it over another. He also serves who rules, and the eldership serves by ruling mutually and together: "Where there is no guidance, a people falls; but in an abundance of counselors there is safety" (Prov. 11:14; see also 24:6).

Rule in the Church, on the Biblical model, is done, then, by a plurality of elders, equal in rank and authority. Exercise of mutual respect and self-restraint among themselves schools the elders in the exercise of leadership in the Body.

3. Complete parity: The distinction in function between the teaching and ruling elder which grew up in the history of the Church has tended to favor the teaching elder (the minister) with a certain superior status over the ruling elder. This carries over into meetings of the eldership and into broader ecclesiastical assemblies. For this discrimination there is no basis in the Bible: "For you have one Teacher, and you are all brethren" (Matt. 23:8) — such is the instruction of the Lord.

4. Procedures: unity, equality, and the search for consensus require certain desirable procedures for elders' meetings, like these:

a. Adhere to parliamentary rules of order (see Chapter 4).

b. Prepare an agenda for each meeting, preferably for distribution in advance.

c. Provide sufficient background information for items on the agenda so that decisions rest upon firm footing.

d. Avoid pushing things through, however urgent or whatever the excuse.

e. Allow ample time for discussion; elicit the views of all who care to speak; be ready to postpone on sufficient grounds for so doing.

f. Behave in all respects as if Christ were present among you — as indeed He is!

SCOPE OF RESPONSIBILITY

The eldership bears a broad scope of responsibility, to which this book is addressed. In brief, your major concerns include:

1. Preaching: supervision of the pulpit and the Word preached. This is the primary function of the Church, and therefore primary supervisory responsibility of those who serve the Lord by governing His Body (see Chapter 12).

2. The Sacraments: the true administration of the Lord's Supper and baptism are marks of the Church. Faithful and proper administration is the elders' responsibility (see Chapter 13).

3. Discipline: the Word preached and made visible in the Sacraments must come to fruition in the lives of all members. Encouragement and admonition, along with discipline and, when required, excommunication are the elder's task (see Chapters 9, 10, and 18).

4. Membership: admission to membership in the local congregation is under the supervision of the eldership (see Chapters 14 and 21).

5. Care and Comfort: the Body of Christ is also the Family of God, and the eldership reaches out for the Family to all of the members of it who are in any kind of need (see Chapters 7, 8, 9, and 15).

6. Congregational activities: the eldership must supervise all of the activities of the congregation, in worship, education, societies and clubs, diaconal outreach (see Chapter 6, 7, and 14).

7. Trends: the eldership must be alert to trends in Church and world, watchful especially against threats to doctrine and life in the fellowship (see Chapters 3, 19, and 20).

The Lord's distribution of varied gifts among the eldership will fit some better for certain of these tasks than others. It is wise to distribute elders' assignments in terms of talents and interests.

Watchfulness over self, both individual and corporate, is always fundamental to other forms of watchfulness.

Appendix A

THE ECUMENICAL CREEDS:

APOSTLES' CREED

This Creed is called the *Apostles' Creed,* not because it is a production of the apostles themselves, but because it contains a brief summary of their teachings. More than any other creed of Christendom, it may justly be called an ecumenical symbol of faith.

    I. I believe in God the Father, Almighty, Maker of heaven and earth.

    II. And in Jesus Christ, His only begotten Son, our Lord;

    III. Who was conceived by the Holy Spirit, born of the virgin Mary;

    IV. Suffered under Pontius Pilate; was crucified, dead, and buried; He descended into hell;

    V. The third day He rose again from the dead;

    VI. He ascended into heaven, and sitteth at the right hand of God the Father Almighty;

    VII. From thence He shall come to judge the living and the dead.

    VIII. I believe in the Holy Spirit.

    IX. I believe a holy catholic Church, the communion of saints;

    X. The forgiveness of sins;

    XI. The resurrection of the body;

    XII. And the life everlasting. Amen.

NICENE CREED

The Nicene Creed is a statement of the orthodox faith of the early Christian Church in opposition to certain heresies, especially Arianism. These heresies disturbed the Church during the fourth century, and concerned the doctrine of the Trinity and of the person of Christ.

I believe in one God, the Father Almighty, Maker of heaven and earth, and of all things visible and invisible.

And in one Lord Jesus Christ, the only-begotten Son of God, begotten of the Father before all worlds; God of God, Light of Light, very God of very God; begotten, not made, being of one substance with the Father, by whom all things were made.

Who, for us men and for our salvation, came down from heaven, and was incarnate by the Holy Spirit of the virgin Mary, and was made man; and was crucified also for us under Pontius Pilate; He suffered and was buried; and the third day He rose again, according to the Scriptures; and ascended into heaven, and sitteth on the right hand of the Father; and He shall come again, with glory, to judge the living and the dead; whose kingdom shall have no end.

And I believe in the Holy Spirit, the Lord and Giver of life; who proceedeth from the Father and the Son; who with the Father and the Son together is worshipped and glorified; who spake by the prophets.

And I believe one holy catholic and apostolic Church. I acknowledge one baptism for the remission of sins; and I look for the resurrection of the dead, and the life of the world to come. Amen.

ATHANASIAN CREED

This creed is named after Athanasius (293-373 A.D.), the champion of orthodoxy over against Arian attacks upon the doctrine of the Trinity. For centuries it has been the custom of the Roman and Anglican Churches to chant this Creed in public worship on certain solemn occasions.

(1) Whosoever will be saved, before all things it is necessary that he hold the catholic faith; (2) Which faith except every one do keep whole and undefiled, without doubt he shall perish everlastingly.

(3) And the catholic faith is this: That we worship one God in Trinity, and Trinity in Unity; (4) Neither confounding the persons, nor dividing the substance. (5) For there is one person of the Father, another of the Son, and another of the Holy Spirit. (6) But the Godhead of the Father, of the Son, and of the Holy Spirit is all one, the glory equal, the majesty co-eternal. (7) Such as the Father is, such is the Son, and such is the Holy Spirit. (8) The Father uncreate, the Son uncreate, and the Holy Spirit uncreate. (9) The Father incomprehensible, the Son incomprehensible, and the Holy Spirit incomprehensible. (10) The

Father eternal, the Son eternal, and the Holy Spirit eternal. (11) And yet they are not three eternals, but one eternal. (12) As also there are not three uncreated nor three incomprehensibles, but one uncreated and one incomprehensible. (13) So likewise the Father is almighty, the Son almighty, and the Holy Spirit almighty; (14) And yet they are not three almighties, but one almighty. (15) So the Father is God, the Son is God, and the Holy Spirit is God; (16) And yet they are not three Gods, but one God. (17) So likewise the Father is Lord, the Son Lord, and the Holy Spirit Lord; (18) And yet they are not three Lords, but one Lord. (19) For like as we are compelled by the Christian verity to acknowledge every person by himself to be God and Lord; (20) So are we forbidden by the catholic religion to say: There are three Gods or three Lords. (21) The Father is made of none, neither created nor begotten. (22) The Son is of the Father alone; not made nor created, but begotten. (23) The Holy Spirit is of the Father and of the Son; neither made, nor created, nor begotten, but proceeding. (24) So there is one Father, not three Fathers; one Son, not three Sons; one Holy Spirit, not three Holy Spirits. (25) And in this Trinity none is afore, or after another; none is greater, or less than another. (26) But the whole three persons are co-eternal, and co-equal. (27) So that in all things, as aforesaid, the unity in Trinity and the Trinity in Unity is to be worshipped. (28) He therefore that will be saved must thus think of the Trinity.

(29) Furthermore it is necessary to everlasting salvation that he also believe rightly the incarnation of our Lord Jesus Christ. (30) For the right faith is that we believe and confess that our Lord Jesus Christ, the Son of God, is God and man. (31) God of the substance of the Father, begotten before the worlds; and man of the substance of His mother, born in the world. (32) Perfect God and perfect man, of a reasonable soul and human flesh subsisting. (33) Equal to the Father as touching His Godhead, and inferior to the Father as touching His manhood. (34) Who, although He is God and Man, yet He is not two, but one Christ. (35) One, not by conversion of the Godhead into flesh, but by taking of the manhood into God. (36) One altogether, not by confusion of substance, but by unity of person. (37) For as the reasonable soul and flesh is one man, so God and man is one Christ; (38) Who suffered for our salvation, descended into hell, rose again the third day from the dead; (39) He ascended into heaven, He sitteth on the right hand of the Father, God Almighty; (40) From thence He shall come to judge the living and the dead. (41) And shall give account of

their own works. (43) And they that have done good shall go into life everlasting, and they that have done evil into everlasting fire.

(44) This is the catholic faith, which except a man believe faithfully, he cannot be saved.

Appendix B

DOCTRINAL STANDARDS OF PROTESTANT CHURCHES:

Baptist and Methodist denominations have not adopted doctrinal standards, although the Southern Baptist Convention did approve a statement of the "Baptist Faith and Message" in 1963.

Lutheran Doctrinal Standards:

> Augsburg Confession and its Apology
> Smalcald Articles
> Luther's Catechisms
> Formula of Concord

Presbyterial Doctrinal Standards:

The following Presbyterian churches subscribe to the Westminster Confession and the Westminster Larger and Shorter Catechisms:

> Associate Reformed Presbyterian Church
> Bible Presbyterian Church
> Orthodox Presbyterian Church
> Presbyterian Church in America
> Presbyterian Church in the United States
> Reformed Presbyterian Church, Evangelical Synod
> Reformed Presbyterian Church of North America

Presbyterian Church in Canada:

> Westminster Confession
> Westminster Larger and Shorter Catechism
> Second Helvetic Confession
> Gallican Confession
> Belgic Confession
> Heidelberg Catechism

United Presbyterian Church:

> Scots Confession
> Heidelberg Catechism
> Second Helvetic Confession

> Westminster Confession and Catechisms
> Barmen Declaration
> Confession of 1967

Reformed Church Doctrinal Standards

Christian Reformed Church:
> Belgic Confession
> Canons of Dort
> Heidelberg Catechism

Protestant Reformed Church in America: same as Christian Reformed

Reformed Church in America: same as Christian Reformed

Copies of these doctrinal standards may be found in the Service or Worship Books of the denominations holding them; also in Philip Schaff's *Creeds of Christendom,* in Arthur Piepkorn's *Profiles in Belief,* Vol. II, in John Leith's *Creeds of the Churches,* and in E. F. K. Muller's *Bekenntnisschriften der Reformierten Kirche* (here, as also in Schaff, the confessions appear in the original languages as well as in translation).

Chapter 3

THE CONGREGATION
IN THE BODY OF CHRIST

The elder faces inward, keeping watch over himself and the congregation in which the Lord has appointed him guardian.

The elder also faces outward, as we have already observed, in that the local congregation is, except in independent and congregational polities, a structural part of a larger denominational body.

It is our conviction, as developed in Chapter 16, that the unity of the Church universal is best expressed in what the Apostles Creed calls "the communion of saints". Such communion embraces the world, and becomes visible whenever and wherever Christians of all denominations work together, as they do in many ways. Here is displayed the oneness of which St. Paul speaks: "There is one body and one Spirit, just as you were called to the one hope that belongs to your call, one Lord, one faith, one baptism, one God and Father of us all, who is above all and through all and in all" (Eph. 4:4-6).

In terms of ecclesiastical polity, or Church law, three basic conceptions of Church government separate large denominational and local communions from official union.

These three conceptions are, briefly:

1. Independents and congregationalists: they see the local congregation as sufficient, ecclesiastically, to itself. They do not acknowledge the governing authority of any broader body, though local congregations may, and do, form general associations for specific practical purposes. Theologically, many of these stand in the Reformed or Calvinist tradition. Baptist congregations will form themselves into conventions, though these generally are without specific confessional base.

2. In views dominant in both the Roman Catholic and various Episcopal bodies, the Lord exercises His rule over the Body by means of a hierarchical structure. Offices are, starting locally, priest, bishop,

archbishop, and — for Rome — the Pope.

3. Presbyterian and Reformed churches locate authority, derived from Christ, in the congregation's eldership. Broader assemblies derive their authority, by delegation, from the local council or consistory or session. The classis, presbytery, conference, and again, the synod, general assembly, general conference can act for the local unit because they are presumed to be but extensions of it. It is out of this context that this handbook is written, allowing for such denominational adaptation as required.

CORPORATE RESPONSIBILITY

Decision, even in the local congregation, must usually be delegated. This means that some participate immediately, while many do not. When decisions are made by broader ecclesiastical bodies, it is easy for the local member to think of such assemblies as meeting "over there" somewhere, dealing with matters of their own. Even the local eldership may not feel itself very much involved in, or responsible for, what broader assemblies do — or fail to do.

This is a mistake.

The Church, even in its various denominational forms, is always a unity. No congregation can exempt itself from involvement in decisions made by broader assemblies. By delegation the local eldership acts in the classis or presbytery. By deputation, the local eldership is present in the broadest body. It is not, "our Church and that, or your, Church" — it is altogether *our* Church.

Watch that you, as elder, feel this way, and communicate this feeling. Issues before the broadest body may seem abstract. They often are matters of church order, of creed or confession, of liturgical forms, and questions of order and discipline unresolved by small bodies. But these, too, affect and represent the Church, the Body of which every member is a living part.

We believe that broader assemblies should confine doctrinal decisions to particular cases, involving specific problems. Theology by assembly is rarely profitable to the Church, and its decisions are usually unenforceable.

There is a general erosion of the sense of corporate responsibility in much of the Protestant Church. Congregations whose polity is by no means independentist behave more and more as if in fact it were. Church Order, as adopted by, and for, the denomination is readily ignored in favor of local preference. This is to be deplored, not in judgment upon congregationalism but because a Church which is only nominally Presbyterian or Reformed is apt to be only nominally a Church. If your congregation is officially a part of a denomination, but in practice functions congregationally, seek the integrity of its becoming wholly one or the other. The house divided against itself, as our Lord says, cannot stand (Mk. 3:24). Our commitment, as to which form we think most condusive to good order, is to the Reformed (or Presbyterian) polity.

Some elders have their vocations in corporate enterprise. There the subordinate executive is indeed responsible for operations assigned to him, but he exercises little authority for the corporation as a whole, and may feel little sense of full participation in it. Perhaps this mentality colors such elders' view of the relation of the local congregation to the broader assemblies.

To counteract isolationism, and to stress the consciousness of the responsibility for the whole which the local congregation should share, we suggest:

1. The eldership should appoint, if it has not done so, a committee on the denominational broader assemblies, say the classis and synod. It will be the task of this committee to acquaint itself, and the eldership as a whole, with the agenda and decisions of the broader assemblies to which the congregation owes allegiance.

2. Encourage the membership of this committee to attend meetings of the broader assemblies, even if not appointed as delegates. Have full reports presented to the eldership in addition to that of the congregational delegates, if such there be.

3. Delegate to broader assemblies the same persons for several consecutive assembly meetings. This will give these delegates a familiarity with issues and procedures which will encourage their active participation in the deliberations of the assembly.

4. Commonly the local congregation delegates its minister along with an elder to the broader assembly. This means that minister delegates acquire a far greater familiarity with the assembly machinery and procedures than can the elder delegate, especially when he attends but once in his term of office. Sending the same elder to several sessions of the broader assembly will offset his comparative unfamiliarty, and permit the assembly to enjoy full participation by all delegates.

5. It is not common for local congregations to instruct delegates as

to what position to take on issues scheduled for the broader assembly. It is assumed that the delegate must remain open to the discussion and the leading of the Spirit. There is prudence, however, in serving the delegate with the wisdom of the full eldership; and before electing their delegate, the elders might want to know his view of matters pending.

6. You should encourage the calling of regional elders' conferences to discuss matters likely to engage the attention of the broader bodies.

7. Consider circulating an occasional newsletter among the elders of your area, one which sheds light upon issues of denominational importance.

8. Be sure to provide financial remuneration of both expenses and salary or wages lost of delegates to broader assemblies.

All of these suggestions, which surely can be amplified by consideration in your eldership, have the same aim: to draw the congregation more and more into active participation as a conscious part of the denomination to which it belongs.

This, too, is a part of your watchfulness, as elders, over yourselves.

Chapter 4.

PRINCIPLES OF PUBLIC SPEAKING AND PARLIAMENTARY PROCEDURE

So you are not a public speaker?

Voice quavers, knees turn to jelly, heart pounds, words flee, ideas die aborning?

Join the club!

There is no other kind of speaker. Only some people learn to master these very natural problems, while other people are mastered by them. We want you, because the Lord wants you, to triumph over such handicaps. Countless others do. So can you.

SPEAKING IS . . .

As natural as breathing.

Speaking in public, that is in a group or before an audience, is simply doing on a larger scale what you do perfectly well at home and among friends. There is no real difference between talking to one or two and speaking to ten or fifty. Your hangup is only you!

In the group, or before the audience, you are thinking of yourself. Stop that! Think only of what you want to say, of whom you want to convince, and of the Lord you mean to serve. This will by no means cure your nervousness with all its effects. There may always be "butterflies" fluttering around inside as your turn to say something approaches. Your business is not to get rid of them; it is to transcend them. All speakers have to.

FORGET YOURSELF

Quit wondering if you are going to make a hit. Or if someone is going to sneer, openly or to himself. Quit thinking at all about your "image". Let the Lord who appointed you an elder worry about that; and you

41

get yourself intent upon doing His business through your voice and ideas. Remember that His sun will rise on time tomorrow morning, no matter how you do as public speaker tonight. And then sail right on into what you want to say — as if you were snugly at home in your living room chatting with family and friends. Millions have done it. So can you.

Fix your mind on what needs saying. Fix your attention on those to whom you are saying it. Forget what you sound like; concentrate on what you want them to hear and believe. If you can talk in private, you can talk anywhere. Even as delegate to a broader assembly. Speak up, man! Yes, speak up like a man! The Lord entrusts you with His eldership; you trust yourself to see it through.

SOME HINTS

1. Be brief; be heard; be seated!
2. Practice. Practice anytime and anywhere you can. Make little speeches on issues you know are coming up at the next elders' meeting, or on whatever interests you. Get used to talking out loud when no one is listening. Imagine your eldership, or your audience out there, hearing you. Throw yourself into persuasion. Feel from your toes the importance of the issue, and what you think about it. Get involved. Gesture. Raise your voice. Look your listeners (in your imagination — and in fact, too) right in the eye.
3. There are three secrets of good speaking, said the great Greek orator Demosthenes: (1) Practice! (2) Practice!! (3) PRACTICE!!!
4. Be prepared. The best balance to nervousness is preparation. Know your stuff. Have thought it through. Know where you stand and why. Come loaded. This is the key role of knowledge and information in public speech. Live with the Bible, study the Confessions, get all the facts on the issue coming up.
5. If you are likely to be discussing your views as against those of others, figure out in advance what *their* arguments are likely to be. Prepare answers: "If he says this, I will say, 'So and so...' " Practice that aloud, alone somewhere.
6. Refuse to be bluffed. Don't let yourself be put down. Argument is not won just by somebody's saying it's so. Proof comes only in one of these three ways:
   a. Through presenting the facts which support the argument.
   b. Through quoting good authority, especially that of the Scrip-

tures or the Confessions.

    c. Through plain reasoning which leads to sound conclusion.

Insist on one or more of these, and be sure you use them yourself.

7. Don't be silenced by something like, "Well, I've studied this and you haven't." Insist on one of the three tests listed in item 6 above.

8. Don't be bluffed by quotations from the Bible in Greek or Hebrew. What cannot be proved in English isn't there.

9. Remember that the Bible is perspicuous — that is, the Bible is clear on the basic doctrines of faith and life. Insist that positions which are said to rest on the Bible have that clarity themselves.

10. When you are about to talk:

    a. Don't worry about the quality of your voice. It's the only one you have. God accepted it when He made you an elder.

    b. Don't expect not to be nervous. It's natural, and is in fact an indication that you are getting ready, like a good race horse, for doing something. Even the best orators are often tense. It may go away when you get started. Try, anyhow, simply to live with it.

    c. Don't worry about your grammar or pronunciation. You'll be understood if you passionately have something to say.

    d. Don't think about gesture or posture. Simply try to avoid doing things with your hands, or taking a position, which claim attention away from what you are saying.

    e. Use enough vocal volume to be heard right from the beginning.

11. Stand up! Speak up! Shut up! Know your point. Make your point. Stop before others quit listening.

12. You have far more speaking ability than you will ever believe. Try getting some of it out and into the Lord's service. Others' right to speak may be education; yours should be sainthood. The Word is best understood through obedience. Obedience is open to all.

BASIC PARLIAMENTARY PROCEDURE

The purpose of parliamentary law is good order. The basic handbook of parliamentary law is *Roberts Rules of Order.* We strongly urge that your council decide to be guided by *Roberts Rules,* if it has not already done so.

The aim of parliamentary law is to set business before the body in a form that can be properly discussed and fairly decided by majority vote. *Roberts Rules* summarize the wisdom gained from several centuries of experience with democratic parliamentary practice. Strict adherence to the *Rules* is by far the best way of arriving at fair and prompt decision.

Following are the commonly used rules of procedure, grouped according to what may be done through them. We set them out in ways that may be easily mastered and quickly referred to. With each rule we give the number of the section in *Roberts Rules of Order* (Revised, 75th Anniversary Edition) where it is more fully explained. You should be able, however, to conduct successful meetings by using the following charts alone. Moreover, each one is set up in such a way that by covering the right hand column with a paper or card you can practice using the motion in its correct form, checking yourself by looking under the card.

FUNDAMENTAL PRINCIPLES

Getting Business Before the Body

Business is set before the body in the form of a Main Motion. Only one Main Motion can be on the floor at the same time.

The Main Motion requires a second. This means that at least two members of the body believe that the matter should be presented and discussed.

After the Main Motion has been made and seconded, the Chair must restate it so that there can be no misunderstanding of exactly what it is. Up to this point, the mover may withdraw his motion (with or without permission of the seconder) if he so decides. After the Chair has restated the Motion, it belongs to the body and may be withdrawn only by its permission.

Reports and recommendations of committees, and resolutions of various kinds can also be used, like Main Motions, to get business before the body.

Discussion

Main Motions are presented for discussion. It is the responsibility of the Chair to keep remarks on the Motion, to permit all who wish to speak to be heard, and to move the discussion along toward the goal of decision.

Disposing of the Main Motion

When discussion has ended, or been closed by vote of the body, the Chair once more restates the motion before the house. He then calls for the vote of those in favor, and then the vote of those opposed, and announces the decision of the body: the Motion is passed, or defeated. The Chair himself, if a member of the body, may vote (if he has not already done so) whenever his vote would change the final outcome.

Ways other than voting the Motion up or down which also remove it from the floor will be mentioned below.

A Main Motion can be modified on the floor by amendment, properly made and passed by majority vote. If the Main Motion combines two or more distinct proposals, it can be divided on request of any member of the body and each part voted on separately.

Incidental and Privileged Motions

While Main Motions are being debated, other matters may arise which require immediate attention. These are brought before the body in the form of incidental or privileged motions, described below.

Parliamentary law secures good order in the handling of business properly before the council. Use it to that end, and the Church will always be the gainer. Parliamentary law is a threat only to those who want to cut corners in getting things done, or preventing their being done, after their own way.

PART I. GETTING BUSINESS BEFORE THE BODY

MAIN MOTION   MAIN MOTION

Purpose: to place business properly before the body

Requires second

Is debatable

Form for Use:

1. You address the Chair:	Mr. Chairman (or Chairperson)
	Madam Chairman (or Chairperson)
2. Chair recognizes you:	States your name
3. You make your motion:	I move that....
4. Another member seconds:	Second, or, I second the motion
5. Chair re-states:	It is moved and seconded that....
6. Chair asks for discussion:	Is there any discussion?
To discuss:	You address Chair
	Chair recognizes you
	You speak your piece
7. After discussion, Chair:	Re-states motion
	Asks all in favor to say "Aye"
	Asks all opposed to say "No"

8. Chair announces decision: The motion is passed, or
                             The motion is defeated
9. Chair moves to next order of
   business

                        (*Roberts* Section 11)

Note: Use the same form for Resolutions and Committee Reports or
      Recommendations.

                    *   *   *

Sometimes the discussion shows that changes should be made in the
Main Motion so that it more accurately represents the matter before
the body. Such changes can be made by means of amendment.

TO AMEND   TO AMEND

Purpose: to change the motion on the floor in one of three possible
         ways: 1) add to it, 2) delete from it, 3) substitute one part
         (but not all) of it with something else
Note: An amendment may be proposed to an amendment already on
      the floor, but only one such an amendment-to-an amendment
      is in order at a time.

                                    Requires second
                                    Is debatable

Form for use:
1. You address the Chair
2. Chair recognizes you
3. You make motion: I move to amend the motion be-
                                 fore us by adding.... (or by insert-
                                 ing...between the words....)
                                 I move to amend the motion be-
                                 fore us by deleting...
                                 I move to amend the motion be-
                                 fore us by striking out...and sub-
                                 stituting....

4. Another member seconds
5. Chair re-states the motion: It is moved and seconded to
                                 amend the motion before us by....

6. Chair asks for discussion
7. After discussion, Chair re-
   states: The motion is to amend the mo-
                                 tion before us by....

All in favor say "Aye"

All opposed say, "No"

8. Chair declares the amendment: Passed - and then restates the Main Motion (or amendment) before the body as amended, and calls for further discussion, or

Lost - and then restates the Main Motion (or amendment) and calls for further discussion

Remember: An amendment belongs to the Main Motion to which it is proposed, and cannot therefore be tabled or postponed by itself

(*Roberts* Section 33)

*   *   *

It may become clear that the business before the body would be served best if the entire Main Motion were reformulated. This can be done by proposing a Substitute Motion, which can be made even though one Main Motion is already on the floor. Remember the "Notes" at the bottom of the next chart about Substitute Motions.

SUBSTITUTE MOTION   SUBSTITUTE MOTION

Requires a second

Debatable/amendable

Purpose: to substitute an entirely new motion (to serve the same purpose) as one already on the floor - is like an amendment to the whole motion

Form for use:

1. You address the Chair
2. Chair recognizes you
3. You make motion: I move as a substitute motion, the following...

4. Some member seconds
5. Chair re-states the motion: It is moved and seconded, as a substitute motion, that....

6. Chair asks for discussion
7. After discussion, Chair re-states: The motion before the house is to substitute...

All in favor say, "Aye"

All opposed say, "No"

8. Chair declares the motion:
Passed - now the substitute motion is before the body for discussion

Defeated - leaving the motion already on the floor up for further discussion

Note: Discussion on the substitute motion can include comments on the other motion for which the substitute is being recommended.

Normally, the substitute motion should intend the same purposes as the previous one for which it is being offered - only better.

The Chair may not itself simply decide to substitute one motion for another.

(*Roberts* Section 33)

PART II. DISPOSING OF THE MAIN MOTION

Motions are made to get business before the body, to discuss it, and to come to some decision about it. The Main Motion is normally disposed of, then, by being passed by majority vote or defeated by majority vote. Problems may arise, however, which call for other handling, through motions like the following:

TO REFER TO COMMITTEE

TO REFER
Requires second
Debatable

Purpose: to save time, get carefully considered advice, get motion out of way

Note: Motion may be referred to either: a standing committee
a special committee

Form for use:
1. You address the Chair
2. Chair recognizes you
3. You make motion:
I move that this matter (the motion before the house) be referred to the Standing Committee on....
(you may add when a report should be made)

OR

48

I move that this matter be referred to a special committee of... members, to be appointed by... (or, to consist of...), with instructions to report at....

4. Another member seconds
5. Chair re-states the motion: It is moved and seconded that the motion before the house be referred to....

6. Chair asks for discussion: Is there any discussion?
7. After discussion, Chair says: The motion is to refer to....
All in favor say, "Aye"
All opposed say, "No"

8. Chair declares the motion: Passed, and declares the main motion referred as instructed, or
Lost, and asks for further discussion of the main motion

(*Roberts* Section 32)

* * *

The Main Motion can be temporarily set aside by moving to "table" it. If not removed from the table before the end of the meeting, the Motion dies. This may, therefore, be a simple way of disposing of a proposal on which the body prefers, for one reason or another, not to vote.

TO LAY ON THE TABLE TO TABLE

Requires second
Not debatable/amendable

Purpose: to lay aside motion, to get rid of motion altogether without voting on it, to test strength of opposing sides
Note: A motion laid on the table can, by majority vote, be taken off the table at any time during the same session.

Form for use:
1. You address the Chair
2. Chair recognizes you
3. You make motion: I move that we lay the motion to... (state motion before the house) on the table

4. Another member seconds

| 5. Chair re-states the motion: | It is moved and seconded that the motion before the house be laid on the table
All in favor say, "Aye"
All opposed say, "No" |
| 6. Chair declares the motion: | Passed, and says that main motion is tabled
Defeated, and asks for further discussion on the main motion |

Note: The motion to table may be made even after a motion to close debate has been carried, or when it is pending (the Chair must be alert to permit a member who may have this in mind to secure the floor before calling for a vote, or even after declaring the vote, on Previous Question)

(Roberts Section 28)

TAKE FROM THE TABLE

TAKE FROM THE TABLE
Requires second
Not debatable/amendable

Purpose: to put back before the house a motion which has, during this same session, been laid on the table (this could be done after a number of members have gone home!)

Form for use:

1. You address the Chair
2. Chair recognizes you

| 3. You make motion: | I move to take from the table the motion to...which was tabled earlier in this session |

4. Another members seconds

| 5. Chair re-states the motion: | It is moved and seconded to take from the table the motion to...
All in favor say, "Aye"
All opposed say, "No" |
| 6. Chair declares the motion: | Passed, and re-states the main motion for further discussion
Defeated, and moves to next order of business |

Note: The motion to take from the table is *not* in order immediately after a motion to table has passed; further business must be transacted first.

(Roberts Section 35)

* * *

It may be desirable to defer discussion of a Main Motion to some later time in the meeting. This is accomplished through the motion to postpone to a certain time. As soon as possible after that time arrives, the Chair calls the postponed motion back to the floor, but may not interrupt other business to do so. If the desire is to get the motion back to the floor at an exact time, then the motion to postpone must include words to that effect, namely to make it a "special order of business" at the time specified. This, however, requires a 2/3 vote to pass. Note that "2/3 vote" *always* means 2/3 of those present *and* voting, unless otherwise stipulated in the body's constitution or by-laws.

TO POSTPONE DEFINITELY   TO POSTPONE DEFINITELY

Requires second

Debatable

Purpose: to postpone discussion of a motion until later in the session (a more appropriate time; when strength for your side is gained, or that of other side is lost)

Note: To "make a special order of business" at a specified time requires a 2/3 vote to pass.

Form for use:

1. You address the Chair
2. Chair recognizes you
3. You make motion:

I move that we postpone consideration of this motion until....

OR

I move that this motion be made a special order of business at....

4. Another member seconds
5. Chair re-states the motion:

It is moved and seconded that we postpone consideration of this motion until...

OR

It is moved and seconded that this motion be made a special order of business at...

6. Chair asks for discussion: Is there any discussion?
7. Chair re-states the motion: The motion is...
    All in favor say, "Aye"
    All opposed say, "No"
8. Chair declares the motion: Carried, and indicates when discussion will be resumed
    Lost, and calls for further discussion of the main motion before the house

Note: A 2/3 vote is counted in terms of those present and voting, and usually will require a show of hands, or rising, which the Chair may ask for.

(Roberts Section 31)

       *   *   *

Sometimes it becomes clear that the Main Motion before the body should not have been made at all. Or sometimes it is desirable to test the mind of the body without bringing the Main Motion itself to a vote. Either of these ends can be achieved through the motion to postpone indefinitely — that is, never to return in this session. Notice that on this motion those who favor the Main Motion will be voting "No" and those who oppose the Main Motion will be voting "Yes" — a neat way for politicians to confuse the public as to their real views (and so used sometimes, though more commonly in the form of "refer back to committee").

POSTPONE INDEFINITELY   POSTPONE INDEFINITELY

    Requires Second
    Debatable

Purpose: to prevent discussion of the motion during the current meeting to test strength of both sides

Form for use:
1. You address the Chair
2. Chair recognizes you
3. You make the motion: I move that we postpone consideration of this motion indefinitely
4. Another member seconds: Second, or, I second the motion
5. Chair re-states the motion: It is moved and seconded that we postpone consideration of this motion indefinitely.

6. Chair asks for discussion:	Is there any discussion of the motion to postpone? (only that!)
7. After discussion, the Chair says:	The motion before the house is on the motion to postpone consideration of the motion to.... (state the main motion) All in favor of postponement say, "Aye" All opposed to postponement say, "No"
8. Chair declares:	The motion to postpone is carried; next order of business OR The motion to postpone is lost; is there further discussion of the motion to....

(Roberts Section 34)

* * *

It may be that everything about a motion has been said long before the body stops talking. To bring discussion to an end, move the previous question — that means the question now on the floor. This is commonly done by calling out, "Question" but can be acted upon properly only if duly moved and seconded as indicated below:

PREVIOUS QUESTION
(TO CLOSE DEBATE)

PREVIOUS QUESTION

Requires second
Not debatable/amendable
Requires 2/3 vote

Purpose: to stop debate and bring the motion before the house to a vote

Form for use:
1. You address the Chair
2. Chair recognizes you
3. You make motion:
    I move the previous question, or
    I call for the question, or
    I move that we close debate, or
    Question

4. Another member seconds

5. Chair re-states the motion: The question is called for, or

The motion is to cease debate

All in favor say, "Aye"

All opposed say, "No"

6. Chair declares the motion: Passed, and calls *at once* for a vote on the main motion before the house

Defeated,and call for further discussion

Note: The call for the question (previous question) should not be repeated immediately after it has been lost - the Chair must decide if sufficient discussion has been carried on since the question was last called for (and lost) before entertaining it again.

(*Roberts* Section 29)

*   *   *

And now, the vote. In small groups the Chair will normally simply ask for a voice vote (*vive voce*). If in doubt, he may ask for a show of hands. In a large group the Chair may ask members to rise for counting. Any member who doubts the accuracy of the Chair's decision as to whether the motion passed or failed may ask (and must be given) a re-count, called "Division of the House":

VOTING:

DIVISION OF THE HOUSE   DIVISION OF THE HOUSE

Does *not* require second

Not debatable/amendable

Purpose: a check as to whether or not the Chair has correctly determined the voice vote - by having the assembly vote by show of hands or rising

Form for use:

1. You call out: Mr. Chairman, I call for a division, or

Division, Mr. Chairman

2. Chair must act on request: A division is called for:

All in favor of the motion raise their (right) hands

All opposed raise their hands

OR

A division is called for:
All in favor of the motion please rise
All opposed to the motion please rise

3. The Chair declares the motion: Passed, or
Lost

(*Roberts* Section 25)

*   *   *

No member, including the Chair, may ask for a vote by ballot or roll-call except by making this a motion which requires a majority vote to pass:

VOTING BY BALLOT

VOTING BY BALLOT
Requires second
Not debatable/amendable

Purpose: to permit, or require, the use of secret ballot
Form for use:
1. You address the Chair
2. Chair recognizes you
3. You make motion: I move that we vote on this motion by ballot

4. Another member seconds
5. Chair re-states the motion: It is moved and seconded that we vote on this motion by ballot
All in favor say, "Aye"
All opposed say, "No"
6. Chair declares the motion: Passed, and appoints tellers to distribute, collect, and count ballots
Defeated, and asks for voice vote (member may ask for division of the house)

Note: It may also be moved to vote by roll-call in the same manner as above.

(*Roberts* Section 25)

*   *   *

A member may wish that the body would change its decision regarding a motion previously passed or rejected. If the motion in question was adopted at an earlier meeting, it may be undone or changed simply by making a new motion at this meeting for decision by majority vote. If the motion in question was passed, or defeated, earlier in this meeting, the following options are available to give the group an opportunity to change its mind. Note that the two motions differ as who may make them, what vote is required to pass, and what is the result if passed.

TO RESCIND

TO RESCIND
Requires second
Is debatable
Requires 2/3 vote

Purpose: to repeal, or annul, a motion passed earlier
Note: May be made by any member any time when floor is open.
Form for use:
1. You address the Chair
2. Chair recognizes you
3. You make motion:

I move that we rescind the motion to....which was passed earlier in this meeting

4. Another member seconds
5. Chair re-states the motion:

It is moved and seconded to rescind the motion to....

6. Chair asks for discussion:

Is there any discussion?

7. Chair re-states the motion:

The motion is to rescind the motion to....
All in favor say, "Aye"
All opposed say, "No"

8. Chair declares the motion:

Passed, by 2/3 vote, repealing the previous action
Lost, leaving the previous action unchanged

(*Roberts* Section 37)

TO RECONSIDER

TO RECONSIDER
Requires second
Is debatable

' **Purpose:** to call back for further discussion and another vote a motion already passed or defeated
Note: This motion may only be made at the same meeting in which the

previous action has been taken, and only by a member who voted with the *prevailing* side (that is, he voted "Yes" if the motion passed, or "No" if it lost). Otherwise the required motion is to rescind.

Form for use:

1. You address the Chair
2. Chair recognizes you
3. You make motion: I move that we reconsider the motion to....
4. Chair inquires: Did you vote on the prevailing side? (If "Yes," then a second is in order)
5. Some member seconds
6. Chair re-states the motion: It is moved and seconded to re-consider the motion to.... (passed, or lost, previously)
7. Chair asks for discussion: Is there any discussion (*only* on the motion to reconsider, not on the previous motion)
8. Chair re-states the motion: The motion is....
   All those in favor of reconsideration say, "Aye"
   All those opposed to reconsideration say, "No"
9. Chair declares motion: Passed, putting the original motion once more before the house - Chair calls for further discussion
   Defeated, making no change - next order of business

Note: Unlike the motion to rescind, the motion to reconsider requires only a majority vote to pass.

(*Roberts* Section 36)

PART III. INCIDENTAL MOTIONS

These motions take care of matters that arise in the course of a meeting. They may be made when other motions are on the floor.

The "Appeal from Decision of the Chair" allows a member to seek the support of the body against a decision made by the Chair. Note, however, that when the Chair's decision is on a point of parliamentary law, it must be *Roberts Rules* and not a majority vote which settles the matter. Appeal cannot be made against parliamentary law, nor can such law be set aside by vote of the body.

APPEAL FROM DECISION OF THE CHAIR

APPEAL FROM THE CHAIR

Requires a second

Debatable

Purpose: permits a member to appeal to the assembly against a ruling by the Chair

Note: No appeal can be made against a parliamentary ruling if that is based on the constitution, by-laws, or *Robert's Rules of Order.*

Form for Use:

1. You call out:

Mr. Chairman, I appeal from the decision of the Chair

2. Some member seconds
3. You may state the grounds for your appeal
4. The Chair may state grounds for his decision

(others may enter the discussion)

5. Chair re-states the motion:

There is an appeal from the decision of the Chair:

Those in favor of the decision of the Chair say, "Aye"

Those opposed to the decision of the Chair say, "No"

6. Chair declares the motion:

Passed - the decision of the Chair stands

Defeated - the decision of the Chair is overturned (and whatever follows from that)

Note: Some groups require that when a decision of the Chair is appealed, the gavel shall be handed to the Vice-president or other officer while the Chair steps down into the body to defend himself.

Note: A mistaken parliamentary decision by the Chair, or by a parliamentarian, can be corrected by quotation from proper authority, and must then be changed - but this is not really an appeal from a decision of the Chair.

(Roberts Section 21)

Each member of the body is responsible for proper parliamentary procedure. When he detects a mistake, he should call it to the Chair's attention by raising a "point of order," on which the Chair must then rule for purposes of correcting the fault.

POINT OF ORDER

POINT OF ORDER
Does *not* require second
Not debatable

Purpose: to call Chair's attention to some mistake in procedure, usually a violation of parliamentary rules of order

Form for use:

1. You call out:

Mr. Chairman, point of order, or
Mr. Chairman, I rise to a point of order

2. Chair asks you to state point of order
3. You do so
4. Chair rules:

Your point is well taken, we shall....
Your point is not well taken, the rules provide (or, the right rule is...)

Note: Point of order may be made while another has the floor, but must be made as soon as the mistake occurs or is observed - member who may have the floor must remain silent until point of order is decided.

Note: If the Chair's decision is not based on proper parliamentary authority, appeal from that decision may be made to the assembly.

(*Roberts* Section 21)

* * *

When you want to set something before the body but do not know the exact parliamentary procedure, you should simply ask the Chair (or the parliamentarian through the Chair) what to do. Never keep silent because you don't know the rule. Find it out! Asking is free.

PARLIAMENTARY INQUIRY

PARLIAMENTARY INQUIRY
Does *not* require second
Not debatable

Purpose: to permit any member to ask what is the correct way for him to do whatever he is wishing to bring to the assembly

Form for use:

1. You call out: Mr. Chairman, I rise to a parliamentary inquiry

2. The Chair: State your inquiry

3. You do so

4. Chair responds (or asks parliamentarian)

Note: No member need ever remain silent because he does not *know*,
or dares not risk trying, the right way to do or say something:
ask!!!

(Roberts Section 27a)

*   *   *

If something a speaker is saying, or has said, leaves you puzzled and in
the dark, ask him what he means. You do so, not directly, but through
the Chair as follows:

POINT OF INFORMATION   POINT OF INFORMATION

Does not require second
Not debatable

Purpose: permits any member to interrupt a speaker for clarification,
or to ask the Chair or anyone else for pertinent information

Note: Members of the assembly do not ordinarily speak directly to
each other: an inquiry is addressed to the Chair, who relays it
to the speaker or other member.

Form for use:

1. You call out: Mr. Chairman, I rise to a point of
information, or
Mr. Chairman, I rise for information

2. Chair responds: State your question

3. You do so: May I ask the speaker....
May I ask....
Can the Chair tell me....

(Roberts Section 27b)

*   *   *

Most meetings have an agenda or order of business. When the meeting
strays from its prepared agenda, or order of business, the Chair should
be reminded of this through the following motion:

CALL FOR ORDERS OF THE DAY

CALL FOR ORDERS

Does *not* require a second
Not debatable

Purpose: to remind the Chair, or the assembly, that the scheduled order of business (or the agenda) is not being followed

Form for use:

1. You call out: Mr. Chairman, I call for the order of the day

2. Chair responds: Your point is well taken, we will now....

        OR

3. Chair responds: State your point
4. You do so   (If Chair rules otherwise, you may appeal to assembly)

Note: Any member may move to suspend the order of the day in order to continue, or to do, something else. This would require majority vote, unless the particular item had earlier been made a special order of business (then a 2/3 vote).

(*Roberts* Secton 20)

*   *   *

There may be rules in your orders of the day, on agenda, or passed as previous motions which interfere, in a given instance, with getting something rightly done. A body may set aside such rules, just for the particular problem at hand. The motion is as follows:

TO SUSPEND A RULE

TO SUSPEND A RULE

Requires a second
Not debatable/amendable
Requires 2/3 vote

Purpose: allows the assembly to operate for limited time under suspension of rules which prohibit participation in debate by non-members, or rules which normally govern the agenda, or other order of business or custom

Note: It is *never* permissable to suspend the constitution or by-laws of the body, *nor* to suspend the rules of parliamentary procedure!

Form for use:

1. You address the Chair
2. Chair recognizes you
3. You make motion: I move that we suspend the rule

which interferes with.... (or, the rule which requires that....) so that we can....

4. Another member seconds

5. Chair re-states the motion: It is moved and seconded that we suspend the rule which....
Those in favor of suspending the rule for this purpose, say "Aye"
Those opposed to suspending the rule say, "No"

6. Chair declares the motion: Passed, and the rule is suspended so that....
Defeated - next order of business

Note: If passed, the motion to suspend the rule applies only to the specific occasion for which it is made; immediately thereafter all rules again apply.

(*Roberts* Section 22)

PART IV.   PRIVILEGED MOTIONS

Some motions may be made while business is on the floor, for purposes of special importance. Following are three of them:

TO RECESS   TO RECESS

Requires a second
Debatable/amendable
(usually)

Purpose: to take some time off, break for lunch or dinner, time to cool off, etc.

Note: If the motion to recess is made while the dicussion of another motion is in progress, THEN a 2/3 vote is required, and the motion is *not* debatable, but it may be amended as to length of time for the recess.

Form for use:

1. You address the Chair
2. Chair recognizes you
3. You make motion: I move that we recess for... (time)
4. Another members seconds
5. Chair re-states the motion: It is moved and seconded that we recess for... (or until...)

6. Chair asks for discussion (UNLESS motion is made while other business is pending)

7. After discussion, Chair re-states:

The motion before the house is...
All in favor say, "Aye"
All opposed say, "No"

8. Chair declares the motion:

Passed - and orders the recess
Defeated - and goes on with business

Note: The Chair should be sure that a motion to recess states the length of time, or indicates when the group shall re-convene.

(*Roberts* Section 18)

QUESTION OF PRIVILEGE

QUESTION OF PRIVILEGE
Does *not* require a second
Not debatable

Purpose: enables any member to ask for removal of disturbances, improvement in temperature or ventilation, better hearing, etc.

Form for use:

1. You call out:

Mr. Chairman, I rise to a question of privilege

2. Chair responds:

State your question

3. You do:

Could the lobby doors be closed, so there will be less noise here? or, Could a window be opened? or, It's too cold in this corner, etc.

4. Chair responds:

Your privilege is well taken (or, granted): will the ushers close the lobby doors, etc.

Note: This form may also be used when a member feels that he, or others, are being abused by a speaker, or when the speaker's language is offensive, etc. The member then rises to: *a point of privilege;* and then if the Chair sustains, the offending member is warned to desist.

(*Roberts* Section 19)

TO ADJOURN

TO ADJOURN
Requires a second
Not debatable/amendable

Purpose: to end this session or meeting

Form for use:

1. You address the Chair
2. Chair recognizes you
3. You make motion: I move that we adjourn
4. Another member seconds
5. Chair re-states the motion: It is moved and seconded that we adjourn
   All in favor say, "Aye"
   All opposed say, "No"
6. Chair declares the motion: Passed, and meeting adjourned
   Defeated, and meeting continues with next order of business

Note: If the motion to adjourn is made and defeated, it is not in order again until there has been some progress in business on the floor; the Chair must decide if the motion to adjourn is being repeated from time to time for purposes of obstruction, and should then rule it out of order (a ruling which can be appealed).

Note: The motion to adjourn loses its special status if it is qualified in any way (like until tomorrow...), or if the group does not have another regularly scheduled meeting and would thus be dissolved — then it is treated like a main motion, subject to debate and amendment.

((*Roberts* Section 17)

PART V.   PRIORITY OF MOTIONS

The rule is that only one Main Motion may hold the floor at one time. But by now you have noticed that many other kinds of motions may be made while the one Main Motion is being discussed. Sometimes it is important to know what rank these motions have in respect to each other. For example, if the motion to table is on the floor, is a motion to refer to committee in order? (It is not). How shall the Chair, and the group, know this? By having at hand a table of priority, or precedence, of motions.

To provide such a table, *Roberts* first divides motions into the broad groupings we have been following: 1)Main Motions, 2) Subsidiary Motions, which apply to Main Motions, 3) Incidental Motions, and 4) Privileged Motions. Each group takes precedence of the one before it. So that, Subsidiary Motions may be made while a Main Motion is on the floor; Incidental Motions may be made while Subsidiary Motions are on the floor; and Privileged Motions may be made while Subsidiary and Incidental Motions are on the floor (generally speaking). Within each main grouping the various motions have their own order of priority or precedence. The following tables are taken from *Roberts Rules,* and furnish a guide to which motions will be in order while other motions are on the floor. It is rare, of course, that very many motions try to occupy the floor at the same time, and members will try to avoid such complication.

CLASSIFICATION OF MOTIONS:
    Main, or principal motions   (Roberts, # 11)
    Subsidiary motions
    Incidental motions
    Privileged motions

*   *   *

Main motions: "A main or principal motion is a motion made to bring before the assembly, for its consideration, any particular subject" (# 11).

Subsidiary motions: "Subsidiary motions are such as are applied to other motions for the purpose of most appropriately disposing of them" (# 12).

    In order of precedence: Lay on the table
                          Previous question
                          Limit or extend limits of debate
                          Postpone definitely, or to a cer-
                             tain time
                          Commit or refer, or recommit
                          Amend
                          Postpone indefinitely

Incidental motions: "Incidental motions are such as arise out of another question which is pending, and therefore take precedence of and must be decided before the question out of which they arise; or, they are incidental to a question that has just been pending and should be decided before any other business is taken up" (# 13).

                      Questions of order and appeal
                      Suspension of the rules
                      Objection to consideration
                      Division of a question
                      Division of the assembly

> Motion relating to nominations
> Requests: parliamentary inquiry, information withdraw a motion, read papers, etc.

Privileged motions: "Privileged motions are such as, while not relating to the pending question, are of so great importance as to require them to take precedence of all other questions, and, on account of this high privilege, they are undebatable" (# 14).

> Fix the time to which to adjourn
> Adjourn
> Recess
> Raise question of privilege
> Call for orders of the day

CONCLUSION

Familiarity with the motions charted above will equip you to use parliamentary law to facilitate business with justice to the full membership. This is what *Roberts Rules* is for.

You may not remember just which motions are not debatable, or which ones require more than majority vote. Most people can't. Keep this book with you for that purpose.

There are various small handbooks to parliamentary procedure. You might care to obtain one, though *Roberts Rules* itself is preferable if you have to Chair meetings.

Obey the law, and the law will serve you.

Chapter 5

THE ELDER AS LEADER

You are chosen to lead the Church.

For you this is not likely to mean public notice, news headlines, or interview on television. We are not talking about political or charismatic leadership.

The elder as leader is the elder who finds the time to get his job done, as effectively and as efficiently as he can. Your success will depend upon your ability to handle time.

PART I. TAKE CHARGE OF TIME

Time is a unique resource. All of us begin with the same amount each day, each week, each year. Time is a totally perishable gift. Your stewardship of time is primary test of your stewardship of the opportunity to serve the Church through leadership.

Though all have the same amount of time every day, some seem to do much in their alloted hours while others accomplish little. Strangely enough, very busy people seem to find time to do more things than do less busy ones. This is why civic projects are so often headed by the busiest people in town — not because they can delegate work, but because they have learned the secret of managing their time. And that secret is open to you: hours are short, but minutes are long!

Take control of your minutes, and the hours will take care of themselves. And at the end of the week you will be pleasantly surprised to discover how much you have accomplished.

DISCOVERY

To get a clear picture of what happens to your own time, you should run an inventory of its use. For this you can't trust your memory.

Many time-wasting habits are by now second nature. We follow them without thinking, and are unaware that precious time slips unused away.

There is no quick way to discover how your time is spent, but there is a simple way. Your ability to follow this way is a good test of your capacity for self-discipline.

Keep a running inventory, day by day, of your use of time for a period of several weeks. Call it a ledger, or a journal, or use an appointment calendar marked off into hours. Be especially precise as to how you spend time not required by your job or profession, inasmuch as this is the time most under your control.

If you keep such a record with care, in a real determination to learn how you can make best use of God's gift of this unreclaimable resource, you will soon have before you a profile: My Use of God's Time!

EVALUATE

Keep in mind the purpose of this investigation of yourself. You want to find out how well you are using the gift of life, especially in the light of the demands which being an elder place upon you.

Do not leap to conclusions as your time-use-profile emerges.

Think out a scale of values: the time required by your job, by your family, by essential recreation; the time due the Church, the community, your social obligations; the time required to stay alert to issues in the news, the issues in your country and community, to issues in the Church; the time essential to Bible study, meditation, and prayer. Consider essentials peculiar to your own circumstances, or those of your family, which require allocation of precious hours.

SET PRIORITIES

Having discovered how your days are spent, and having reflected on how your time should be allocated, set down a list of priorities for your own use of the years — that is, the minutes — God gives you.

Always allow sufficient time for your work, and for your family. Your work is your present financial resource, and your future. Your family all too soon is grown and gone.

What you are trying to isolate, and put to better use, are wasted minutes. Especially those which dribble away in waiting: for meals, for transportation, for appointments. Time to be thinking, taking notes, writing a card, making a phone call, jotting down something to remember to do later. It is in wasted moments, not in big blocks of spare hours, that you will find time to mine for service.

ELIMINATE NON-ESSENTIALS

Aside from putting hitherto wasted moments to use (driving to work is a good time to pray, for example), sort out and get rid of activities you could just as well, or better, get along without. Only you can decide on these. But if you are to do full justice to your calling, to your family, and to your work as leader, some things may have to give. Surrendering a "pastime" — almost a sacrilegious word! — may seem hard at first, but in the long run both you and the Church will benefit by hours better spent. Try it and see!

ACT

Having decided how to use your time more efficiently, do it!

Good intentions so frequently fail to mature into fruit because we let slip until tomorrow what we should be doing today.

Try to plan your use of time, and stick to your plan.

If you have a number of things to get done, plan the most difficult or unpleasant first. You will find that getting these behind you liberates you for doing the rest.

DELEGATE

If the demands on your time are in fact greater than you have hours available, involve others. Seek out persons in your elder's district to help with visiting, and to do so in your place. Tap some suitable young adults to function as Big Brother or Sister to youngsters in need. Take care of the shut-ins through the energies of the deacons and others. Enlist your wife to do calling in your place. Leadership is getting the job done, not necessarily doing it all by yourself.

SOME FURTHER HINTS

1. Learn to use, and rely on, a pocket notebook. Relieve your memory thus of dates, appointments, needs, ideas, etc., while at the

same time you keep a record of your calls, plans, and projects.

2. Keep simple records at home. Use a file card system — a recipe box will serve very well. Keep track of the families in your district. A record of special days in their lives will remind you to send cards or to make a call. It will help you to remember names, and to keep track of those who may be drifting away. Such a file may be passed on to your successor when you retire from the active eldership.

3. Carry things through. Let your notebook and records remind you of promises made, or things left unfinished at a previous visit, etc. Find the time to finish the job!

4. Re-evaluate your time-habits occasionally. Have you fallen back into wasting precious moments? Or found new pastimes?

5. Be careful, in all this, to enslave time to your leadership, not yourself to time. Remember that order is a condition for freedom, and that good order is simply the right use of time. Enjoy your better use of this precious resource. God invests time in us so long as we live; our best use of it becomes His return on that investment.

PART II. THE EXERCISE OF LEADERSHIP

Leadership involves not only such control over yourself and the use of your time as to get your job done, but it also means the involvement of others in the callings of the Church. Leadership, seen from this perspective, is: the art of successfully achieving desired results through and with the energies of others. Leadership draws others into the common cause. This, too, is part of your responsibility — and opportunity — as elder.

Some are born with the gift of natural leadership of others, and often become successful politicians. You may, or may not, take easily to leading others. But the essentials of leadership required of the elder are accessible to you, if you prayerfully seek to master them. These essentials may be treated in the following order: planning, organization, giving direction, coordination, and control.

PLANNING

Planning is programming to achieve clearly stated results. Planning looks clear-eyed ahead. Planning sets goals, and then envisions them — tries to see in advance how they will work, what problems may arise, etc. Planning is day-dreaming with a purpose — a very good use for otherwise wasted moments!

A plan governs the use of time and energy.

Don't make the mistake of thinking that planning is required only for "big" things, like a new sanctuary or program of outreach. Plan all your work as elder. Plan your visits, your approach to problems, your evaluation of church programs, your use of other people, the Bible passage you will read, the texts you will quote, the answers you will give to likely questions. And, of course, as an eldership, plan what the Church should be doing in every aspect of its activities.

Here are some hints. Apply them, as needed, to your plans as individual elder and as member of the eldership:

1. **Gather facts and information.** Don't go into situations, if you can help it, blind or uninformed. Where applicable, learn things like these: what was done before? who were involved? what were the results? what is being done like this elsewhere?

2. **Analyze and reflect.** Consider the information you have acquired, and its effect on your plans. Be thus led to seek other information.

3. **Foresee.** Give free rein to your ideas: if **this**, then what? Keep your feet on reality, and don't go off on a guessing game — least of all as an excuse to do nothing. But try to foresee results of what you are planning to do, and how you are planning to get it done. This is a real test of good planning. Something, again, that can be done in moments otherwise wasted.

4. **Set goals and results.** What, specifically, are you planning to do, and to get done? If you have followed the previous steps, this should be easy. If it is not, then reconsider what has gone on before. Do not set goals in a vacuum, or put them out of touch with where you are and what resources you have.

5. **Consider alternate courses of action.** Reflect on all the ways open to attaining your goal. The results you achieve may depend on your alertness to several means, even detours. Weigh alternatives. Choose the best, but remain open to change if that becomes desirable.

6. **Evaluate and check.** Keep an eye on where you are, and where you are going. Be sure that what is being done moves toward the goals you have set. Be prepared to change, to pause, even to start over.

Obviously, a brief mental review of the steps outlined above will suffice for many simple tasks. But more complex objectives should be planned in writing, perhaps by sub-committee, and must be carefully mapped out. Costly and time-wasting mistakes can thus be avoided or minimized. Solicit, of course, the cooperation of God the Holy Spirit in every step of either the most simple or the most complex process.

ORGANIZING

This involves defining duties, positions, relationships, and the assignment of personnel. Organization fits people and activities together in the best ways to get work done effectively.

No matter how small the congregation, or how routine the tasks, organize you must. To say, "We do things informally here" usually can be understood to mean, "We are not very efficient, nor very effective." Organization is the only alternative to aimless drift.

The congregation requires organization in terms of duties, positions, assignments, relationships, responsibilities, evaluation. And the elder must himself organize his own work and that of all those responsible to him. Let there be organization charts for standing relationships in the Church.

There must be descriptions for all positions within the congregation, which clearly define:

1. **Relationships**: what you are responsible for
   whom you are responsible to
   who is responsible to you
   what authority you have

2. **Results**: what are the job goals?
   what are your activities?
   what are the means of evaluation?

Such a job description, or job profile, should be the product of combined thought and planning by all who are concerned, and should be subject to change when improvement is possible or redefinition is desirable.

GIVING DIRECTION

Directing is leading, supervising, motivating, delegating, and evaluating the work of those you are called to lead. The leader is actively directing when he sees to it that the efforts of each individual involved are focused on the common objective. This implies that the leader has a plan, and that all who work with him understand it. Here the presence, or absence, of a plan makes all the difference between success and failure.

The degree of vigor and initiative displayed by you as leader will infect and stimulate those working with you. Let your enthusiasm show. It will be contagious.

COORDINATION

Coordinating is that phase of directing which unifies, *in proper sequence*, the participation of a number of workers. Coordination flows out of keeping an eye on the goal and on the whole of what is being done. Here, again, proper planning in advance pays dividends. Work gets done in time, and at the right time. Energies are harmonized.

The eldership must recognize that coordination of the congregation in the achieving of goals and purposes of the Church can be frustrated by keeping a cloak of secrecy over what the elders are doing. Decisions should, so far as possible, be openly arrived at, and clearly explained to the congregation. Let there be a constant flow of information from the eldership to the people, and of reaction from the people to the eldership.

When the programs of the Church develop opposition or contention within the Church, coordination requires a resolution of such tensions. To this end we offer the following suggestions:

1. Recognize that many conflicts flow out of misunderstanding; strive to correct that.

2. Always seek an atmosphere of integrity and honesty as between the eldership and the congregation, and within the eldership and the congregation. Keep it all on the table.

3. Avoid bringing things to an either/or situation if at all possible; give all parties a way out which does not require compromise of truth or principle.

4. Be fair and objective; insist upon that from others.

5. Be a good listener, but keep talk on the subject.

6. Compromise need not involve loss of integrity or surrender of principle, if both sides can discover prejudice and stubbornness in themselves, as usually there is. Fix the attention of both on the desirable end of working together.

7. Keep the pressure on for a resolution. Assign responsibilities for other courses of action, diverting attention away from differences.

8. If the tensions mount, a committee may be appointed to bring opposite sides together. Be sure that the committee has a purpose and knows what it is; to this end, we suggest:

    a. Define the committee's goal.

    b. Be sure that it has an agenda and sticks to it.

    c. Appoint members carefully — they must be "right" for the job.

    d. Evaluate progress.

    e. Aim to get the job done and the committee disbanded.

9. The elder himself aids coordination by:

    a. Setting a good example of cooperative effort

    b. Seeking out the participation of others, even those with whom he may differ in some matters

    c. Keeping an eye on results, and exuding confidence and determination

Keeping all shoulders to the wheel, whatever the project in hand, requires constant and often self-effacing leadership. Let this characterize you.

PART III.　COMMUNICATION

Communication as used here means the meaningful exchange of words and the emotions that surround them.

Words are no doubt the most important factor in making communion possible among human beings, indeed in making us human and in getting God's work done in the world.

Here are some things to bear in mind about the sharing of thoughts and feelings by means of words:

1. Understanding only occurs when there is a common sharing in the meaning of words. Be sure that you say what you mean, and grasp what is meant by the words spoken to you. This may take some explanation and some questioning. This is especially important in visiting the family, and in dealing with matters of difference and discipline.

2. Not only what we say, but also how it is said conveys meaning.

3. Face to face conversation is less likely to lead to misunderstanding than that by phone or mail.

4. Keep your remarks simple, and keep them short.

5. Concentrate on what the other is saying. Avoid letting your mind wander, and take care not to let the words you hear fall into preconceived patterns of what you think the other believes.

6. Be able to hear, and try to understand, words critical of your own views, even of your "sacred cows" and deeply held convictions. Until you do this, communication comes to a dead end in these instances.

7. Remember that communication depends upon empathy, which is

the ability to put oneself in the shoes of another.

8. Gain a reputation for being a fair, understanding, compassionate, and trustworthy listener. It will draw people to you in times of their need.

PART IV.   MOTIVATION

Motivation is that inner force which causes the individual to release his own unique resources toward achievement. What motivates one may leave another untouched. The springs of human behavior are mysterious.

The Christian is open to appeals to obvious sources of motivation, namely his love of God and neighbor and his gratitude for free and unmerited redemption in Jesus Christ. The Church leader should be conscious of the fact that obedience can be promoted by an atmosphere or climate that motivates. The creation of such an atmosphere should be the conscious goal of preaching and of teaching in the congregation.

Comprehensive planning for the congregation coordinates the efforts of all its agencies in the motivation of obedience to the will of God, and the desire to learn more and more of His revelation.

The Church has always prized the proclamation of the Word of God as the genuinely motivating force for the true Christian life. Recent experiments and studies confirm the relation between high levels of performance in commerce and industry and the spread of information among personnel. All organizations discover the importance of spreading knowledge in terms of motivation.

Trust the preaching and the teaching of the Word to fire the congregation with a zeal for participation in the projects for which you are called to give leadership.

And then give that zeal the leadership it requires and the Church so badly needs.

PART II

KEEP WATCH OVER THE FLOCK

PART II.
"KEEP WATCH OVER THE FLOCK"

Tools for the elders' evaluation of the public worship services, including responsibility for the liturgy, preaching, prayer, praise, and special services, with some common questions discussed. Specifics for revitalizing home visiting. Being most helpful in promoting sound marriages and Christian homes, both before and after the wedding and when children come. Dealing with divorce and remarriage. Including the single parent, and child, in the Family of God. Being a resource for the unwed mother, her child, and her parents. Maintaining constructive relations with juveniles at odds with the Church. Practical ways of promoting obedience to the Word among the membership, including guidance to the elder as personal counselor. Concluding with suggestions based on Matthew 18 for healing wounds opened by the sin of one member against another.

Chapter 6.

PUBLIC WORSHIP

The Lord requires attendance at the Sunday worship services: "Forsake not the assembling of yourselves together" (Heb. 10:25). Those who obediently assemble in response to His command do not meet alone: "For where two or three are gathered in my name," the Christ declares, "there am I in the midst of them" (Matt. 18:20). It is significant that the Lord's name is, according to St. John, "Word" (Jn. 1:1). To gather in His Name, then, is to gather about His Word, the Holy Scripture. It is such gathering, to hear the Word read and preached, that identifies the true Church of Jesus Christ. And in the Holy Word the Lord is present to His own.

The elements of the Sunday worship service are together called the liturgy. Supervision of the contents of the liturgy is the heavy responsibility of the eldership. It is from the worship service as center that the Church radiates its influence into life. The strength of obedience at the center is reflected in waves of influence reaching out into the world.

To supervise well, the elder must consider carefully what each element in the liturgy is *for*. He will observe that the service may be thought of as a dialog. God speaks to man; man speaks to God — through the intermediary, usually of God's chosen ministry. The right of any element to a place in the liturgy depends upon its contribution to this dialog.

We begin by asking:

WHAT IS WORSHIP?

In the broad sense, God is worshipped whenever His commandments are obeyed: "For this is the love of God, that we keep his commandments" (I Jn. 5:3). Again: "If you love Me, you will keep My commandments" (Jn. 14:15). It is for this lifetime of daily obedience that

81

the Scriptures are given (II Tim. 3:17, "that the man of God may be complete, equipped for every good work"), and the Church is instructed to teach all believers "to do all that I have commanded you" (Matt. 28:20). All other worship is useless: "In vain do they worship Me, teaching as doctrines the precepts of men" (Matt. 15:9, quoting Is. 29:13).

The life of obedience, called the life of love in the Scriptures, depends then upon sound instruction. Such instruction constitutes the purpose of worship in the narrower sense for which the congregation gathers into Sunday services.

The Church must never suppose that the Sunday worship services are ends in themselves. Nor must it be imagined that attendance upon them, in obedience to divine command, satisfies God's demand for life-long worship. The Lord warns repeatedly in the Scriptures against hoping to substitute Sunday worship services for the worship of daily obedience:

"When you come to appear before Me, who requires of you this trampling of My courts? Bring no more vain offerings; incense is an abomination to Me. New moon and sabbath and the calling of assemblies — I cannot endure iniquity and solemn assembly....When you spread forth your hands, I will hide My eyes from you; even though you make many prayers, I will not listen; your hands are full of blood....cease to do evil, learn to do good; seek justice, correct oppression; defend the fatherless, plead for the widow" (Is. 1:12-13; 15; 16-17).

"Do not trust in these deceptive words: 'This is the temple of the Lord, the temple of the Lord.' For if you truly amend your ways and your doings, if you truly execute justice one with another....then I will let you dwell in this place...." (Jer. 7:4-5; 7).

And the Christ echoes His prophets by saying: "Not everyone who says to me, 'Lord, Lord,' shall enter the kingdom of heaven, but he who does the will of My Father who is in heaven" (Matt. 7:21).

The true worship of God, through daily exercise of love, is what life is all about. This is the teaching of the Scriptures. Constant schooling in what true worship is, and inspiration to seek after it, is what the Sunday service is all about. In your supervision of congregational life, you are responsible before God for daily worship. In your supervision of the Sunday services, you are responsible for the liturgy.

THE LITURGY

Think of liturgy as the table of contents for the Sunday service. Morning and evening liturgies may not be identical. Some services will contain one or both of the sacraments, the Lord's Supper and baptism. The test to be applied to each element of the worship service remains, however, always the same: how does this part of the service contribute to the overarching purpose for which God calls the congregation together, namely to "learn to do good" (Is. 1:17)? By putting this question, and requiring an adequate answer to it, the elder supervises the liturgy of the Sunday worship services.

THE WHOLE PERSON

Bear in mind that the life of daily obedience involves the total person: "You shall love the Lord your God with all your heart, and with all your soul, and with all your mind, and with all your strength" (Mark 12:30). Love implicates the whole believer. So will the adequate worship service. There must be, as central, the illumination of the mind through the Word read and preached. There must be also the appeal to the will, so that what enters by the ear emerges in the life. And to facilitate the transformation of Word heard into Word done, there must be appropriate firing of the emotions which are the engines of behavior. Mind, will, and feelings are laid hold of in the true worship service. The liturgy is planned to make this so.

"MOMENTS" IN THE LITURGY

The worship service moves through a series of phases, or "moments". To be aware of these, and the purpose of each, is to understand what goes on in the service as God beholds it.

In chronological order, these moments are:

1. The assembling of the congregation together. An air of order and due solemnity becomes the people of God: "All things should be done decently and in order" (I Cor. 14:40).

2. The divine greeting, called the "Salutation". God has required coming; He now greets those who have heeded His call. This greeting, like all other words of the service spoken as by God's lips to His people, is said by God's appointed servant, the ordained minister. Contents of the salutation may vary, but should take their origin from

Scripture. "Our help is from the Lord, who made heaven and earth" is derived from Psalm 121:2. The greeting may further contain blessings drawn from St. Paul's salutations in various of his letters: "Grace, mercy, and peace from God the Father and Jesus Christ our Lord" (I Tim. 1:2), and the like. The salutation combines an acknowledgment of who it is that calls the congregation to assemble, and the grace and love in which He is disposed to His people.

3. Here may begin the congregation's response to God's greeting in song, united confession of creed, union in the Lord's Prayer, or opening prayer by the minister for the people.

4. The moment of confession of shortcoming, repentance, and absolution follows:

a. The believer is led to see himself, and his weekday worship of God, in the light of God's demands upon him, as summarized in the two "great commandments" to love God above all, and his neighbor as himself (Matt. 22:36-40).

b. Humbled by the law he has not fully kept, the believer acknowledges his failure, confesses his sin, repents, and turns to God-in-Christ for his cleansing and forgiveness.

c. Liberated from the burden of failure by divine absolution pronounced from the Scriptures by the minister, the congregation rededicates itself to the weekday worship of God.

d. This rededication is given content and focus by the hearing of the divine commands as contained in the Decalog.

e. The congregation is now free to enter upon the heart of the service prepared to hear, and to will to do, the obligating Word of God.

5. The reading and preaching of the Word together constitute the fundamental mark of the true Church, and that moment in the service for which the people are primarily called together. A separate discussion of the elder's relation to the preaching appears in Chapter 12.

6. Prayer and praise intertwine among the other elements of the service. A separate section is devoted to each, below.

7. The moment of the offering, wherever placed in the liturgy, enables the believer to demonstrate his thankfulness and commitment by returning for God's use a part of all that God has given him.

8. The benediction closes the service. In words taken from the Scriptures, the minister lays God's blessing upon those now departing to do His will in weekday worship. A common benediction is that prescribed by God to Aaron and his sons for the people of Israel: "The Lord bless you and keep you: the Lord make His face to shine upon you, and be

gracious to you: the Lord lift up His countenance upon you, and give you peace" (Num. 6:24-26). Another benediction commonly used is taken from St. Paul: "The grace of the Lord Jesus Christ and the love of God and the fellowship of the Holy Spirit be with you all" ((II Cor. 13:14).

9. At those services when the sacraments of baptism or of Communion are celebrated, an appropriate form including prayer and perhaps sung or spoken praise together constitute this moment in liturgy (see Chapter 13).

The content of each moment, or element, of the liturgy is to be judged by its contribution to the purpose for which the worship service is commanded by God: "For we are His workmanship, created in Christ Jesus for good works, which God prepared beforehand, that we should walk in them" (Eph. 2:10). Bearing this principle in mind, in the light of all that has been said thus far, the elder should be able to cut through the maze of liturgies and liturgical experiments often urged upon a congregation on grounds that the people must be reached, youth must be pleased, the modern taste must be cultivated, etc. It is God who calls His people to assembly, and it is He who decides why they come and what is expected of them in and after so doing. As God's appointed overseer, the elder is responsible for how well God's purposes are carried out.

PRAYER

God speaks to the congregation through the lips of His minister. The congregation speaks to their God through the same lips, and may also address Him with united voice in the Lord's or other Scriptural prayer. The solemnity of address to the living God is cheapened by the assumption that anyone filled with emotional fervor or gifted with easy flow of words is qualified to pray for the congregation in the worship service. The Church may choose to pray in this manner at weekday prayer services. The Lord's instruction, however, to all but His ordained ministry is clear: "And when you pray, you must not be like the hypocrites; for they love to stand and pray in the synagogues and at the street corners, that they may be seen of men. Truly, I say to you, they have their reward. But when you pray, go into your room and shut the door and pray to your Father who is in secret; and your Father who sees in secret will reward you" (Matt. 6:5-6).

Congregational prayer may take four forms, some separate from others in the liturgy: a) confession and public repentance, b) praise, c) commitment and re-commitment, d) petition for aid and blessing. The reading of the Law, in both its summaries and in its form in the Ten Commandments, as noted above, sets the context for prayer of confession and repentance, of re-commitment, and petition for blessing.

Jesus goes out of His way to teach His Church how to pray (Luke 11:1-4; Matt. 6:9-13). Elders will find it worth their while to reflect on the model laid down in the Lord's Prayer as a standard by which to judge congregational prayer through the lips of the ministry. The model prayer reminds us of such things as these:

1. God is addressed as "Father," but as "our" rather than "my" Father. One Father makes all believers one family, brothers and sisters of each other.

2. "In heaven" points to the exaltation of God, and discourages chumminess and too much informality in addressing Him. The appropriate mood is one of awe, fear, respect. Father is not buddy! "Hallowed be thy name."

3. "Thy kingdom come," which is immediately explained as, "Thy will be done," becomes the first priority of the believer. Once again, it is evident for what purpose God assembles His people to pray, namely that they may be qualified and inspired to seek first His kingdom, that is the doing of His will "on earth as it is in heaven." The aim is total and absolute commitment, a standard of performance as high as heaven itself.

4. Only then does the prayer turn to congregational self-interest: "Give us this day our daily bread." Having committed themselves to getting God's will done on earth, believers may ask material blessings with which to carry out their commitment. The gifts asked for are gifts to be used in obedience, or they are not legitimately asked for at all.

5. But, obviously, not all of God's gifts are properly used toward bringing in His kingdom. The believer then is in debt for blessings given him by God but put to our selfish use: "Forgive us our debts," therefore. How else shall we ask again for blessing?

6. The ground of the believer's plea for forgiveness is the believer's own performance: "as we forgive our debtors." The Lord emphasizes this: "For if you forgive men their trespasses, your heavenly Father also will forgive you; but if you do not forgive men their trespasses, neither will your Father forgive your trespasses" (Matt. 6:14-15). He further emphasizes the same lesson in the parable of the debtor servant, who was forgiven by his master but declined to forgive those

in debt to him (Matt. 18:22-35). Forgiveness of "our debts" to God is to be passed along in kind, or will not really be received.

7. Surrounded as we are by blessing, the believer knows that he easily falls into many kinds of temptation. We may give obedience to other gods instead of the true God; and/or, we may put self-interest over concern for others. Knowing all this, we plead: "Lead us not into temptation, but deliver us from evil." No other rescue will do.

8. The prayer ends with doxology. "For thine is the kingdom...," is an expression of utter confidence that God is able to do all that has been asked of Him, indeed that He "is able to do far more abundantly than all that we ask or think" (Eph. 3:20).

The Church is never restricted to the words of the model prayer each time the congregation goes to prayer. But the alert elder will perceive in the Lord's Prayer guidelines for how, and for what, believers ought to petition the Father. Adding to these guidelines other Scriptural injunctions regarding the form and content of prayer, the elder is equipped to oversee this intimate part of the worship service.

PRAISE

Thanksgiving flows naturally from believing lips. The Psalms bubble over with praise and exaltation. So do the Epistles of the New Testament.

Undergirding praise is a subtle theology of which the elder must be aware. He may ask himself questions like these:

1. Why praise in the worship service?

Not only because the believer's life is of grace, and therefore a blessing, despite whatever hardships may encumber it, but also because praise properly identifies the source from Whom all blessings flow. God therefore requires praise: "Let all who take refuge in Thee rejoice, let them ever sing for joy" (Ps. 5:11). Again: "Sing psalms and hymns and spiritual songs with thankfulness in your hearts to God" (Col. 3:16). God, as giver of life and all that in it is, requires our acknowledgment of His beneficence in praise.

2. How praise in the worship service?

No doubt principally in song. Words, preferably chosen from the Scriptures, set to appropriate music and sung by the congregation.

And also in words read together, chanted together, recited together.

3. With what words?

Suggested above is that the words used in praise be from the Bible. Some Churches restrict singing to the Psalms, versified and set to solemn, stately music. Others permit also hymns drawn from other parts of Scripture, or reflective of the believer's experience. Our preference is for words drawn from the Bible, best of all those drawn from the Psalter. God is then adored in words inspired by His own Spirit. How better praise Him well?

4. How is praise related to the purposes of the worship service?

Praise inspires obedience. It does so in two ways: a) by acknowledging that God is the giver of all blessing, even of life itself, and is therefore fully deserving of "interest" on His investment in us, and b) because music and rhythm engage the feelings which add momentum to the will, raise courage, stimulate love.

Praise becomes in truth a pledge to obedience. God is not truly praised for all His blessings in the worship service if these blessings are not then turned to His service in weekday worship. Praise from the pew comes to testing in life.

Praise validated in obedience insures eternal possession of divine gifts. The believer, having acknowledged by praise that God is donor of life and all its gifts, gives spiritual form to his possession of material goods by using them in accord with divine commands: "Lay up for yourselves treasures in heaven, where neither moth nor rust consumes and where thieves do not break in and steal. For where your treasure is, there will be your heart also" (Matt. 6:20-21). Praise is a promissory note drawn on investments being made in heaven, or praise is noise (I Cor. 13:1).

In short, true praise depends upon self-denial: "He who does not take up his cross and follow Me is not worthy of Me" (Matt. 10:38). A self-denial which is made joyous in the praise of acknowledging God as Giver of all.

It is important that the congregation be made aware of the theology of praise, lest singing and thanksgiving become routine and, far worse, become a judgment upon those who heedlessly engage in them. The eldership is responsible for seeing to it that such cannot occur, at least not through ignorance.

SOME QUESTIONS ANSWERED

1. **How does a choir fit into the liturgy?**

Some churches reject the choir altogether on the ground that the congregation should praise God either in unison together or through the lips of the ordained ministry. This view finds no justification for a third party. Other churches believe that God must be pleased when trained voices blend in harmonious praise in the name of all His people. It may further be argued that music well performed does stimulate appropriate emotion, which is a legitimate element in the worship service as pointed out above. Between these points of view the Bible gives no clear decision, and the eldership will have to make its own determination. To be avoided, however, is the use of musical performance solely as entertainment, for this makes of the worship service an end in itself.

2. **What about visiting groups of singers? other musicians?**

In the worship service, these certainly can become a "third party" as between God and His people in *this* congregation, a third party to whom what truly liturgical role can be assigned? Encourage such groups to come before or after the formal service, on Sunday afternoons or on weekdays when truly inspirational entertainment is surely in order, but normally the service has a unity of its own built around the twin participants: God and this congregation of His people (including, of course, visitors and non-members who are joined as one with the congregation).

3. **What about organs and music not accompanied by words?**

This is an old question, generally settled now in favor of the organ and music played without accompanying words. But hidden in the long discussion of instrumental music in the Church is the ancient theory that music does convey moral feelings on its own, not all of them elevated feelings; and the belief that music can very subtly slip these feelings into the soul of the listener without his being aware of its influence. Music alone, it has long been thought, can corrupt if it is sensual, secular, sexually stimulating, depressing, and the like. At least being aware of this alerts the elder to a watchful ear as to what is played during transitions in the worship service. And those churches which forbid instrumental music are not without some grounds for so doing.

4. **Should the eldership supervise the content of music sung in the service?**

By all means. Heresy has long slipped into the Church by way of seemingly pious hymns, popular religious songs, and the like. Once again, music slips past the sentinels of the mind, carrying with it doctrines the mind on the alert might not approve. Words must be doctrinally defensible; music must be qualitatively fitting. This is the elders' responsibility. No element in the worship service is neutral in its effect upon the whole.

5. Is there a role for unordained members in the liturgy?

There is, as members of the Body. Together the Church sings, prays, makes confession, pledges obedience, reads responsively. But as individuals, there is no appropriate role for the membership in the liturgy of the worship service. How the congregation may arrange prayer meetings, special gatherings on weekdays, and the like, is the eldership's to decide. The lay individual is not appointed by God to speak for Him to the congregation, nor for the congregation to Him. This unique role is, as we have explained in Chapter 12, only by divine appointment verified by the Church. Under unusual circumstances, when no minister can be present, elders or deacons may perform ordained functions, but this is the exception. For a discussion of the priesthood of all believers, see Chapter 17.

CONCLUSION

It is important that the congregation be schooled through the preaching as to the purpose of the worship service, and the role of each element in it. Here begins the outward-reaching influence of the Church in the world. The eldership should ever be on the alert that the service be fitted to God's purposes in requiring it.

Chapter 7.

VISITING THE MEMBERSHIP

A new and appreciative look must be taken at an old practice: elders' visits to parishoners' homes: house-visiting. Experience has long shown that family visits build strong churches. Such visiting should be done on schedule, covering the congregation each year, if possible.

We consider the following aspects of house-visiting:

Why?

The Lord provides for his Body in the visiting ministry of the eldership what the secular world tries to duplicate through encounter groups and the like. The confidence, security, and togetherness which can be created by carefully planned and conducted family visiting draws the Church together into the local communion of saints — a communion all seek and one which the secular therapist cannot give.

The Word specifies the dual responsibilities of both believer and elder which come to expression in such visiting: "Obey your leaders and submit to them; for they are keeping watch over your souls, as men who will have to give account" (Heb. 13:17). Both the visited and the visitor will one day have to settle their respective accounts with the Lord, who keeps close watch over any two or three gathered in His name (Matt. 18:20).

Visiting is a part of the Church's program for schooling the believer in faith and obedience. As such it may be considered a logical extension of the Word preached.

A regular program of family visitation promises the following benefits:

1. It extends the care and supportive concern of the Church into the homes of the membership. "Therefore," writes the Apostle Paul, "encourage one another and build one another up, just as you are doing. But we beseech you, brethren, to respect those who labor among you in

the Lord and admonish you, and to esteem them very highly in love because of their work" (I Thess. 5:11-13).

2. Family visiting provides ways to determine the precise needs of the congregation, and thus give focus to preaching, diaconal assistance, teaching programs, and further attention to specific problems. Visiting takes the pulse and temperature of the Body.

3. It allows the elders to assess the people's reaction to the preaching, the teaching, and all other functions of the Church.

4. Visiting establishes a meaningful relationship between eldership and congregation apart from emergency situations, and makes handling difficulties the easier.

5. It provides a way to detect problems in the bud, and perhaps to nip them there.

Always assuming, of course, that both elder and believer take these visits as more than social occasions.

Before Visiting

It is the minister's responsibility to make family visiting most useful by preaching from time to time on its significance from a suitable Biblical text. The congregation must fully understand, and systematically be reminded of, the values for Church and member implicit in well-conducted family visiting: what they may expect from the elder, and what he may expect from them — and how the Lord is served through both. The minister may well set family visiting in the context of the key role played by the Christian family in the rearing of the young and the stability of society. Texts like the following apply: I Thess. 5:14; Heb. 12:15; I Peter 5:2.

The eldership may decide to structure family visiting around one or several themes for a given season, to be introduced by appropriate preaching. Or the visiting elders may decide to highlight a topic or topics on their visits. Some suggested themes or topics follow:

1. The Family
   a. Biblical view of the family
   b. Worshipping as a family, table devotions, singing, prayer
   c. Ways in which members relate to each other
   d. Special problems of one-parent families, and the Church's concern
   e. Working parents, absence of mother from the home, traveling father

    f. Discipline in the home

    g. Nurture of growing children, entertainment, church attendance

    h. Christian education

2. The Church

    a. Why the Church gathers to worship on Sundays, as a family

    b. The role of preaching and of listening

    c. The liturgy, what and why

    d. Participation in Church activities

    e. Financial contribution to the Church.

3. The following general subjects could be developed into similar topics:

    a. The Bible

    b. Christian growth, the Christian daily life

    c. Prayer

    d. Afflictions

    e. Special problems of youth

    f. Stewardship of goods and talents

    g. Values

    h. Faith and works

    i. Providence and human responsibility

    j. Missions and evangelism

We make these practical suggestions for the conduct of family visiting:

1. This is a team effort. Usually the minister and an elder, or two elders, constitute the visiting team. Be sure to plan matters like these: who is to take the lead in opening subjects? who will read the Word? offer prayer? close with prayer? Who makes the necessary arrangements? Who takes the initiative in leaving? Planning is the key to a good visit.

2. Make each visit a matter of prayer.

3. Ascertain in advance, if possible, what special problems or needs are likely to be encountered, and plan on response to these.

4. Know the names of all in the family, occupation, school levels, etc.

5. Be certain to be expected, with the visit pre-arranged by phone, bulletin announcements, or the like.

6. Yet, despite careful planning, avoid the "canned" rehearsed appearance. Think things through, but trust the Lord for words to speak when the visit is taking place.

During the Visit

Remember that you, as elder, go in the name of, and on errand for, the Lord of the Church. Make the visit serve Him and His Body and He will lend authority and power to your words.

Some practical suggestions for conducting the visit:

1. The Bible places high value on healthy family relationships (Eph. 6:1-4, for example). Make this, therefore, a *family* occasion, inviting both parents and children to gather 'round for this short hour.

2. Be cheerful at arrival. Wait to be invited in. Wait to be seated. People can be touchy about such things. Get off on the right foot.

3. Keep the good humor, courtesy, modesty, love all the way. Remember that children especially may dread family visiting, and must be won by sincere attention to their concerns.

4. *Work* at involving all family members in the visit. Do so with sympathy and understanding. What you do not already know about their interests and occupations, as appropriate to the purposes of your visit, try to learn — but keep the conversation aimed at spiritual realities.

5. If you intend to open with reading Scripture, select the passage before hand and bring your own Bible. Perhaps a short, crisp comment on the reading will get things going. Do not, however, start with a sermon(ette).

6. Generate discussion by avoiding questions which demand only Yes/No answers. For example, in discussing personal relationships with the Lord, tongues may be loosened by mentioning ways in which the Christian does grow in the knowledge of God: through the preaching, personal Bible study, church school, affliction, tensions, temptations, prayer, obedience.... Ask which benefits the most, and why? the least, and why? Other means of grace? Or again: rather than inquiring whether the member is enjoying the preaching (which tempts a critique of the minister — which must, of course, be dealt with in its proper setting), the elder may ask, "Why do you suppose that the Bible emphasizes preaching so much?" And, "How does one get the most out of the sermon?" And, "How might one prepare himself best to appropriate the Word preached?" This manner of approach will bring about a fruitful and often stimulating visit.

7. Let the closing prayer indicate that you have heard the needs, concerns, joys of *this* family. Pray by name for those who require this, always tactfully.

8. Don't overstay your welcome. There will be another day.

9. Decline controversy. If the family has a genuine complaint about the Church, the minister, the liturgy, hear it and promise to report to the eldership. If the matter is serious, arrange to have it aired at appropriate time and place. Avoid, also, seeming to sweep criticism under the rug, and whitewashing faults. There is no better way than that to lose credibility with the member.

10. Be aware that some member of the family might have a matter he wishes to discuss privately. Sense this. Make arrangement for it on another occasion.

After the Visit

Reflect personally on what you can learn from the visit: better ways to open, to develop discussion, to sense problems, to advise, encourage, admonish. Pray over the visit. Confess your mistakes; ask blessing on your efforts.

The eldership as a whole must turn visiting into congregational profit by:

1. Reports and discussion: strengths, weaknesses, problems real and potential among those visited since last meeting. Gifts for service in the Church discovered during the visits. Potential for wider service. The "state of mind out there" as revealed by the visiting. The spiritual level. Concerns and challenges to be met from the pulpit.

2. Reactions to the Church revealed in the visits: criticisms, just and unjust; suggestions; appreciations; pointers to new ways, higher goals.

3. Visiting techniques: an especially successful approach; one to be avoided hereafter; something to be tried again for another look.

Summary

Family visiting can be tedious and boring for visitor and visited alike. It can also be the glue that binds the congregation closer and closer together as elders and people come better and better to know and understand each other.

It all depends on you, and your solicitation of the aid of the Spirit in this important aspect of an elder's calling.

Chapter 8

MARRIAGE AND THE FAMILY

The home is the cornerstone of society. A stable and progressive society grows out of stable and creative homes.

Marriage is the foundation of the home. A stable and creative home grows out of a healthy marriage.

Christianity is the heart of a healthy marriage. Thus through the home the Church makes incalculable contribution to society. This makes marriage one of the primary concerns of the eldership.

PART A. CHALLENGE AND OPPORTUNITY

The elder must first of all envision the profound challenge set before man and woman by the divinely ordained institution of marriage. *Compared to this challenge, all other callings are more selfish and less fulfilling.* In marriage, as the Bible clearly teaches, man and woman most nearly live out the relation between Jesus Christ and His Church (as we shall see below). The Old Testament also compares God's relation to Israel, His chosen people, to that of marriage.

You must avoid the mistake of thinking of marriage as just one relationship among many, or of the home as just one institution among many. Marriage and the home are unique. To no other human institution does the Bible compare God's relation with man in the same intimate way.

Avoid also the radical feminist perspective that views marriage as hardly meriting comparison with a "career" for the liberated woman. To the contrary, success in marriage is as significant in terms of what it means to be truly (that is, Christianly) human as being a Governor or President is in terms of being a politician. True, one can be human without being married, just as one can be a politician without rising to the top; but the challenge of marriage and the home is the most exacting, and exciting, open to men and women.

ESTABLISHED AT CREATION

Marriage was instituted by God "in the beginning".

God formed man "out of the dust of the ground" (Gen. 2:7). He then formed woman out of the man's rib (Gen. 2:23). Eve was bone of Adam's bone, and flesh of Adam's flesh. No more intimate relation could have been made than was thus made, man and woman of one flesh. Small wonder that the male and the female are irresistably drawn together.

Eve was expressly made by God to be Adam's helper, associate, in the mutual obedience laid upon them by God in the Garden of Eden (Gen. 2:18). The relation between man and woman, since the beginning, is not one of superiority/inferiority, but one of headship/assistance. God established the roles in which each sex finds its fulfillment in becoming what male and female are intended to be. God sets the form in which man and woman serve Him in His world. The eldership must take care that modern movements, however widespread, do not shift the Church from the Biblical basis on which she stands.

Note that Eve was not formed from Adam's lower limbs, as if to be his servant; nor was she formed, as was one of the gods in Greek mythology, from man's head, as if to be his guiding mistress. Eve was made from the region of the heart, to love and to be loved (Gen. 2:21). And it is in love that man and woman harmonize their respective assignments in God's world and family.

Because they were made of one flesh, man and woman are said to become one flesh again in marriage (Gen. 2:24; Matt. 19:5; Eph. 5:31). St. Paul argues from this fact to the husband's unceasing obligation to love his wife: "For no one ever hates his own flesh" (Eph. 5:29). In keeping with this call "from the beginning," boy and girl, come to age of discretion, leave their parental homes, marry, and begin another home by becoming one flesh.

The great solemnity, and mystery, of marriage take root, then, from God's original creation of man and his helpmeet. No one can take marriage too seriously, and the elder must see to it that this understanding of marriage permeates the congregation and is taught from the pulpit.

ONE FLESH

Marriage reflects a oneness which is most clearly manifest in sexual union.

The act intended by God to engender new flesh is the act which binds man and woman together. This is the ground for the Lord's rejection of sexual promiscuity and adultery. While God permitted polygamy in the early history of mankind, the ideal set before us by the Bible is monogamy. And the union of flesh, through sexual intercourse, outside of marriage is forbidden. St. Paul sums up the Biblical commandment as follows: "The body is not meant for immorality, but for the Lord, and the Lord for the body . . . Do you not know that your bodies are members of Christ? Shall I therefore take members of Christ and make them members of a prostitute? Never! Do you not know that he who joins himself to a prostitute becomes one body with her? For, as it is written, 'The two shall become one' " (I Cor. 6:13;15-16).

The unity of flesh which underlies marriage is reflected in the union of sex. This union is reserved for marriage, and marriage alone. This the Church must teach, and the elders counsel, day in and day out. "For the desires of the flesh are against the Spirit, and the desires of the Spirit are against the flesh . . ." (Gal. 5:17)—and the task of the Church is to promote the desires of the Spirit, while offering understanding in love to all who fail and repent of their failure. "Go," says Christ to the adulteress, "and sin no more" (John 8:11).

CHRIST AND THE CHURCH

What, then, are the roles assigned by God to man and woman in marriage?

They are modeled by the relation between Christ and His Bride, the Church, as revealed to us most clearly in Paul's letter to the Ephesians, Chapter 5:21-33. These words should be well-known in the congregation, from constant reference, teaching, and preaching. For the sound marriage, and Christian home, are of utmost importance in our times.

The Church is the new Eve, Mother of Believers as Eve was mother of mankind. And like Eve, the Church too, has her symbolic origin in the new Adam's side. From Christ's side, as He hung on the cross, flowed out mingled blood and water after the thrust of the soldier's spear. These obviously symbolize the sacraments of the Church. Washed in the water of baptism, the believer is joined by the Spirit to Christ's Body. Fed by the living Word of God, symbolized in the sacrament of the Lord's supper and the blood which flowed from the Lord's side, the believer grows in grace and obedience. So the new Eve springs, as it were, from the place where the first Eve was taken (see, also, Chapter 13 on the Sacraments).

The relations of the new Adam, Christ, to the new Eve, the Church, become model for the relations between the Christian man and wife.

The headship of the husband is now understood as the headship of Christ over the Church. His is a headship indeed, and involves authority, too. But it is a unique headship which has nothing to do with an exercise of superiority or dictatorship or tyranny. St. Paul puts it this way: "Husbands, love your wives, as Christ loved the Church . . ." And how, then, did Christ love the Church? Paul continues, "and gave Himself up for her" (Eph. 5:25).

Marriage begins in the courtship of romantic love, the desire of one for another inherent in being, originally, of one flesh. And a marriage founded on a romantic love which endures will enjoy one of the elements of health and strength. But another love is exhibited by Christ for the Church. Not the love which demands, but the love which fulfills itself only in giving, even to the gift of life itself. This is the love required of husband for wife: "Husbands, love your wives, as Christ loved the Church . . ."

Out of such giving, such total giving of self, properly flows the headship in the family which the Lord lays upon the husband. This, too, follows the divine pattern in dealing with us. God *first* gives, and *then* exercises authority.

Notice these examples: God first creates His world, provides in it a marvelous garden, and gives all to man—and only then lays down law for man's obedience (Gen. 2:16-17). Again, God first liberates Israel from Egypt by awesome displays of His power, and leads His people to safety—and then gives Moses the Ten Laws by which Israel shall serve Him (Ex. 20; Deut. 5). Once more, God in Christ first assumes human flesh, suffers, and dies upon the cross—and then the resurrected Christ gives instruction that the Church shall teach believers to do all that He has commanded (Matt. 28:20). Always the same order: *first* the giving, and *then* the exercise of authority.

And this is the pattern which Paul lays upon male headship in marriage: first, and always, the total giving of self for the good of the

62073

family, and then the right to final decision where the welfare of the family is concerned. It is obvious that if the husband's total devotion is matched by that of the wife, the making of decisions will commonly arise by mutual agreement as to the best for the whole. The relation between the Church and her Lord is not one of constant struggle, ongoing tussle, and persistent wrangling. Rather, the more the Church realizes how much her Lord has done, and does, for her welfare, the more participation in His will becomes her joy and self-realization. So it must be in the home.

For the wife is, indeed, required to "be subject to your husband, as to the Lord" (Eph. 5:22). Why? "For the husband is the head of the wife as Christ is the head of the Church" (Eph. 5:23). Paul puts it this way in his letter to Corinth: "But I want you to understand that the head of every man is Christ, the head of the woman is her husband, and the head of Christ is God" (I Cor. 11:3). The divine order is hierarchical, not democratic.

Once again, however, in a marriage based on self-sacrificing love, like Christ's love, the wife finds her role in the family liberating, not confining. It must always be remembered that the Biblical pattern is not arbitrary. It is divinely ordained. Despite the claims of women's lib, and vocal feminism, the human being—male and female—will find true selfhood only in obedience to man's Creator and Savior. So the Church must teach, and discipline. Countless happy Christian marriages, and creative homes, testify to the divine wisdom. It is not in the Christian home that husband and wife are constantly at each other's throats. It is, rather, in those families overtaken by spirits of the age and seduced by false standards of equality. We become who we are meant to be only in strict obedience to the Lord's commands. Every effort to take "sexist" language out of Scripture, or to reduce Biblical commands to products of the writer's culture ("sitz im leben," as it is called: situation in life) doom their advocates to failure and their followers to futility.

Let the voice of the Church be heard in the wilderness of modernity: marriage is of the Lord, and as lived according to His commands will produce the strong and liberating homes upon which civilization urgently depends. Especially so when easy divorce has so much devaluated the popular understanding of what true marriage is.

THE INTRUSION OF SIN

Of course, sin intrudes upon the Christian family. There may be need for counsel and instruction. This the Church must abundantly provide, from the pulpit, in special classes, and by the counsel of the eldership. Set the goal, light the ideal, and never slacken your enthusiasm for the truly Christian home!

Admonish the husband who behaves like a ruling monarch. Admonish the wife who behaves like a rebellious child. Teach, pray, help, and never give up on the home; it is the fount of society.

We make the following suggestions for your work:

GENERAL PRINCIPLES

1. An appreciation of the high calling of marriage and home-making ought to be a part of the child's earliest instruction in the home itself. Some understanding of what building an enduring Christian home requires ought to be part of the child's upbringing. For in it he also senses his own responsibilities toward the family. In short, the quality of the next generation of Christian homes takes root in the early upbringing of boys and girls. This the Church must constantly stress: "Train up a child in the way he should go, and when he is old he will not depart from it" (Prov. 22:6). This applies also to the child's perception of what being part of a Christian home requires of—and does for—him.

2. The Church should weave instruction regarding marriage, sex, and home-making throughout its entire youth curriculum. Keep before young people the challenge of marriage, the requirements of purity, and the high calling of making the truly Christian home.

3. The pulpit should never neglect preaching about the home for long. Let the challenges and problems of family living be kept constantly before the congregation from Biblical instruction inspired for this purpose. The eldership should see to this work of the pulpit ministry.

4. Young couples who contemplate marriage should receive special attention from both ministry and eldership. The aid of Christian counsellors can be enlisted in pre-marriage classes sponsored by the Church. Let everything point to the utter seriousness with which the Church views marriage and the home.

5. Take account of the incessant pressure of the times to make sex a

passing, animal entertainment. Draw on your own experience to know just how tempting this can be. Circumstances make sexual gratification easy, and the pill has made it "safe" in a purely physical sense. Reckon, however, with the fact that God's law written upon the human conscience never quite leaves illicit sex entirely "safe". Be open to troubled young people who are tempted and need advice, or who have yielded to temptation and need counsel. They will approach you only if you admit to being human enough to understand, and loving enough to help rather than condemn. Let the Word judge, while you strive to build up courage, hope, rededication.

BEFORE THE WEDDING

We have already stressed preparation for home-making in early childhood. Now for those who are ready to contemplate marriage, try to instruct as follows:

1. Marriage belongs, not to the partners, but to God. He need not have made us as He did, but in fact the family is natural to man and without it there would be no society, and no means of raising children.

2. Marriage is, therefore, entrance upon a trust. A trust implies two parties: God and the couple. Both have an interest. To meet that mutual obligation is to succeed in this highest of all mutual callings. Constant reference, therefore, is to be made, not to self-interest or self-will, but to God's interest and His commands for the Christian life. Focus concern "out" rather than "in" and self-realization will come to both partners as a precious by-product. Implied in the trust-relationship is a final accounting. Those who take marriage upon themselves must one day give account of their stewardship. They can do this only if they marry in the determination to draw their strength from the Lord, through His Word and in the Church.

3. Be sure that the young couple understands the principles of marriage expounded especially by St. Paul in Ephesians 5, and discussed above.

4. Be alert to the problems likely to arise from marriages involving mixed faiths. Be sure that the couple understands the obligations laid by the Catholic Church, for example, upon the raising of children in the case of Protestant-Catholic marriage partners. The time to face such issues is before the wedding.

5. Still more, bear in mind St. Paul's admonition: "Do not be mismated with unbelievers. For what partnership have righteousness

103

and iniquity? Or what fellowship has light with darkness? What accord has Christ with Belial? Or what has a believer in common with an unbeliever?" (II Cor. 6:14-15). Love sometimes stimulates the believing would-be partner to suppose that the unbelieving one can be "converted" after the marriage takes place. Experience suggests that this is not necessarily so, and the Bible expressly forbids such marriages. Here great caution and understanding are required. Undertake to instruct the unbeliever, showing by your own love what the Church offers. Be sure, however, that a "conversion" is genuine. If true love is present, the couple will undergo the delay to achieve the better marriage in the end.

6. Marriage is forever. Christ says: "So they are no longer two but one. What therefore God has joined together, let no man put asunder" (Matt. 19:6). "No man" includes, of course, the marriage partners themselves. And the Lord goes on to warn, that "whoever divorces his wife, except for unchastity, and marries another, commits adultery; and he who marries a divorced woman commits adultery with her" (Matt. 19:9). This follows from the nature of marriage itself, and must be carefully contemplated by those who plan on undertaking its exciting challenge.

7. The couple must realize that romantic love is not sufficient to make marriage successful. There must be, from the beginning, the self-sacrificial love displayed by Christ for His Church, and the self-denying love required of the Church for her Lord. True marriage sustains true love by practicing it. The home grows on love, as love is displayed in the true home. Often it must be by act of will, running counter to emotion, that the marriage move ahead. And the persons involved must learn to distinguish between love as "feeling" and love as "commitment". Christ did not enjoy His incarnation; He did it out of His deep will-to-love. Marriage will not be all peaches and cream; the family grows out of obedient commitment to the roles given by God to each parent.

8. Explore with the couple their concepts of money management, of time usage, of roles outside the home, of raising children. On the one hand, all this cannot be settled in advance; on the other hand, at least the means of coming to such decisions ought to be explored. The use of money will be especially likely to cause difficulties. What lifestyle does each expect? Who will handle the family income? On what priorities?

9. The elder must bear in mind that, in fact, he is often better able to

discuss these matters with the young couple than is anyone else. He stands outside the pressures from friends and families, and yet he represents the larger family of God whose love must surround the family now being planned.

10. Remember, too, that the channels of communication, and mutual trust, now being opened between the young couple and you as representative of the Church must be so inviting, so sincere, and so understanding, that after the wedding you, and the Church, will be thought of as familiar friends. You, too must love!

AFTER THE WEDDING

Life is learned by living. So is marriage. And the Church, through you, should reveal its continuing interest in the newly-weds' progress. Telephone, drop by, send a note or card. Be available. Become a kind of "Big Brother" to the newly founded families in your district, not to interfere or to offer unwanted advice, but just to show the interest which love knows how to take without becoming a nuisance. The good which such interest may do might not be known to you until the Judgment Day.

Here are some suggestions:

1. Recommend open communication between husband and wife. Many problems start and grow because they remain beneath the surface of the marriage. Some persons speak up much more readily than others, but it is often just the reticent who should air their thoughts. Encourage the couple to talk over problems before they fester. Something put into words is already partially resolved.

2. Remind them, as occasion arises, of St. Paul's admonition: "Let not the sun go down upon your wrath" (Eph. 4:26). Tempers will flare. Try to put the fire out the very same day. Refuse to retire angry.

3. Emphasize the importance of family devotions, and the usefulness of having these at stated times. In these the couple consciously invites the Lord to share their development of a Christian home. Bible reading and prayer, at stated times, contribute much to Christian growth.

4. Stress this matter of *growth*! The Word is given us, St. Paul writes, that we may be "equipped for every good work" (II Tim. 3:17). This means that what the Word requires us to do, we try to do — at once. If God asks prayer, then pray; if praise, then sing; if giving, then give. Read the Word to grow by it. Such ought to be your counsel to everyone: "Man does not live by bread alone, but by every word that proceeds out of the mouth of the Lord" (Deut. 8:3; Matt. 4:4).

5. Relate the couple to the Church. By your interest, let them know that they can use the Church, can count on the Church, can call on the Church in all kinds of need. And be sure that they find in the congregation the welcome and help, if needed, and invitations to use their talents which will give balance to their family. Urge upon the new family the necessity of contribution to the support of the Church, both financially and by attendance and participation. Encourage them to feel, at once, a part of the Body, and to work at being a vital part of it. We feel wanted, often, where we want to be. Be sure that the ministry frequently reminds the Church of its obligations as family to families.

WHEN CHILDREN COME

The home rounds out in the arrival and raising of children.

The life of the child falls into merging periods: babyhood, young childhood, early schooling, adolescence.

The earliest years are thought by some students of childhood to be the most important years for pointing the child to the way of the Lord. The early years are trying years, especially for the young mother. Her burdens seem more than doubled when the first baby arrives. How she manages a second and third, besides, as the years hasten by, only God the Spirit fully knows.

Mother, then, needs encourgement in patience, ability to see the developing adult in the demanding baby she must so much care for. Father needs inducement to share in household tasks he may not think his own. Care of the child should be the concern of both parents — though just what division of labor and responsibility prevails is theirs to work out.

Your interest as elder is in the child's early exposure to prayer, to praise, to evidence of faith, to acquaintance with Jesus as companion and Lord. What the child retains from family devotions he seems too young to understand may surprise the parent later on. Love is more readily caught than taught, and the parents' behavior toward each other, as well as toward the child, registers deep in the fledgling's soul.

In short, the elder and the Church are deeply concerned that the child be raised in a "Christian" home, where the Lord and His Word are daily companions. Bible stories, hymns and psalms, sturdy faith and loving conversation and behavior are to the child's soul what good food, cleanliness, and adequate shelter are to his growth in body.

We believe in early attendance upon worship services. How long the child should go to nursery, if provided; how long to youth "church," if provided: these are matters for the parents and the congregation to have solid views on. We believe that when the child can attend regular worship services without creating disturbance, he should be there, with his family. Do not be too ready to say sermons are "over his head," or prayer "doesn't mean anything to him yet," or "it's too long a time for sitting still," and the like. For generations children sat through far longer services than are today common, and came to adolescence and adulthood with knowledge and sense of piety we well might envy.

EDUCATION

Do not hasten children off to nursery school unless you know what for, should be, we believe, the elder's sage advice.

No school can provide what the companionship of mother provides, nor give the individual attention she can give. The mother who chooses work outside the home in exchange for sending her children off to nursery school makes, except in cases of absolute necessity, a poor bargain. She robs the child to enrich her husband and herself — and the robbery is spiritual while the enrichment is only material. The Lord does not thank a parent for giving things in exchange for companionship and love.

When school age arrives, let the choice be carefully made. It is desirable, indeed indispensable, that the values held high in the home not be undermined in the classroom. This may imply the choice of Christian or parochial school. The Church should share, when necessary, in the added expense this involves.

The eldership should be fully acquainted with the value systems and philosophy of life implied by what goes on in all the classrooms which children of the Church attend. Know, and discuss together, what passes for "education" in your community. And let your voice be heard, and your weight be felt, where false values and mistaken views govern the upbringing of children. Do not be bluffed out of the arena of public education by cries for the "separation of Church and state". This separation can be fully honored, institutionally, without removing religion from public life and schooling. Decline to let Truth be pushed aside just because the state, rightly, does not support one faith over another. The Truth of the Decalog, for instance, is not only religious; it is inherent in the nature of man, and is written on every conscience. Honesty, not religion, testifies to this. Do battle to secularism where it tries to govern the spiritual growth of the child, getting wherever you can a fair and objective hearing for what religion means in human life and history.

Meanwhile, support Christian alternatives in schooling, and you should join the struggle — in our opinion — to avoid "double taxation" of Christian parents by seeking tax support of religious schools, strings-free.

ADOLESCENCE

The paths of youth are beset with thickets of temptation. The world's standards enter the home via communications media. Peer pressure to do what everybody does falls heavy upon the young. To go with the crowd seems almost mandatory, into sex, alcohol, drugs, and other dissipations. No one is immune. Often Christian families deeply burdened with their children's problems prefer to keep silent about them. The elder must try to penetrate this protective facade for the benefit of home, child, and Church.

An alert eldership discovers what goes on among youth, and especially among the Church's youth. You need not yourself plumb depravity to its myriad forms, nor indulge temptations as such. You need only keep an eye and ear open to learn what the world is like, and how that world impinges insidiously upon the lives of the young. Discuss as an eldership what today's "youth culture" is. Get accurate information from police and other sources as to the extent of alcohol and drug abuse in your community. *Know* your city or town! It's where your young people are growing up!

Then discipline yourself to meet your youth with understanding, and in genuine love. School yourself to be firm without being censorious. It will do no good to nag, or to threaten. No use saying, "Now, when I was young...." No one cares. Your only reliance is on the Word, and the Spirit who applies the Word.

We make these suggestions (see also Chapter 14):

1. Looking back from the problems posed by adolescence, parents can see very plainly their missed opportunities when the children were young. There's no use in your saying, "I told you so," but you can use the temptations of today's adolescents in your counseling of the

parents of very young children: prepare them, now, for the day and the hour of need!

2. Be sure that the pulpit draws, too, out of the day's subtle temptations of youth for stress upon keeping the Christian home sound and healthy. Face parents who give almost all attention to "getting" with the question: what are you doing, now, to create the kind of warm and loving home that raises children against the day of the beast?

3. Be early with your own interest in the young. Try thus to avoid picking up, later, the tearful pieces.

4. Be certain that everyone in the congregation perceives, and is constantly reminded from the pulpit, that children are the gift of God, and that raising them in His fear is the awesome reponsibility of home, school, and Church. Discourage all family arrangements which remove the mother, even only part time, from the home. Father and mother together must know, and behave as if they fully recognized, that the child is God's most precious gift — and responsibility — that the family can receive.

5. Bear in mind principles like these:

a. Children learn by example. Parents must themselves be models of the kind of integrity, honesty, fairness, patience, and love which they hope their children will learn. There is no substitute for doing what you say, being what you want the child to be.

b. Parents must work at developing in the child a due respect for God and His commandments, and an understanding of the role of Christ and of His Spirit in helping them obey.

c. Parents must be consistent in the treatment of the child, and in treating all of their children fairly. Differences in treatment, due to differences among the children, must be explained and understood, so none will think the parent partial or prejudiced.

d. Maintain family discipline firmly in love. Require respect and obedience and participation in family duties.

e. Expect, with understanding, the child's sharing some responsibilities for the running of the home.

f. Let punishment, when necessary, be swift and just.

g. Teach due respect for money without stressing materialism over spiritual values.

h. Encourage the development in each child of his own devotional life.

i. Always remember that as God loves us, so we must love others, especially those whom He gives to parents for upbringing.

Marriage is the highest adventure in self-realization given to man.

Raising children is the noblest calling set by God before us, as families and as Family of God.

Set all of the problems and heartaches which marriage and child-rearing occasion in the light of His Word, surrounded by prayer. There is no other way.

PART B.   DIVORCE AND REMARRIAGE

DIVORCE

The Lord forbids divorce: "What therefore God has joined together, let no man put asunder" (Matt. 19:6).

But divorce occurs at a steadily increasing rate, not only outside the Church but also within the fellowship. The Church is obliged, therefore, to deal with divorced parents. In doing so, the elder must constantly remind himself that divorce is not unique among sins. The Lord forbids sinning altogether, and commands perfection of His disciples: "You, therefore, must be perfect, as your heavenly Father is perfect" (Matt. 5:48).

Yet sin mars the life of each Christian, who finds himself more and more saying with St. Paul, "Jesus Christ came into the world to save sinners, of whom I am chief" (I Tim. 1:15). This does not mean that the Church therefore accepts sinfulness, let alone glosses it over or ignores it. The Church deals with sinners patiently and in love, seeking always the consciousness of sin, the need of repentance, and the will to reform and go forward in obedience.

The elder who represents the Church in dealing with divorced persons must always remember that he, too, requires constant forgiveness for, and persistent reformation of, his many failings.

In this frame of mind, deal with the divorced in the light of these suggestions: (we are using the term *divorcee* for either husband or wife)

1. Divorce is often a shattering personal experience. No matter how much blame the one party lays upon the other, each endures some sense of personal failure and loss of self-esteem. Questions like these nag constantly: what might be wrong with me? Could I have done more to avoid the rupture? Were the faults which I found unbearable in the other somehow reflections of faults within me? Even if the other partner broke the marriage by sexual infidelity, might I have driven

him or her to that extreme by coldness or indifference? Was I too busy with things outside the home? Too involved with the children?

2. These and like unanswerable questions may plague the divorcee's mind. And there are, besides, the numbing memories of the tensions leading up to the split, and of the divorce proceedings; the lost friendships, the alienated in-laws, and fears concerning the children's ability to accept things as they are, or their preferring the other partner.

3. If you foolishly suppose that these emotional hangovers can be dispensed with in a visit or two, you should leave the handling of the divorcee to someone else. Building a bridge back into society, and into the congregation, will take much patience and a long time. Expect to be received coolly, and kept at some distance until you can make very plain in attitude, word, and deed that the Church comes through you to understand and to help, not to condemn and find fault. Read for yourself from time to time the account of Jesus and the woman taken in adultery (Jn. 8:1-10) when the temptation to sit in judgment upon the divorced overcomes you.

4. If there are children in the broken home, refer to the Section which follows, "The Single Parent".

5. Enlist the aid and interest of others in the divorcee's broken life, and be sure that the minister visits regularly.

6. Try to interest the divorcee in Church activities, beginning with regular attendance at worship services. But do not be discouraged if such interest is at first sporadic and irregular. It takes time for the divorcee to discover whether or not the congregation is in fact ready to accept him or her, and can exchange greetings without a critical and judgmental look. This is a test of the congregation's ability to love, and this they should be made to understand — in regard, of course, to all who have obviously failed in any of many ways.

7. Inquire into the financial stability of the home, especially if the divorcee is a mother and the children are young. Perhaps diaconal aid is required. Perhaps legal advice is necessary as to alimony payments and child support. Find out for yourself what the community offers victims of the broken home.

8. Be patient. The scars of divorce go very deep, for what was one flesh has been rudely divided. The healing of mind and spirit will be long in coming, and may never be fully accomplished. Try to keep the divorcee's eye and mind fixed upward on the understanding, loving, and forgiving Lord, who Himself says, "I came not to call the righteous but sinners" (Matt. 9:13). Help the divorcee to seek His constant

companionship through His inspired Word.

9. Be persistent. Don't take your first success as winning the battle. Keep an eye on the family, and on its integration into the congregation. We too quickly forget sorrows which may only be glossed over in public. Stay around, even if only to be available on call. Be a place to come to, and respond when that occurs.

10. Obviously, all this is more than a one person job. The congregation must embrace the broken ones, and this must be stimulated by constant instruction from the pulpit. The Church must be prepared to handle crises long before they arise. Seeing to that is an important part of your responsibilities.

AND REMARRIAGE

Handling the realities of divorce becomes doubly complicated for the Church when a divorcee once again falls in love and contemplates remarriage "in the Lord".

The Church is confronted by the plain teaching of Jesus: "I say unto you that every one who divorces his wife, except on the ground of unchastity, makes her an adulteress; and whoever marries a divorced woman commits adultery" (Matt. 5:32). And the commandment is without exception: "You shall not commit adultery" (Ex. 20:14).

When sexual infidelity has disrupted a marriage, the innocent party may remarry without adultery.

But if the divorce has not been based upon marital infidelity, and in the case of the adulterous partner, remarriage would result in violation of the seventh commandment for both partners to the new marriage.

This teaching of Scripture has always confronted the Church with grave decisions. Is there room in the household of God for the remarriage of divorcees guilty of severing the living flesh of a previous marriage? Or should the Church advise the victims of divorce to choose the hard way of celibacy, referred to by our Lord when He says, "There are eunuchs who have made themselves eunuchs for the sake of the kingdom of heaven. He who is able to receive this, let him receive it" (Matt. 19:12)?

The Lord implies that there are some who cannot so control their sexual passions as to live the celibate life; and St. Paul writes: "But if they cannot exercise self-control, they should marry. For it is better to marry than to be aflame with passion" (I Cor. 7:9). And though the Apostle's reference here is not specifically to the divorced, the Church will find the description apt also to many of them.

What then?

We make these suggestions:

1. Discover the official position of your own denomination on the re-marriage of divorced persons, especially of those guilty of disrupting the previous union. It is your duty to teach and to practice these guide-lines. If your denomination has taken no position, or if your congrega-tion is not bound by the presbyterial system, the eldership must come to a common mind.

2. Remember, in dealing with remarriage, that an act of marital in-fidelity does not, often, break a marriage. This means that the wound caused by the sin of adultery can be healed, and a marriage continued. And this suggests that the sin of adultery which does break one mar-riage can be healed in another. Do not be too quick to speak of the re-marriage of divorced persons as "continuous adultery". Consider, rather, that the former sin can be confessed, repented of, and left behind in a good remarriage.

3. Remember, further, that only one sin is unforgivable, and that is the mysterious sin against the Holy Spirit (Matt. 12:31). Those who have fallen against the seventh commandment, and who have even destroyed a marriage bond by so doing, can find forgiveness. Having done so, to the satisfaction of the Church, the best advice some of them could be given might well be to contract another marriage relation-ship, all the better schooled by the past to make this one succeed.

4. Experience abundantly teaches that remarriage by divorced persons can be richly blessed, and can provide a genuinely Christian home for raising both the children half-orphaned by divorce and those given by God to the new family.

5. If, then, it is the decision of the eldership to endorse the remar-riage, be sure:

a. That the partners to the new contract recognize and repent of sins that led to the previous breakdown, and will be especially alert to avoiding them hereafter.

b. That both partners know complete forgiveness, and enter upon the new relationship with their souls eased of the guilt of past failure. Let them "marry in the Lord" in full expectation of His blessing.

c. That both are fully committed to the self-sacrifice required to make marriage succeed.

d. That the new family intends to become an active and living

113

part of the Church, and that the Church is so prepared to receive them.

6. Stay close to the new family. Be sure it is warmly received into the Church. Let them know that you are always as close as the telephone and as interested as the ruling elder should be.

7. As you struggle with this whole complicated problem, do not ask more of others than you demand of yourself. Different persons fall into temptation to different sins. Some are victims to their passions, others to greed, and still others to pride. Divorce often revolves around yielding to passion, even to lust. Grievous as such sin is, and awful as its consequences can be in the home and upon the children, it is no more to be censured than other violations of the law, and its victims are to be loved no less. It was Paul himself who cried out, "I do not understand my own actions. For I do not do what I want, but I do the very thing I hate." What then? He looks above and beyond himself, "Who will deliver me from this body of death? Thanks be to God through Jesus Christ our Lord!" (Rom. 7:15; 24-25). So may it be for those who, wiser and sadder, try marriage for a second, or even a third, time. Bear with them in His strength!

PART C. THE SINGLE PARENT

The family is sometimes spoken of as a "circle". The symbolism points to the security, solidarity, protective character of the closed group.

Sometimes this circle is shattered, from within by death or from without by divorce. The single parent is left with the care of home and children. The Church must make special effort to understand and minister to such single parent families.

Take note:

1. In the absence of the mother, the heart of the family is gone. Children naturally lean more heavily on the mother than on the father, and find in her an awareness of their needs and moods which many fathers lack. There is, really, no replacement for mother, even by remarriage, but the Church can help by providing child care, hired assistance, warm meals on occasion, and time out of the house for the children in summer and on weekends. The elder should keep in touch with the home, giving or finding help when needed.

2. In the absence of the father, financial problems may loom, the male strength is lacking, and the mother is obliged to discipline entirely on her own. The deacons should be alerted to financial needs,

care for the children should somehow be shared, and the mother should know that loving concern is always as close as the phone.

SPECIFIC SUGGESTIONS

1. First of all, recognize the potential need. The single parent family often presents a brave front. The children seem to be growing happily. And the Spirit often does provide against the missing adult member by drawing the others in the family closer together. But be alert for needs, and especially crises, behind the scenes.

2. Have the Church consider a "Big Brother" and "Big Sister" program, one in which adults, *on schedule* provide escorts for the children to sporting events, parties, entertainment, the beach, etc.

3. Support the single parent, especially the mother, in handling discipline by talking with her and encouraging her in love. The single parent needs the child's affection, and often hesitates to risk that by requiring obedience against the child's initial resistance. Try to help bridge the gap between parent and child if this becomes serious.

4. Alert the single parent against too much compensation for discipline, or loneliness, by way of material gifts to the children. Evidence of love there must be, also in gifts and things; but the child must not be raised to measure all affection in terms of goodies.

5. There may be real economic hardships in this kind of family, especially if the mother is left alone and not well provided for by insurance or alimony. Try in every way to keep the mother in the home if the children are young, enlisting the diaconate and civic agencies in support of the family. If the children are older, help secure at least part-time work for the mother. Be prepared to find financial assistance in the children's education, especially higher education, if that becomes necessary.

6. By your concern, and that of the Church, counter as much as possible the inevitable loneliness of the single parent. Counsel against hasty decisions, unwise friendships, escape entertainment. Let the love of the Church, shown by you and those of the Body whom you can interest in the home, balance off the temptations of unwisdom and emptiness.

7. In homes broken by divorce, look for conscious, or more often unconscious, efforts by the remaining parent to encourage dislike of the missing one. Even where this seems merited, caution against it, for it will give the remaining parent a bad image in the mind of the child,

and may encourage the other parent to retaliate during permitted visiting periods. Bygones are bygones, so far as the broken family is concerned, and best left that way.

8. Try always to fix eyes forward in the broken home: "But this one thing I do, forgetting those things which are behind, and reaching forth unto those things which are before, I press toward the mark for the prize of the high calling of God in Christ Jesus" (Phil. 3:13-14).

PART D. THE UNWED MOTHER

Violation of the seventh commandment becomes public with the pregnancy of the unmarried woman. As soon as this pregnancy is known, the elder has obligations to carry out, assuming this is a Church family.

1. Resist advice for abortion. Be sceptical even of medical or psychological advice to terminate the pregnancy. Even if your congregation, or denomination, or you yourself are not wholly in the "pro-life" movement, consider that the Lord has His ways in these matters, too, and the longterm effects of abortion upon the mother may leave her forever saddled with guilt.

2. Be cautious about advising a hasty marriage. Be sure that:

   a. There is genuine love upon which to base a home.

   b. There is sufficient potential for maturity to anticipate a good home.

   c. There is some financial base upon which a home can be sustained. Lacking any of these conditions, a marriage might be far worse that the life of the unwed mother, both for her and for the child.

3. Be cautious about recommending immediate adoption after birth. Much here depends upon the mother's parents, and her own attitudes and maturity. If there is parental support, and the mother can foresee the restraints upon her freedom imposed by child care, keeping the baby is best for all involved. There is rarely as profound a relationship as that between parent and natural child.

4. On the other hand, be careful not to commit mother and child to the whim of grandparents who, at first, delight in the thought of another baby in their home, while the mother will want her freedom and the child may outwear his welcome. Then, it may be, immediate adoption is in order.

5. If the parents are bitterly at odds with the whole thing, holding their daughter as little better than á prostitute, you have a twofold

task:

a. Reconciliation of parents and child, along the lines that all of us do sin, all require forgiveness daily, and the parents continue in sin if they are unforgiving while the child's sin is behind her.

b. Realistically, the attitude of the parents also enters into the question of adoption. Only if the Church will assume support responsibilities should you unconditionally advise keeping the baby.

6. The adoption question is complicated by the doctrine of the covenant. If the baby is being born into a Christian home, the covenant line holds. And both mother and grandparents may feel obliged to carry out their covenant commitments by raising the child after the Lord's commandments. Some adoption agencies, however, guarantee placement in Christian homes, and both grandparents and parents can then exercise their responsibility by support of the Church and of agencies for Christian education and social welfare. The covenant is not lost through adoption. The promise of the Lord holds sure. But those who are most intimately concerned must make up their minds as to their duties here. Help them as best you can. This can be the hardest element in the whole matter.

7. The unwed mother has her own concerns over the attitude of the Church toward her and her sin. Make clear that sin can be repented of, and forgiven. After this, there remains no real barrier between the Church, on the one hand, and mother and baby on the other. You must then help bridge the gap. You must see to it that all members of the congregation do so, too: "Who are you to pass judgment on the servant of another? It is before his own master that he stands or falls. And he will be upheld, for the Master is able to make him stand . . . Then let us no more pass judgment on one another, but rather decide never to put a stumbling block or hindrance in the way of a brother" (Rom. 14:4;13).

8. This means that after reconciliation with the Church through repentance, the mother should present the baby for baptism if the child is retained by her, and if she by reason of membership is eligible to do so.

9. The road of the unwed mother, and of her child, is not easy, even though single-parenting of this sort grows more common. Keep in touch. Pray. Love!

PART E. DIFFICULT MEETINGS

It may happen that the eldership as a body meets with the juvenile at odds with the church. The future of that youth's relation to the people of God may hinge upon the wisdom, under grace, of your handling the situation.

We recommend:

1. Your goal: "Do not be overcome by evil, but overcome evil with good" (Rom. 12:21). There is nothing the Devil hopes for more than that this young person leaves your meeting humiliated, embittered, mumbling hotly to himself of "hypocrites".

2. To outwit the Devil in such instances, seek first of all to understand what has been going on in the mind of the young person alienated from the Church. Listen. Inquire gently. Encourage frank expression, even if it involves criticism of the Church, of the ministry, of yourselves, of you. Accept in advance the fact of universal imperfection, also in the handling of this matter so far.

3. Avoid, on the one hand, implying your superior holiness. You are not called to compare your behavior with that of the person before you. You are trying to understand, and cure, his delinquency, whatever it be.

4. Avoid, on the other hand, foolishly trying to get onto his wave length. Don't suggest that you would naturally be on drugs, indulging in fornication, disobeying parents, getting into difficulty with the law—all if you were young today, as is he. He will detect you for a phony. You are you, and he is he; and you have to go from there.

5. Having tried very sincerely to discover, and to understand in his terms, what makes him "tick," your task is firmly to set the requirements of the Lord against his behavior. Your aim is not to humiliate, but if necessary it is to humble. Your aim is not to embarrass, but it is to bring to confession of guilt and repentance. But if this is to be done well, time may have to elapse between the first interview and the turning to correction. Perhaps the eldership needs time to try to see into the delinquent's lifestyle and problems and pressures before change can even be suggested.

6. Do not be pressured into hasty action by some who argue that the Church's reputation is at stake, tongues are wagging, everybody is wondering, what will people say, etc., etc. Do the right and your congregation's reputation will take care of itself, especially in heaven where the truth is fully known.

7. If there be a delay between interviews, appoint a committee or the delinquent's district elder to keep in touch with the erring one, and to be sure that he attends the next scheduled interview.

8. Consider how long it has taken the Lord to get you to where you are on the ladder of perfection, and be prepared to suffer along with someone who may now be where once you were.

9. Begin each session which deals with delinquencies with the reading of I Corinthians 13, especially noting: "Love is patient and kind . . . Love does not insist on its own way; it is not irritable or resentful . . . Love bears all things, believes all things, hopes all things, endures all things . . ." (I Cor. 13:4;5;7). Remember that if the delinquent does not experience firm but understanding love in the eldership of the Church, he will be at a loss as to where to find it; and the Devil, coming as an angel of light, will seduce him with counterfeit affection.

10. Always bear in mind that the confrontation which will win the day must be between the Word of the Lord and the delinquent, not between the elders and the youth, nor between you and his faults. Let the Word stand forth, garbed as it is in sacrificial love, and pray that through it the Lord will work His will with you as willing instrument.

11. Remember personally in prayer, at every elders' meeting, those delinquents whose cases are pending before the body.

Chapter 9

PROMOTING OBEDIENCE

PART A. FRUITS OF OBEDIENCE

The teaching Church never graduates her pupils. Education under the preaching of the Word continues all the believer's life. The Church's goal never changes: "that we may present every man mature in Christ" (Col. 1:28). This is the Church's pedagogical task. Its oversight is the primary responsibility of the eldership.

Maturation in Christ is always a combination of hearing and doing, of doctrine and life, of Word and obedience. Truth enters by way of ear and eye, is received in the soil of faith, and bears fruit in countless acts of love. The Word leaves God through inspired revelation and returns to God in the form of obedient living, the cycle for which it is sent thus made complete.

God instructs His people from the pulpit. Preaching His Word is, therefore, first mark of the true Church.

Overseeing the pulpit, and working alongside it, the eldership is assigned the task of promoting congregational obedience: "Exhort one another every day, as long as it is called today, that none of you may be hardened by the deceitfulness of sin" (Heb. 3:13).

The elders further carry out their assignment through regular family visiting, care for the sick and elderly shut-ins, and general supervision of the Body.

OVERSIGHT FOR OBEDIENCE

The elder will note that St. Paul, as himself an overseer of the Church, does not begin his epistles with outright appeals for good works. His practical suggestions conclude his letters. He begins with instruction in sound doctrine, and thus confirms an already established Biblical principle: good works flow from sure knowledge. The path to sound living runs through sound doctrine. The Bible itself achieves the goal of its revealed teaching in obedient behavior: "All Scripture is inspired by God . . . that the man of God may be complete, equipped for every good work" (II Tim. 3:16-17).

The Church schools the believer in doing good works because this is why redemption is given: "For we are His workmanship, created in Christ Jesus for good works, which God prepared beforehand, that we should walk in them" (Eph. 2:10).

Obedience, then, roots in knowledge of the Scriptures. The elder's first concern is that the congregation *know* the Word. Lacking such knowledge, trying to do good works would be like trying to make bricks without straw. Appeal to will and emotion waits upon approach to the head.

KNOWLEDGE

What the believer must know is summarized in the creeds and confessions of the Church. Here begins the road which leads through the strait gate and along the narrow way to life eternal (Matt. 7:14).

The way pointed out by the Commandments begins with the knowledge that, "I am the Lord your God, who brought you out of the land of Egypt, out of the house of bondage . . ." (Ex. 20:2). The parallel passage in the New Testament, the Great Commission, begins with the knowledge that through Christ the believer is still rescued from Egyptian bondage to the world, the self, and the Devil: "Go, therefore, and make disciples of all nations . . ." (Matt. 28:19). Men are discipled by instruction in revealed doctrine: the knowledge of God as Creator and Sustainer, and the world as His; the knowledge of Jesus Christ as Redeemer, and the believer as His; the knowledge of the Holy Spirit as active Agent, applying God's work in Christ to the believer's redemption through faith working in obedience.

CONDUCT

God leaves no doubt as to what are the good works He saves the believer to do. They are defined negatively in the Decalog, and positively in the two great commandments which each summarize one table of the Decalog. One sentence summaries of God's will are given by the Prophet Micah: "He has showed you, O man, what is good; and

122

what does the Lord require of you but to do justice, and to love kindness, and to walk humbly with your God?" (6:8), and by the Lord Himself: "So whatever you wish that men would do to you, do so to them; for this is the law and the prophets" (Matt. 7:12).

The Bible is itself inspired commentary upon the will of God for man thus summarized in the Law written with His own finger on tablets of stone. Congregational obedience to the teaching of the Scriptures is the elder's abiding concern. It is what the Bible means by "love".

IN PRACTICE

Scriptural teaching on the life of love is far too abundant to outline here, but some pointers may be taken from the Word, as follows:

1. As touching humility, the believer is not to think of himself more highly than he ought to think, but with all lowliness of mind to think others better than himself (Rom. 12:3; Phil. 2:3). The poor and unknown are to be as highly esteemed as the rich and powerful (Rom. 12:16; Jas. 2:1-4).

2. As touching human relations, the believer is to live peaceably with all men so far as possible, give no grounds for offense, and believers are to live at peace with one another (Rom. 12:18; II Cor. 6:3; Heb. 12:14).

3. As touching love, believers are to bless their enemies, make prayers and supplications for all men, and must be tenderhearted, forgiving one another as Christ forgives them (Matt. 5:44; I Tim. 2:1; Eph. 4:32).

4. As touching purity, believers must let the presence of Christ stand guard over their thoughts, meditate on elevated themes, let no corrupt words or foolish talk proceed from their mouths, and hate even to touch what is tarnished by sensuality (Phil. 4:7-8; Eph. 4:29; Jude 23).

5. As touching joy and contentment, the congregation is to give thanks continually, to joy in God through the Lord Jesus Christ, to rejoice in the hope of His coming, and to be content in whatever state providence assigns them (Rom. 8:28; Phil. 4:4-6,11).

6. As touching their deportment, Christians are to live blamelessly before the world so that their good deeds will not be evil spoken of; they are to be epistles of Christ, known and read of all men (Rom. 12:17; 14:16; II Cor. 3:2).

7. As touching their words, they should speak evil of no man nor

123

bring a railing accusation against any. They should be at all times ready to believe the best of every person. They should be ready to hear, slow to speak (Titus 3:2; Jude 9; I Cor. 13:7; Jas. 1:19).

8. As touching temperance and self-control, they must not obey the dictates of the flesh. They should have appetite and passion under control at all times and be temperate in all things lawful (I Cor. 9:25-27; Rom. 8:12).

9. As touching good works, they are to be zealous in their practice, doing good works to all men, especially those of the household of faith (Gal. 6:9; Titus 2:14).

The diligent elder, schooled from the pulpit by the diligent pastor, knows that the Scripture also contains countless practical instructions for parents, children, employers, employees (master, servants), preachers, elders, listeners, rich, poor, husbands, wives, rulers, subjects—for every calling and situation.

The path to eternal life is so plainly marked that no one need guess about anything pertaining to the life of holiness and thankfulness. Posting these markings is the task of the Church, under oversight of the eldership.

The justification in Christ which is the heart of the gospel works in the justified by faith, and out of its working emerges the life of thankful obedience to the commands of the Lord. So intimate is the connection between gospel and obedience, that both St. Paul and St. Peter speak of divine judgment against those who "obey not the gospel" (II Thess. 1:8; I Pet. 4:17).

PART B. THE ELDER AS COUNSELOR

You, as an elder, are inevitably a counselor.

Your efforts to encourage godly living will encounter many Christians bogged down in family and marriage problems, or beset by anxieties, insecurity, wrong priorities, self-centeredness, etc., etc. Cure must be preceded by counsel.

This brings the elder face-to-face with the immense claims and pretensions of the counseling industry. For such it is, an industry reaping profits in wealth and prestige for a professional clique. Until he has examined the largely hollow "front" of this industry, the elder is apt to feel himself incompetent to counsel. This is a serious mistake. It is the elder, and not the secular counselor, who is given the key to mental health and personal growth. Bear these things in mind:

1. Widespread confusion reigns in the counseling industry. There is no consensus as to what is: mental health, mental illness, normality, the goals of life, and how these goals are to be sought. Trial and error are rampant in secular counseling, while counselees pay through the nose at one office after another.

2. Despite its many forms—sensitivity sessions, T-groups, psychoanalysis, dialog, sex therapies, etc.—secular counseling is frequently ineffective. The patient may get the advice he wants to hear; may find simply a well-paid listener; generally effects such cure as occurs on his own. Considering the resources the secular counselor brings to his work, as noted below, this low rate of "cure" is not all that surprising. Reflect on it. Check with those who have undergone "therapy," and see the results. Count, for example, marriages "saved" against marriages broken, often on the advice of the counselor.

3. The love, concern, and practical experience as a Christian which the elder brings to counseling are themselves the highest, and indispensable, qualifications for constructive advice. These qualifications are yours. Stand on them, and let no one bluff you with college or university degree, diploma, foreign languages, etc.

4. You know that it is the Word of God rather than the words of psychiatry which bring light ("The entrance of thy words gives light" Ps. 119:130), and spiritual healing ("Speak the word, and my servant will be healed" Luke 7:7), new birth ("He cried with a loud voice, 'Lazarus, come forth!' and the dead man came out . . ." Jn. 11:43-44), and guidance to right living ("Thy word is a lamp to my feet . . ." Ps. 119:105). Be prepared to bring this Word to the solution of the counseling problems you encounter, and God is prepared to do the rest: "My word that goes forth from my mouth . . . shall accomplish that which I purpose, and prosper in the thing for which I sent it" (Is. 55:11). Recognize secular counseling for what it is: an attempted substitute for the Word.

5. It is well to acquaint yourself with trends in secular counseling. Briefly, there are three main streams and innumerable cultisms:

   a. *Psychoanalysis:* exploration of the counselee's past to account for his behavior, feelings, attitudes. By surfacing things long forgotten, the psychoanalyst hopes to "liberate" the "patient" from their influence. Chief name here is Sigmund Freud, who divided the personality into three facets: the *id,* or hidden drives and suppressed desires; the *ego,* or conscious self who lives and acts; the *super-ego,* or conscience, which suppresses the *id,* sets impossible goals, inspires

125

guilt and anxiety. By transferring his guilt to the *id*, for which he is not responsible, the "patient" achieves liberation from restraint, anxiety, frustration. This is the theory.

b. *Behaviorial therapies:* designed to reinforce socially desirable conduct and discourage undesirable conduct by way of punishment, reward, fitting human behavior into the categories of cause/effect science—on the assumption that persons are controlled, and can be modified, by scientifically discovered techniques. Chief name here is that of B.F. Skinner, who teaches that if man surrenders the illusions of freedom and dignity, he can be molded through behavior-modifying techniques into whatever society wants man to be. The future of mankind depends, for these theorists, upon the application of science to biological evolution.

c. *Humanistic therapies:* assuming that the counselee must effect his own cure, these techniques rely upon dialog, sensitivity sessions, encounter groups for bringing to the surface all of the client's inner drives, hates, loves, desires where he may behold them through the eyes of others, and change accordingly. Leading names here are: Rogers, Maslow, May.

d. *Fringe groups:* of all kinds, offering release of all inhibitions, cure of all hang-ups, and so on.

The hold that the counseling industry has upon the public will not be broken overnight. One obvious reason is that secular counseling relieves the "patient" of responsibility for his behavior. He is "ill". What "mental illness" makes him do can hardly be his fault. Moreover, his "cure" may involve further indulgence of desire, passion, hatred, egotism. With these things going for it, the counseling industry has a bright future. Only those who have seen it from the inside and experienced its emptiness can fully estimate its threat to society. And from there the elder can learn the power and validity of counseling from the Word in contrast.

WHY COUNSEL?

1. Just as the hungry man can hardly hear the Gospel for the rumbling in his stomach, so the burdened counselee needs advice before admonition. The problems of life take up so much spiritual space as to leave little room for truth, unless that truth be first focused on the problems. Counseling clears the inner eye to perceive redeeming truth.

126

2. Counsel because the Church must also be the communion of saints, that is a sharing of one another's burdens (Gal. 6:2). Sometimes burdens may be so personal and so private and so devastating that only the eye of the elder can be exposed to them. But if the elder's ear is deaf, the sufferer may well drift into the counseling industry.

3. Counsel because thus you encounter at first hand the dark shadows cast by the Devil in the world. You will be driven to the only effective antidote against the Devil's inroads, the living Word of the living God.

HOW COUNSEL?

1. Listen. Listen with all your heart. The lure of humanistic counseling lies in its being "client-centered," that is, being willing to listen. Speech is man's unique gift from God. Just to formulate problems in words is already the beginning of therapy. So, listen, patiently and long.

2. Avoid snap judgment. Generally avoid judgment altogether: "Judge not, that you be not judged" (Matt. 7:1); "Who are you to pass judgment on the servant of another?" (Rom. 14:4). Learn from the Lord Himself to avoid hasty judgment (Jn. 12:47-50). As you enter into the Word with the counselee, let the Scripture expose and condemn fault and weakness, for you too are not without sin.

3. Keep certain guiding principles in mind, bringing them out as you sense the appropriate time, like these:

a. To be truly human, one must accept full responsibility for his own behavior. Only machines are subject to cause and effect. You do the counselee no favor by helping him dodge such responsibility. On the contrary, the beginning of therapy is acceptance of personal responsibility for the counselee's own role in the creation of his problems. Help him get his own behavior out of any cause-and-effect cycle. Choice is his. Responsibility is his.

b. The faults of others do not excuse our own. The Golden Rule is not, do to others as they do to you, but do to others as you would have them do to you (Matt. 7:12). Where the counselee's problems arise from neglect of this divinely inspired advice, try to help him understand this.

c. With an understanding of one's own responsibilities and faults comes the call to confession and repentance—confession to God, if not to the elder, and the choice of God, rather than self, as Master. Here

127

emerges the importance of acknowledging personal responsibility for behavior: God can forgive only those transgressions we confess as our own. So long as the counselee blames others for his misbehavior, he has no sins to confess and God, therefore, none to forgive. Which leaves him in his plight.

d. Instead, therefore, of exploring the counselee's past, sex life, childhood frustrations, current angers and resentments, the elder will concentrate his attention upon developing the counselee's understanding of his own situation before God and His Law. Rather than fix his eye inward, upon self and feelings and past, the elder fixes the counselee's eye outward, on the healing Word of God. Introspection is only pseudo-therapy. Lasting cure is to be had only at the hand of the Lord.

e. There may indeed be circumstances in the counselee's life, at home or at work or in school or among friends and acquaintances that do need correction, that do contribute to misbehavior. Express your understanding of these. Resolve to correct what you can, or what others can. Bring the attention of the eldership to bear, when possible, on these matters. But all this, while very important in maintaining the confidence of the counselee, does not detract from his personal responsibility for reaction to them.

f. Finally, conduct depends upon belief. As we believe, so we act. The elder must, therefore, try to instruct the counselee in the fundamentals of the Christian faith. These are the basis of every believer's life, and the problems of counselees simply stress their importance.

Chapter 10.

SIN AND RESTORATION

When Christians violate one of the Commandments in relations with each other, the one who breaks God's law sins against his brother. The sin may be intentional; it may be as by accident. The sin, in the eyes of the doer may not seem a fault at all. Frequently the wrong-doer has to be shown from the Scripture that he is guilty of sin.

Sin brought Christ to the cross. He therefore takes sin within His Church very seriously, and requires the Church through the eldership to do the same. Sin injects poison into the bloodstream of love. Sin when public, reflects shame upon the Church. Jesus deals very specifically with the confession, repentance, and if possible restitution which sin involves. The Church, acting through the eldership, is obliged to carry out His instructions.

THE MANDATE

Christ deals with the sin of one against another from two points of view: 1)that of the wrong-doer, and 2) that of the wronged.

1. To the wrong-doer, Christ says: "If you are offering your gift at the altar, and there remember that your brother has something against you, leave your gift and go, first be reconciled to your brother, and then come and offer your gift" (Matt. 5:23-24). This teaching is from the Sermon on the Mount which is the code of behavior required of the redeemed. It echoes the voice of the prophets who persistently teach that God rejects the worship of unclean hands (Is. 1:12-17; Is. 58:1-14; Jer. 22:13-17, etc.). Observe that the obligation is laid upon anyone whose brother even thinks him guilty of wrong-doing: "that your brother has something against you...". First clear that up, perhaps by showing the brother that in fact you did him no ill. Then come to the worship service, and strive once more to serve God every

129

day. The Church's role here is to make the Lord's demand well-known in the congregation. The eldership must see to that.

2. To the wronged, Christ says: "If your brother sins against you, go and tell him his fault, between you and him alone. If he listens to you, you have gained your brother." The one who thinks he has been wronged must confront the wrong-doer, personally and alone. This is not an option among Christians; it is a command. Wrongs may not fester; grudges may not be developed; gossip is forbidden: "Go and tell him his fault, between you and him alone." How much internal tension and alienation would be avoided if this were done, and at once! The Church must be taught this, and reminded of it. Elders see to that!

"But if he does not listen, take one or two others with you, that every word may be confirmed by the evidence of two or three witnesses." These others may already be acquainted with the situation, may have observed the wrong-doing. They may be elders or deacons. They may be mutual friends. The intent is two-fold: 1) to persuade the wrong-doer that indeed he did sin against his brother, and 2) to verify later, if necessary, just what was said, and how. Again, the opportunity to ease tensions in the Church, to draw off poison from its inner life, to liberate the wrong-doer and the wronged from the grip of sin and bitterness. Be sure the congregation knows that this second step is also the command of its Lord. Sin within the Body must be rooted out as quickly as possible: "Therefore, putting away falsehood, let every one speak the truth with his neighbor, for we are members one of another. Be angry, but do not sin; do not let the sun go down on your anger, and give no opportunity to the devil" (Eph. 4:25-26). Only the Adversary is served by reconciliation delayed, by grievances gnawing at the soul.

"If he refuses to listen to them, tell it to the Church; and if he refuses to listen even to the Church, let him be to you as a Gentile and a tax collector" (Matt. 18:15-17). Now the eldership is fully involved as binding arbitrator. A tension within the Church is now brought before the Church, as represented in the eldership, to be rooted out. The Body must be cleansed, an obstacle to growth removed. This is obviously the extreme step. It must be preceded by strenuous efforts to effect reconciliation: "tell it to the Church" is not only to convey information but to enlist the Church's authority in effecting correction of the fault through acknowledgment, repentance, restitution if possible. Evil triumphs when it generates more evil in reaction; it is overcome only by good (Rom. 12:21). Such victory is the aim of the Church, and is the goal of the eldership as they become involved in the sin of one brother against another. If all efforts fail, however, excommunication is required. The sinner is to be expelled from the fellowship, as alien to the Body as the Gentile was to the Jew, as the Roman tax-collector was to Israel.

1. *The ground:* refusal to acknowledge a fault and, therefore, to repent. It is not for the sin itself that expulsion from the fellowship occurs; all members sin, against God if not always against each other. Excommunication is the awesome judgment passed upon the unrepentant.

2. *The reality:* "Truly I say to you, whatever you bind on earth shall be bound in heaven, and whatever you loose on earth shall be loosed in heaven" (Matt. 18:18). In a time when one can move from one congregation to another, and be "saved" by countless gospel crusaders, the force of excommunication is easily obscured. But the Lord's Word is sure. What a congregation, through its eldership "binds" on earth shall be "bound in heaven". The excommunicant who ignores this solemn promise may flee to other "prophets," but will find their assurances as false as those condemned by the true Prophets: "They have healed the wound of my people lightly, saying, 'Peace, peace,' when there is no peace" (Jer. 6:14; 8:11). Again: "Because, yea, because they have misled my people, saying, 'Peace,' when there is no peace; and because, when the people build a wall, these prophets daub it with whitewash; say to those who daub it with whitewash that it shall fall" (Ezek. 13:10-11). The congregation must be instructed in the Church's awesome responsibility, and the binding authority which goes along with it. Nor is excommunication at odds with love. It is the exercise of love because to love the Lord is to obey Him: "And this is love, that we walk after his commandments" (II John 6). Flight to another communion from excommunication is not, therefore, from un-love *to* love. It is a flight *from* love, approved only by false prophets, and condemned by the Lord.

3. *The purpose:* the restoration of the erring one to fellowship with the Lord through fellowship in His Body: "As many as I love, I rebuke and chasten; be zealous therefore and repent" (Rev. 3:19). St. Paul writes to Timothy: "By rejecting conscience, certain persons have made shipwreck of their faith, among them Hymenaeus and Alexander, whom I have delivered to Satan that they may learn not to blaspheme" (I Tim. 1:19-20). Rejection finds its goal in re-acceptance. Re-acceptance comes by way of confession, repentance, and if possible

131

restitution.

4. *The process:* the steps involved in excommunication will be specified in your denomination's Church Order or congregational handbook. Usually there are these: 1) the imposition of "silent censure," in which the member is advised not to partake of Communion nor participate in official functions of the congregation, like the congregational meeting. 2) If no amendment follows, the congregation is notified that a member (unnamed) is under silent censure, and asked to pray for his reconciliation. 3) If no amendment then ensues, the congregation is informed of the member's name, and prayer once more solicited — and made in the worship service. 4) If all this fails, announcement is made to the Body of the deletion from its fellowship of the erring one. Once more ardent prayer is made, and the eldership solicits members in joining them in keeping contact with the errant person.

PRACTICAL SUGGESTIONS

When the charge of wronging another comes before the eldership, these steps should be followed:

1. A committee of two or three elders is assigned to visit those involved. They explain the role the Church must now take in the matter. They seek to learn all relevant information and report it back to the eldership. The first of these tasks will be all the easier if the eldership has been faithful in requiring the pulpit to teach the congregation what is implied by the Church's responsibility for members' behavior toward each other. The second — getting all the facts — is indispensable to rendering a fair judgment. Acute interest in all the circumstances indicates to the participants that the Church takes its responsibility in great earnest.

2. The information reported by the committee of two or three is discussed by the whole eldership. If questions remain, or arise, they must be satisfied by further contact with one or both of the parties. They may be invited to meet with the eldership in person to explain their sides of the matter. No decision can be made before each elder is fully satisfied that all relevant material is before him.

3. The eldership must reach a decision as to the guilt or innocence of the one charged with wrong.

4. A conference is now arranged with the appropriate party: a) with the guilty, if such is the determination; b) with the wronged if his charge is not sustained. The intent is restoration. The Bible must be brought to bear in pointing the way through acknowledgment, confession, repentance, and restoration of fellowship. Teaching and prayer characterize this meeting. In parting, the committee should encourage the member to contact them to make the next step toward reconciliation.

5. If such contact does not occur, the committee arranges another visit. Once again there is instruction, admonition, prayer: "Brethren, if a man is overtaken in any trespass, you who are spiritually minded should restore him in a spirit of gentleness. Look to yourself, lest you too be tempted" (Gal. 6:1).

6. In all these contacts, the emphasis falls upon acknowledgment and repentance, rather than upon the original fault itself — unless the member continues to live in sin.

7. If no change occurs, the eldership will move to the first step in excommunication, the imposition of "silent censure". This must be communicated personally to the member involved. These steps will be found useful:

a. Read some verses from the Scriptures which convey the utter seriousness of the matter: "If he refuses to listen to the Church, let him be to you as a Gentile and a tax collector" (Matt. 18:17). "Obey your leaders and submit to them; for they are keeping watch over your souls, as men who will have to give account" (Heb. 13:17).

b. Point out that the decision of the eldership focuses not, first of all on the offense but on refusal to acknowledge and repent. The elders represent the Church, not the aggrieved party.

c. Read the decision of the eldership. Encourage acceptance. Offer prayer if possible. Be prepared to accept anger and recrimination without reply in kind.

d. Inform the member of the impending step if he declines to repent: "As for those who persist in sin, rebuke them in the presence of all, so that the rest may stand in fear" (I Tim. 5:20). Keep open the opportunity, if possible, for further visits before this last step is taken.

e. If all fails, full and public excommunication must take place. Even thereafter the elder's rule must be St. Paul's: "Do not look upon him as an enemy, but warn him as a brother" (II Thess. 3:15).

BEAR IN MIND

1. Discipline visits should be made by two or three elders: "Any

charge must be sustained by the evidence of two or three witnesses" (II Cor. 13:1).

2. The minister wisely does not participate in these visits, in order that the member may turn to him for counsel and advice. As minister of the Word, the pastor may well exert effective influence upon the member's decision to take the elders' advice.

3. If possible, visits should be by prior appointment. If none can be made, they may be unannounced.

4. All involved must be much in personal and corporate prayer for the success of their efforts, and the doing of justice in what may be very complicated differences of view and opinion.

GENERAL DISCIPLINE

Christians not only remain all their lives in Christ's school, but their beliefs and lifestyle are disciplined by His Word. The scope of the Church's guardianship is broader than sins of one member against another as discussed above. Errors in belief are reflected by faults or shortcomings in behavior. The Church therefore disciplines its members' faith. The procedure will be the same as outlined earlier. Matthew 18 applies to the Church's handling of known or suspected deviations in doctrine: 1) the charge is first discussed by the eldership, however it becomes known; 2) a committee is appointed to call on the presumed offender to ascertain if his views are as supposed, and if so to acquaint him with the elders' judgment on these views; 3) he is invited to appear before the eldership for a discussion of the differences between them; 4) if the eldership continues to hold the members's views as in error according to Scripture and creed, he is called upon to repent of his error; 5) if he declines, then after further effort at instruction, steps toward excommunication must be initiated. Complete unanimity of doctrinal views is unlikely, even in one congregation. The eldership must distinguish between differences which can be permitted and those which require correction or discipline. Best guide to these latter beliefs are the Church's official confessions. Membership in the Church is through confession. His membership is questionable who cannot wholeheartedly subscribe to the Confessions such membership implies.

Violations of the Commandments, private or public, require discipline — in the manner already indicated. Once again, the perfect life is beyond the reach of everyone. The eldership must decide what behavior requires admonition and discipline. Elders must remember that discipline is one of the marks of the true Church, a mark not clearly displayed by many congregations in these times. Failure here is itself a sin which the Church herself must repent of.

Always bear in mind that sin, or fault, or shortcoming is first of all disloyalty to God. Fresh from his sin with Bathsheba (II Sam. 11-12:25), David writes: "Against Thee, Thee only, have I sinned, and done that which is evil in thy sight..." (Ps. 51:4). His sin against man was in fact sin against God. So, too, the prodigal son confesses to his father: "Father, I have sinned against heaven and before you" (Luke 15:21). The congregation must learn from the pulpit that sin has always this vertical dimension, and is therefore subject to discipline by the Lord's Body through His appointed eldership.

Church and elders themselves fall under divine disfavor when they confine discipline to select sins while ignoring violations of divine command by those who may be wealthy or powerful: "My brethren, show no partiality as you hold the faith of our Lord Jesus Christ, the Lord of glory," writes St. James, and goes on to condemn preference for the rich over the poor (Jas. 2:1-7). And the inspired Apostle warns the Church: "But if you show partiality, you commit sin, and are convicted by the law as transgressors" (Jas. 2:9). He here echoes God's instruction to the people of Israel: "You shall do no injustice in judgment; you shall not be partial to the poor or defer to the great, but in righteousness shall you judge your neighbor" (Lev. 19:15).

The Church is on the lookout for sin because the sinner marches to a different drummer than do the obedient. To "repent" is to find this out, and adjust one's step to the rhythm of divine law. Sin robs the Body of witness. Sin robs the believer of peace. Sin robs the pulpit of power. Sin, that is, which is persisted in, which is not acknowledged, repented of, and put behind the sinner. It is to this end that the eldership must take its call to exercise discipline with utmost seriousness, an attitude prescribed by the Scriptures.

PART III

CHOSEN BY THE SPIRIT

PART III

"OF WHICH THE HOLY SPIRIT HAS MADE YOU GUARDIANS"

The elder holds an office he did not institute in a Body not his own. The Holy Spirit appoints to this challenging and awesome opportunity, and how such appointment can be most effectively facilitated in the local congregation.

Chapter 11.

BY DIVINE APPOINTMENT

Any office has its author-ity from its author. In a democracy political office has its authority from the people; they create and fill that office by way of constitution and political process. The people author the office, give its holder his authority, and require an accounting of his stewardship.

'Tis not so in the Church.''

The Author of the office of elder in the Church is God. Elders have their author-ity, therefore, from Him. They exercise their authority effectively only in conformity to His Word. God holds them accountable to Himself. All this we have already drawn from the Scriptures.

GOD FILLS THE OFFICE

The Ephesian elders to whom Paul was speaking were no doubt appointed by himself, or may have been elected from a slate of nominees chosen by the Apostle. Each man now hearing Paul's voice vividly remembers when his name was added to the roll of that great company chosen across the centuries, from the dawn of Israel's history, of elder-leaders of the people of God. A company in which you who read these lines as elder or elder-designate are also now enrolled by name. Your office was not authored by man, nor created only yesterday.

But to those elders of Ephesus who remember their appointment through Paul's hand, the inspired Apostle now says: "God the Holy Spirit made you guardians." Clearly, he goes out of his way to stress two things: a) he, Paul, was only the means, while God was the active Agent in their appointment; and b) God in a very specific sense, as "God the Holy Spirit".

So then. So now.

The means to your selection as elder was election by the congregation. The active Agent in your selection was God Himself. He not only ordained the office of eldership, He fills it.

Paul stresses "God the Holy Spirit" to impress upon the mind of all elders an awesome truth. Yours is not only an office instituted by God long ago; you now occupy that office by the active and efficient working of God then and there in your selection.

God is tri-une, three Persons in one — and one Person in three. When the Bible speaks of God as Father, the stress is on God as creator and sustainer of all that is and will be. When the Bible speaks of God the Son, the stress is on God as Savior and Redeemer of His people. And when the Bible speaks of God as Holy Spirit, the stress is on God's governing activity and dynamic energy in all that happens in His creation, including human history. God was thus active, Paul is stressing, in the appointment of just those men before him, and not others, to the eldership of Ephesus. And God was no less present and active in your selection to this same office in your congregation. The Author of the office, and the Author of your occupying it, are one and the same: the Triune God! Keep this awesome truth ever in your mind, on your heart, and before your conscience.

GOD REQUIRES THE OFFICE

Certain truths follow from what has been said so far:

1. God the Holy Spirit is administratively active in the Church through the eldership. God uses the office He has established and filled to effect His will for order in the local congregation and the Church at large. The eldership is God's board of directors in the Church, His means for channeling the active power of His Spirit administratively into the Body. Good order is not by accident. It is effected through an eldership conscious of its Author-ity and responsibility to the Word.

2. Churches which have no eldership lack God's instituted means for effecting His administrative will. Such churches will evidence either the looseness of everyone's going his own way, or the domination of one or a few strong-willed members or charismatic "leaders".

3. The eldership is the administrative hub of the congregation, and, through classes and synods, of the Church at large. This means that *all* congregational activities fall under jurisdiction of the eldership. They are appointed to oversee the Church in action and obedience. And

through them the Spirit chooses to energize the Body in corporate action. To evade the elders' supervision is to avoid the Spirit's participation. Clubs, groups, the choir, classes in doctrine, societies, and the like must all seek the blessing of the elders' supervision.

4. The eldership is not responsible to the congregation as a politician is to his constituency. The elders have their author-ity from God, not the congregation. To God's will as revealed in His Word the eldership is alone responsible. But of course to such responsibility the congregation may call their elders both by word and in prayer.

5. The health and effectiveness of the Church in the world will be in large measure dependent upon the dedication, courage, and perseverance of the eldership. As goes the elder, so goes the Church.

GOD SETS THE QUALIFICATIONS

It is not surprising that for the office He has instituted God sets the qualifications for admission and retention there. These qualifications are explicit in His Word. The congregation must bear them in mind in acting as the means through whom God selects His overseers. The elder-candidate must bear them in mind as he contemplates a call to stand for election or appointment to this office.

The demands laid by the Scriptures upon all Christians are laid also upon the eldership — both teaching and ruling. Through Paul's letters to Timothy and to Titus, however, the Lord sets down specific requirements for appointment either as teaching (preaching) or ruling elder. You will notice that in his first letter to Timothy, Paul speaks of the elder as "bishop," that is, as overseer:

"The saying is sure: If any one aspires to the office of bishop, he desires a noble task. Now a bishop must be above reproach, the husband of one wife, temperate, sensible, dignified, hospitable, an apt teacher, no drunkard, not violent but gentle, not quarrelsome, and no lover of money. He must manage his own household well, keeping his children submissive and respectful in every way; for if a man does not know how to manage his own household, how can he care for God's church? He must not be a recent convert, or he may be puffed up with conceit and fall into condemnation of the devil; moreover he must be well thought of by outsiders, or he may fall into reproach and the snare of the devil" (I Tim. 3:1-7).

Observe that, in writing to Titus, the inspired Apostle uses the terms "elder" and "bishop" interchangeably, as we have observed

143

before:

"This is why I left you at Crete, that you might amend what was defective, and appoint elders in every town as I directed you, if any man is blameless, the husband of one wife, and his children are believers and not open to the charge of being profligate or insubordinate. For a bishop, as God's steward, must be blameless; he must not be arrogant or quick-tempered or a drunkard or violent or greedy for gain, but hospitable, a lover of goodness, master of himself, upright, holy, and self-controlled; he must hold firm to the sure word as taught, so that he may be able to give instruction in sound doctrine and also to confute those who contradict it" (Titus 1:5-9).

These are high qualifications. They set guidlines for the congregation in the nomination and choice of elders; they set guidelines for the eldership in setting goals for their own conduct.

The elder must avoid, here, both a false pride and a mistaken humility:

1. *A false pride:* do not too quickly suppose that your appointment by the Spirit, through the congregation, to your high office endorses all your behavior as fully in accord with the Spirit's requirements. What the Lord sees in you is the aspiration to become, year by year, more of what He expects His elders to be — this is why He gives the guidelines. What the Spirit inspired Paul to set down regarding the elder serves as a measure for mutual watchfulness by the eldership, and by the congregation. You will serve the Lord and His Church best so long as you recognize that, in meeting His standards, you have not arrived but are on the way. God will bless that attitude.

2. *A mistaken humility:* do not refuse nomination to the eldership if, in the judgment of the congregation you merit that honor, by letting Paul's high measure of the office discourage you. Recall the comfort of the Psalmist: "As a father pities his children, so the Lord pities those who fear Him. For He knows our frame; He remembers that we are dust" (Ps. 103:13-14). He has observed in you the will to do His will, not the perfect doing of it. So long as your aspiration is to be, as best you can, what the Lord requires of stewards in His Church, do not hesitate to take this office, even though you may know, as perhaps others do not, of your shortcomings.

PROFILE OF THE ELDER

We draw the following profile of what the elder ought to seek to be from the prescription given above:

1. The elder is to be male. This qualification is under attack in many quarters. Paul is accused of writing under the cultural influence of his times, when, it is said, women were considered inferior to men. We point out, however, that in fact it was common for women to be priestesses in the pagan religions of Paul's time, and he was, therefore, rather opposing custom than obedient to it. It is said that the churches now neglect other instructions of Paul's, like women's wearing veils (I Cor. 11:10) or leaving their hair uncut (I Cor. 11:15), and why, then, still respect Paul's limiting of the eldership to men? We point out that disobedience to one requirement affords no valid grounds for disobedience to another, and that Paul anchors his teaching on male headship in the Church in creation (I Cor. 11:8-9; I Tim. 2:13), in the fall (I Tim. 2:14), and in the relation of Christ to His Church (Eph. 5:22-24). And Peter supports the same teaching of male headship in the Church with reference to Sarah's obedience to Abraham (I Pet. 3:6; Gen. 18:12). There can be no doubt, finally, that in the passages quoted from St. Paul the Holy Spirit expressly allots the office of elder to men, for only they can be husbands.

2. The elder must be mature, and not a new convert. He must be describable by terms like these: temperate, sensible, dignified, hospitable, gentle, generous, not a victim to drink or greed or bad temper.

3. Some demonstrated ability to manage a family well. He who serves the Lord well as head of his own household thus commends himself as likely to serve the Lord well as one of the leaders of the Household of God.

4. The elder must be apt to teach. This qualification applies most emphatically to the teaching or preaching elder. This is his primary task. But the ruling elders should also share in the instructional program of the Church, though some will be more gifted than others for the classroom. In any case, the elder should so well acquaint himself with sound Christian doctrine that he can obey the command: "Always be prepared to make a defense to any one who calls you to account for the hope that is in you, yet do it with gentleness and reverence" (I Pet. 3:15).

5. Good reputation. It is desirable that the elder be well thought of in his community, with a reputation for honest dealing, openness to others, respect for those who differ, participation in community affairs. This does not imply that the elder has a repute for running

with every wind that blows, never standing for anything controversial. It only means that, by God's standards, the elder is entitled to be well thought of among men.

PREPARATION FOR THE ELDERSHIP

The Church requires preparation of its teaching elders. In this the Church does well.

But the Church should also concern herself with the preparation for office of her ruling elders. This concern is long past due. We think of options like the following:

1. Allow up to a year between election and installation of the elder. During this time he can thoughtfully prepare for his term of service. He may observe eldership meetings; accompany experienced elders on calls and visits; be invited to study problems confronting the congregation and denomination; attend sessions of broader assemblies; work his way through manuals like this one; be diligent in the study of the Scriptures and the Confessions.

2. Seminars and conferences on the eldership and its functions should be organized by congregations and classes or presbyteries or districts. Evening courses might be offered by Bible colleges and other instructional institutions.

3. An elders' newsletter might be circulated in a given area, edited by an experienced elder, perhaps one in retirement from his vocation. It could deal with issues before the Church, with special problems in oversight of the Church and ways to handle them, with stories of successful methods in training the youth, and accounts of challenges to sound doctrine, etc.

Courses and guidebooks to witnessing for Christ abound. The Church should give equal concern to training those who lead the Body into which converts come.

ON CHOOSING YOUR ELDERS

The whole congregation has a vital interest in the selection of both the teaching and ruling elders. The choice of teaching elder, or minister, is governed by congregational or denominational regulations. We make the following suggestions for the choice of ruling elder:

1. The nomination must be carefully made by whatever body is

entrusted with this responsibility, the session, consistory, council, board....

2. While reluctance to serve as elder must sometimes be overcome, if possible, by challenging the proposed candidate to this high service, nominees should normally be willing, when requested, to stand. It may be, however, that highly qualified candidates are modestly unaware of their talents; encourage such to accept nomination.

3. Paul advises, "Know them which labor among you, and are over you" (I Thess. 5:12). This suggests that sufficient time must elapse between the announcement of nominations for the eldership and their election to office. The congregation has a right to know how each man stands on issues before the Church at the time. A profile in a newsletter would be helpful, giving details of the nominee's background, education, vocation, family, interests, etc.

4. A slate of possible nominees might be presented to the congregation for the selection of the final list of nominations from which, later, the elders shall be elected. In this manner, the people are involved from the first in the selection of their leaders.

5. There is reason to believe that elders in the early Church were accorded life tenure. Just as, it appears, ministers were wedded to one congregation for life. There are those who hold for life tenure for the eldership today. The Bible gives no specific direction. The options are obvious:

　　a. Highly qualified elders should serve as long as possible, growing in wisdom and usefulness.

　　b. Rotation, however, does relieve the Church of the burden of less qualified elders, and opens the office to others who might be better servants.

　　c. Even the most gifted do begin to display the weakness of age if life lasts long. Will they know when they should take inactive status?

We assume that your congregation or denomination already has a policy, as to tenure, and we see no strong reason for advocating its change.

PART IV

FEEDING THE CHURCH

PART IV

"TO FEED THE CHURCH OF THE LORD"

The elders' responsibility and ability for oversight of the primary mark of the true Church — preaching the Word. Awareness of the disciplines of congregation and text in sermon preparation and delivery. Getting and keeping a strong ministry. Exercising some influence upon theological education. The nature and administration of the sacraments of Holy Communion and Baptism, with some questions posed and answered. Practical suggestions for the elders' taking a responsible role in the Church's schooling of her youth. An awareness of the temptations thrust upon modern adolescents, including homosexuality. A series of detailed guides to visiting the aged and using the skills of the retired, to calling on the sick, the dying, the bereaved. Ministry to the families of the mentally retarded, and how to stand with the mentally ill.

Chapter 12.

PREACHING AND PREACHER

The primary task of the Church is the preaching of the Word of God.

The primary task of the elder, therefore, is oversight of the preaching.

To meet the obligation of preaching, the Church selects, trains, examines, and ordains men called by the Spirit to the ministry of the Word of God. Deeply involved in all this is the eldership of the Church, acting in consistories and councils, in assemblies, in classes and synods, and on boards of education. Still more deeply involved, however, is each elder in the local consistory which is responsible for what is said from the pulpit. To fulfill this high obligation, the most important in the Church, the elder must acquaint himself with what preaching should be, and how it can be evaluated.

PART A. PREACHING

WHAT IS PREACHING?

Preaching is the hallmark of the true Church. The Reformation signals preaching as the fundamental mark of the Church. Where the Word of God is truly preached, there indubitably *is* the true Church. Where this is not the case, there indubitably is *not* the true Church!

Jesus Himself came preaching (Matt. 4:17), sends His disciples out to preach (Matt. 10:7), and lays the obligation of preaching upon the Church in the Great Commission (Matt. 28:18-20). He also indicates what the intent of Preaching is: "teaching them to do all that I have commanded you" (Matt. 28:20). Paul sums up the preaching task of the Church in his testimony before King Agrippa and the Roman governor Festus: "Wherefore, O King Agrippa, I was not disobedient to the heavenly vision, but declared first to those at Damascus, then at

Jerusalem and throughout all the country of Judea, and also the Gentiles, that they should repent and turn to God and perform deeds worthy of their repentance" (Acts 26:19-20). In which the great Apostle but echoes His Master, whose ministry began thus: "From that time Jesus began to preach, saying, 'Repent, for the kingdom of heaven is at hand'" (Matt. 4:17) — which is to say: desist from allegiance to self and obedience to the gods of the times — get a new Master, and become obedient to the laws He lays down in His revelation for His subjects. The call to repentance from ungodly ways, and the application of God's revelation to daily life is what preaching is called to be.

The Church ordains her ministry. Only those should enter her pulpits who have been chosen, trained, examined, and duly appointed to the ministry. Only to those who thus enter upon the heritage of the Apostles is the promise still given: "He who hears you hears Me, and he who rejects you rejects Me, and he who rejects Me rejects Him who sent Me" (Luke 10:16). The elder's responsibility is to see to it that he who stands in the pulpit is himself so disciplined by the Word that he fulfills the conditions necessary for the Lord's awesome promise to come true.

To accomplish this, the elder must require that the minister subject himself to a dual discipline:

THE DISCIPLINE OF THE CONGREGATION

Preaching is not done in a vacuum. Preaching is not lecturing, that is the teaching of abstract, unapplied truths. Preaching is the exposition and application of a part of the inspired Scriptures to the daily life of the congregation.

To interpret, understand, exegete the Bible the minister must be busy in his study. At his hand should be all tools essential to Biblical interpretation, tools with which his training should have made him thoroughly familiar for just this purpose. The elder does well to get some inkling of what these exegetical tools are, and how they are used. An informative hour might well be spent on these in elders' meetings. As regards his scholarly tools, the minister is to be free. He is not the servant of a priesthood of scholarship. Governing all his thoughts is the determination to hear the Word. And the Word is final.

As free as the minister is from the ruling fads in scholarship, so bound he is by the needs of his congregation. Peering over his shoulder

154

as he studies, as he formulates application upon application of his chosen text, are the urgent demands of his people, who are the people of God. This is the discipline under which sermon preparation is carried out. It is in this city, this neighborhood, these homes, businesses, occupations, professions that the Church is called to "teach them to do all that I have commanded you". This is the discipline which must prevail in sermon development. The text must come alive in life, or the promise "he who hears you hears Me" cannot prevail. Christ did not come lecturing.

A sermon unaware of, or unconcerned with, the daily lives of the congregation may be a lecture, but will never set foot on the ground of people's experience. However beautifully phrased, however exegetically correct, however doctrinally faultless, a sermon which leaves it to the congregation to make application of the text to their daily lives is like an electric circuit which is never quite closed — no current flows from the life-directing Word to the life-living children of God.

Only out of a sought-after awareness of his people's daily lives, only under the discipline exerted upon him by their daily requirements, should the minister's weekly sermonic preparation be pursued.

THE ELDER

It will not be difficult for an alert eldership to observe, from their own experience under the preaching, whether or not such discipline has entered the minister's study and worked there. The lay, untrained, non-theological eldership has every right to sit in judgment, indeed must sit in judgment, upon the ordained, trained, theologically-educated ministry. Why? Because the ultimate test of true preaching is the closed circuit from Word to believer's obedience: does the Word of God speak through this minister's lips to my condition? Does God address me where I live? How does He here lay demands upon my behavior? How encourage me? How enlighten me in His truth? What daily obedience, through grace within my reach flows, or should flow, from this proclamation of the Gospel?

The wise elder not only must, but certainly can, evaluate, criticize if necessary, and give guidance where required concerning the minister's obedience to the discipline which the needs of the congregation ought to lay upon his preparation of sermons in the quiet of his study.

155

THE DISCIPLINE OF THE WORD

In the pulpit, the minister comes under quite another, even weightier discipline than just discussed.

In the pulpit, the minister is wholly under the discipline of the Word. Here there is no place for catering to the whims of the people, avoiding hurt feelings if the truth be spoken in love, bending to popular pressures or the threats, real or implied, of wealth, pride, or power. The minister is liberated by the Gospel from these enemies. He is solely the Lord's man, standing solely by His calling and in His strength.

Now the minister's obedience is to his text. He is to say, in terms of the congregation's needs, what God wants conveyed (as his study has developed that) through this text to this people at this time. He is to bring out the full impact of the text by copious reference to related passages of Scripture, for the Bible's best interpreter is the Bible itself. The Bible is an organism, a living unity. Texts are not isolated twigs detached from a mighty tree, but they are living limbs fed, and supported by the whole.

The sermon may illumine the text by scholarship, enhance its meaning by relevant information, made clearer by learning in languages and history — but the Word is never to be subordinated to these, nor corrupted by them, nor deflected from its plain meaning. Nor may the Word be obscured from the people's comprehension by some show of education. The Bible is, as the Reformers always insisted, perspicuous — that is, perfectly clear in all that pertains to salvation along the Way, the Truth, and the Life. No mists of learning dare becloud that clarity.

THE ELDER

Can the non-theologically trained elder also sit in judgment upon this aspect of the minister's obedience, namely upon his obedience to the text and associated Scriptures?

He must.

It is with sound doctrine that sound living begins.

To exercise doctrinal judgment, of course, the elder will be obliged himself to open the Word, in season and out. You, too, must "search the Scriptures daily, to see if these things were so" (Acts 17:11). Reading a snatch of the Word, in spare moments otherwise wasted,

156

will in the long run pay dividends in knowledge. An elder who is un-acquainted with the Bible, and willing to leave it so, may have attained age in years but not in wisdom, and should not have accepted election to his responsible office. Let your own library boast a shelf or two of commentaries, showing unmistakable signs of use.

THE CONFESSIONS

Happily the elder who conscientiously seeks to evaluate the doctrinal content of the sermon does not rest upon his own resources alone.

Across the centuries the Church has summarized, just for your use now, the content of the Word in the great creeds and confessions — some of them the symbols of your own communion. Differences among the confessions mark off doctrinal boundaries between the denominations. Be sure to know and study your own. Fully acquainted with these, you are able to assess the doctrinal integrity of the sermons you hear.

The confessions serve the Church as touchstones for truth and error — and thus qualify the elder to perform his assigned task of oversight of the preaching. Knowledge of these guidelines will qualify your judgment with more accuracy and authority than you may suppose. The confessions are precious documents. Resist all efforts to degrade or nullify them. Into her confessions and creeds the Church has carefully woven some of the golden threads of living doctrine which bind the Scriptures into organic whole. Master them, and let them master you.

Intuitions schooled by the Scriptures, formulated by the confessions, and infused by experience in the Christian life alert the elder at once to sermonic digression from the Word, and make the combined elders' advice invaluable to the sensitive minister.

Confessions are, it is true, man-made. They can be mistaken. And the Church holds the possibility that new insights into the Word will require modification of the symbols. And the route for such change is open to all serious students of the Bible.

Most often, however, deviation from the Confessions is the work of the Devil masquerading as "an angel of light" (II Cor. 11:14). And doctrinal lapses made from the pulpit should be taken very seriously, admonished, and corrected.

The eldership should devote scheduled meetings to increasing their familiarity with their denomination's creeds, confessions, catechisms.

PART B. THE PREACHER

When the congregation's pulpit becomes vacant, another minister must be found. Let the process be one of all deliberate speed.

KNOW YOUR NEEDS

The eldership should together develop a composite idea of the kind of needs your congregation has, and then a clear idea of the kind of man you should seek.

Some needs are obvious, and so are some standards. The minister must meet the requirements set down by the Word (see Chapter 11). He must be able to preach. It is, indeed, far more important that he preach well than that he be Mr. Nice Guy for social occasions — though both qualifications are desirable. He must be a man of courage, of conviction, and inclined to study hard. His commitment to the Lord, to the Scriptures, and to the doctrinal standards of your denomination must be transparent and unquestionable.

Such nominees for your pulpit are hard to come by. Congregations who have them generally want to keep them. And so, armed with an awareness of their needs, the eldership scans the churches and new theological graduates for possible candidates.

Some cautions:

1. No man is perfect. You must set priorities among your demands, beginning with power in the pulpit.

2. Be looking for potential as well as for maturity. Be prepared to develop your own leader out of someone who shows likelihood of growth and openness to guidance and advice.

3. Beware of the this-worldly prospect whose seemingly chief concern is with housing, salary, fringe benefits, and economic security. The minister above all cannot serve both God and Mammon (Luke 16:13). The congregation will be the victim if he tries.

4. Reckon seriously with the probability that a really courageous preacher may not be altogether popular in the congregation he now serves. He may even be thought heretical by some who are unaware of the indictments the Word brings against popular forms of disobedience.

5. Be prepared, then, to make independent choices. Get the information you want, in the light of your needs and desires, and come to your own judgment.

CHOOSING THE CANDIDATES

Using all the ways in which news gets around, the eldership comes finally to a list of possible candidates for your vacant pulpit. Quietly sending one or two of your membership to hear them preach is a wise foresight. Appointing a small committee to take the following steps will save time:

1. Make a discreet inquiry if the men on your list would, and could, probably accept a call from your congregation if extended.

2. If so, develop and send to them a profile of your congregation, including such information as: size, growth trends, composition as to age and education and general economic status, vitality of Church life, organizations, annual budget, salary and housing offered, and your vision for the congregation under dynamic leadership from the pulpit. (It is becoming common that a housing allowance rather than housing itself be offered).

3. If he is challenged by your profile, the candidate should be asked to submit both his reactions to it, and a profile of his own, including: professional training, interest in continued study, conception of the ministry, the size of his personal library and the magazines he subscribes to and reads, his understanding of the role of the congregation, his reaction to salary and housing offer, his family and the place his wife will take among the people, his commitment to the Christ, the Scriptures, and the confessions of your denomination.

4. Based on the elders' evaluation of this information, either the relation is further developed or politely dropped.

5. Consider asking for some sermon tapes recently recorded of the candidate's preaching. Arrange for a personal interview. Determine whether or not to recommend him as one of a slate of candidates to the congregation. Probably one or two other potential nominations are being simultaneously developed.

6. When two or three nominees are thus obtained, the eldership schedules a congregational meeting at a time when most members are likely to attend.

7. When the meeting is held, the chairman of the eldership will preside. The Lord's blessing and guidance is invoked. The chairman of

the selection committee fully acquaints the membership with the profiles of the candidates. Absentee ballots are accepted, if this be approved by majority vote, for counting on the first ballot only. Discussion of the candidates is permitted, but beware of its slipping into rumor-mongering. Voting is limited to members in good and regular standing, and is done by secret ballot. Thus the nominee is chosen.

8. The eldership extends the call to the elected candidate. If accepted, they arrange for his reception, and installation, and then the elders embark with him upon that mutual ministry of teaching and ruling eldership so crucial to the life of the congregation.

SERVING THE MINISTRY

Open, constructive relations between the teaching and the ruling elders are of incalculable importance for the prosperity, spiritual and temporal, of the congregation. Dedicate yourself to complete success here.

Some suggestions:

1. Let the Word set the tone of your relations with the minister, and govern them. Here, if anywhere, the mutual commitment of minister and elders to obedience is put to the test. Open your first meeting with a reading of say, I Corinthians 13 or parallel passages from St. John or the Psalms — and solemnly resolve in the presence of God and His Word to walk together in the light of this inspired lamp. Always be prepared to set potential tensions under the scrutiny of the Word: "For the word of God is living and active, sharper than any two-edged sword, piercing to the division of soul and spirit, of joints and marrow, and discerning the thoughts and intentions of the heart" (Heb. 4:12). Remembering the Apostle's further admonition: "And before Him no creature is hidden, but all are open and laid bare to the eyes of Him with whom we have to do" (Heb. 4:13). Let this chastening truth guide those meetings where minister and elders may not at first see eye-to-eye. Yours must be a model relationship before the whole congregation.

2. Serve the minister by ruling well, including the oversight of his faith and life.

3. Dedicate yourselves to helping the minister to grow. Let him respond by recognizing the need all men have of continuing willingness to develop and learn.

4. Stand firmly at the minister's side when criticism comes, even if you then must advise him against some fault of his own. Make the eldership the place where the minister can come for support, for honest discussion, for free admission of error and mistake. Yours must be a solidarity in continual search for livelier obedience to the Word.

5. Don't peddle tales out of school, and don't lend an open ear to rumor. Keep secrets a secret, and keep controversy open and above board. If charges are made against the minister, be sure that Matthew 18 is scrupulously followed (see Chapter 10).

6. Keep foremost before you the welfare of the minister and his family. Don't let congregational demands upon his time and energies rob him of the joys of being a good husband and available father.

7. Protect his time for sermon preparation and study. Assume until shown mistaken that he knows how to use time, and will constructively do so. If this is indeed mistaken, guide him in better use of time and talent. Be patient, but firm. Preaching well is his first obligation.

8. Provide adequate funds, besides his salary, for the purchase of books and subscriptions to magazines. Look for them when you visit him in his study.

9. Project plans for leave to be used in study or travel. Treat him like a professional, so he can respond in kind.

10. Don't oblige, or permit, the minister to do and be everything in the congregation. Assist in teaching catechism or church school. Get assistance wherever needed to ease his conscience for work undone by reason of overload. All this will be repaid from the pulpit — if you picked the right man.

11. Don't oblige him, or his wife, to come hat in hand for obvious work that needs doing for the parsonage, or the lawn, or for facilities in the church. Foresee needs, and provide generously for them. On the other hand, warn against too frequent refurbishings and too elegant furnishings. Jealousies are far easier to stimulate than to cure.

12. Pay a decent salary, sufficient so that the prudent minister can set aside a little for emergencies.

13. Anticipate that solid, Biblical preaching will stimulate reaction. You cannot encourage the one, and expect to avoid the consequence. The minister's Lord said it long ago: "Remember the word that I said to you, 'A servant is not greater than his master.' If they persecuted Me, they will persecute you; if they kept My word, they will keep yours also." And the Lord goes on to explain why the courageous pulpiteer will generate opposition, even among those of his own household and congregation: "If I had not come and spoken to them, they would not have sin; but now they have no excuse for their sin" (Jn. 15:20-22). There is no reason to suppose that human nature has changed since these prophetic words were spoken. The eldership must be prepared, then, to receive complaint if they strongly encourage the minister to preach the whole Truth. Be totally committed then, to:

a. Stand foursquare behind your minister, so long as he is preaching from the Word.

b. Require that every charge against him be supported by the Word, or be dismissed.

c. Refuse to be threatened. Church growth is not the measure of courage in the pulpit. Some congregations will probably grow smaller if the whole Truth is preached to them. If you can't live with that, don't urge the minister to preach the whole counsel of God, acknowledging as you do so that this is desertion of your own duty. A timid eldership will make for a tepid witness from the pulpit; and a tepid witness from the pulpit will guarantee an insignificant Church, small matter how fast it grows.

14. There is nothing in the Bible which promises a life of ease, or of freedom from persecution, to the children of God. As you take the eldership seriously, and the minister with you takes preaching seriously, everyone will find out why that is so. Then find solace in the Beatitude: "Blessed are you when men revile you and persecute you and utter all kinds of evil against you falsely on My account. Rejoice and be glad, for your reward is great in heaven, for so men persecuted the prophets who were before you" (Matt. 5:11-12). Bear in mind also the Lord's awesome prediction, applicable to the minister and to you, that, "a man's foes will be those of his own household" (Matt. 10:36). Christianity is serious business. As you and your ministry make it more and more so, do not be surprised if opposition rises from within the congregation. Stand firm: "Be watchful, stand firm in your faith, be courageous, and strong. Let all that you do be done in love" (I Cor. 16:13-14). Notice that there is no contradiction between standing firm and strong and courageously, on the one hand, and love, on the other.

THEOLOGICAL EDUCATION

The Church rarely is satisfied with the work of the seminary. Sometimes this reflects grounds for just dissatisfaction with the products the seminary produces. Frequently there is doctrinal suspicion loose in the churches, and this may indeed be an accurate appraisal of the seminary's position.

As an elder you are deeply concerned with the quality of seminary education. This quality has two aspects: 1) absolute loyalty to the Scriptures and the confessions of the denomination which the seminary serves; and, 2) competent schooling in the disciplines essential to the pulpit ministry.

But how shall the elder satisfy himself as to his doubts, or make his influence effective for change?

We make these suggestions:

1. Try to interest your denomination, and the governing body of your seminary, in a program of rotation of the seminary faculty out into the churches. Faculty members frequently enjoy sabbatical relief from teaching, and are able to leave their homes for study elsewhere, and even abroad, for periods up to one year. Why not have them also rotated out into the denomination to serve in your congregation, for example, living in quarters provided by you, and on regular salary paid by your congregation, as associate pastor for a year? The gains on both sides, to seminary and Church, are obvious.

2. Invite seminary faculty members to make lecture tours of the denomination, where views may be heard, questions asked, doubts put to test or to rest.

3. Dispel the myth of "scholarship" for yourself and your congregation. Learning has its uses, as discussed above in this chapter. But the Bible is understood only in obedience, and sainthood is therefore as open to the humblest member of your congregation as to the most degreed of your seminary faculty. Where the Word hits the roads of life, it is sainthood more than degrees that matters. Oblige the learned to talk the language of obedience, and you will soon detect how loyal their views are to Scripture and creed.

4. The Church is the "market" for the seminary. You exert your influence by governing the demand for the seminary's exports. In the long run this is bound to tell. No school can ignore its market indefinitely. Keep your standards high; don't excuse deviations in doctrine and exegesis with the apology that, "He's only a student and will learn better some day." Require that the graduate you call to your pulpit knows "better" now!

CONCLUSION

There is no more important aspect of your task as elder than fruitful and creative relations between the teaching and the ruling leadership of the congregation. Devote much time, thought, prayer, and study of the Word to making your best contribution here!

Chapter 13.

THE SACRAMENTS

Salvation is wrought by the Holy Spirit through the Spirit-breathed Word. Christianity is an aural religion — the Good News enters the soul by way of the ear. And Christianity is an oral religion — the Good News is proclaimed by the human voice.

Protestantism generally views the sacraments as instituted by God to give confirmation of oral/aural proclamation through other senses: sight, taste, touch. In the sacraments the believer sees, tastes, touches that which he has already heard and accepted. The sacraments are often called, therefore, "the visible words of God," and are restricted by the Church to those who have received faith through the Word.

The Protestant churches administer two sacraments — the Lord's Supper and Holy Baptism. These, the Protestant believes, are the only sacraments specifically instituted by Christ Himself; and in this Protestantism differs from Roman Catholicism with its seven sacraments.

Elders should be aware that the Church has, over the centuries, been more divided by bitter dispute over the nature and use of the sacraments than over any other theological controversy. Sensitive to this, the wise elder will strive to head off differences on the sacraments which may arise in his own congregation by seeking immediate resolution of problems as they emerge. You will find that the Bible gives few specific directions as to the meaning and administration of the Lord's Supper and of baptism. This has given rise to infinite dispute, and calls for wise handling of questions raised about them.

We offer the following suggestions:

PART A. THE LORD'S SUPPER

Biblical reference to the Supper occurs in only two contexts, the institution of the sacrament (Matt. 26:26-28; Mk. 14:22-24; Luke 22:17-19), and St. Paul's criticism of the Corinthians for abusing it (I Cor. 11:23-26). The elder will find little specific guidance in these passages for administering the Supper, and should acquaint himself well with the positions taken by his own denomination on the following issues:

THE THEOLOGY

The sacraments are a means of grace. The bread and the wine of the Supper not only memorialize Christ's suffering and death, in accord with His command, but also feed the hungry and thirsty soul. How this nurture is accomplished, and whether or not the elements (bread and wine) are more than symbolic, is not clarified by the Scripture. Let the experience of the believer, who finds himself fed and refreshed, be sufficient guide to your discussion; avoid argument over transubstantiation (the elements actually become the body and blood), and consubstantiation (the body and blood come "with and under" the elements) versus symbolism (the elements only symbolize the realities) and some halfway position between these (the elements retain their nature, but do spiritually become His body and blood). The Church has been rent enough by fruitless disputation over abstract matters like these.

FREQUENCY

The Bible gives no guidelines as to how often the Supper should be celebrated. Practice in Protestant churches varies widely. No doubt your congregation already has established its policy. Be careful that agitation for change does not engender a full-fledged dispute over the Supper.

Arguments for, and against, frequent communion are obvious: some will say that they need such nourishment often, perhaps once or even more in a week; others will counter that such frequency tends to rob the sacrament of its unique character and makes it mere custom.

There is a wide variation among churches and denominations in the frequency of celebration of the Supper. Inasmuch as the Bible gives no specific guidance, wisdom and, sometimes, compromise must prevail. We are satisfied with the general Reformed practice of quarterly communion, that is once every three months — with the addition, in

166

some congregations, of special occasions like Good Friday and Easter.

SACRAMENT AND WORD

With some variation, Protestantism generally insists upon setting the celebration of the Supper in the context of preaching the Word. To this position we strongly adhere.

However obviously the bread and the wine symbolize the broken body and shed blood of the Lord, the full significance of Christ's atoning death can only be conveyed by the Word preached. The visible words only reinforce the Word spoken. This relationship must not be broken.

Administration of the sacrament must either follow upon the preaching of the Word, or be followed by it.

DISTRIBUTION OF THE ELEMENTS

The elder should think through for himself what is "spoken" by the way in which the Supper is administered, considering matters like these:

1. *Who should break the bread?*

Accounts of the Lord's institution of the Supper indicate that He broke the bread, and He compared His breaking of it to His body, broken for the believer. This suggests that the bread should be broken, now, by the Lord's spokesman in the congregation, the minister. Sectarian groups have long passed among themselves the loaf, each breaking off his own morsel. This practice occurs in some Protestant churches. In our judgment the symbolism is violated when "broken *for* you" becomes "broken *by* you".

Commonly, the bread is cut into small pieces before the communion service, and the minister only breaks one symbolic piece before the congregation. Perhaps this is a necessary concession to time, but you might consider the symbolism of the minister, like a father, breaking bread for the family to eat, one piece at a time from the loaf which symbolizes the unity of the Body.

2. *How is the bread distributed?*

Both the elders and the deacons have served, in the history of Protestant churches, to convey the bread and wine to the believer in the pews. This is not, we believe, a role for the laity. Where the congregation comes forward to receive the bread, they will do so from

167

the hand of the minister(s).

3. *How handle the wine?*

Recognition of the risks of spreading illnesses through the use of a common cup has led many congregations to distribute the wine in individual small glasses. The eldership must decide whether the gain in hygiene costs a loss in the symbolic meaning of drinking together from one vessel, and if so which weighs the more heavily. We are satisfied with individual glasses.

4. *Grape juice instead of wine?*

There has been dispute as to whether or not the fruit of the vine used by Jesus in instituting the Supper was in fact fermented into wine, or was, rather, grape juice. We believe that what the Bible calls wine was in fact *wine*. Those who have conscientious scruples against alcoholic beverages, and those who out of concern for alcoholics in the congregation, want to celebrate the sacrament with unfermented juice should do so on these grounds, not on mistaken exegesis of the Bible. The Scriptures do not insist upon wine, any more than upon whether the loaf be white or brown, be Western bread or Eastern cake. Let the wisdom of the eldership decide this question, no doubt with adequate explanation to the congregation. Perhaps a seating arrangement could be worked out so that those wishing to partake of the symbol for Christ's blood can do so according to conscience and conviction, with grape juice in some sections and wine in others. Read, in this connection, Paul's advice in Romans 14, verses 13-23, summarized in his saying, "Do not, for the sake of food, destroy the work of God" (v. 20).

5. *Should children partake?*

There is a growing movement in some Protestant churches to include children in the Supper. This we cannot endorse.

Paul warns the Corinthians, and thus us also, against partaking of the elements in "an unworthy manner". He requires that, "a man examine himself, and so eat of the bread and drink of the cup. For anyone who eats and drinks without discerning the body eats and drinks judgment upon himself" (I Cor. 11:27-29).

Is a child so able to "examine himself"? Not, we believe, so long as he is in fact a child.

When, then, does the child become adult enough to examine himself? When, we believe, he is old enough for the Church to accept him as as adult member upon public confession of faith. Churches differ as to when such public confession is permissable, that is when confession can be made in full knowledge of what is being confessed.

We believe, however, that such confession is prerequisite to partaking of the Lord's Supper. Some indication is given, we believe, as to maturity by the age of discretion recognized in civil law, usually around the age of eighteen.

OPEN OR CLOSE COMMUNION?

Are all believers, who have joined a local congregation, entitled to partake of the Supper? Is this true not only in the believer's own congregation, but also when he visits another?

Bear in mind that the answer to these questions will reflect your own estimate of the importance of the sacrament. Is the Supper important enough to supervise closely? Or is it so ordinary as to leave supervision aside? Consider these things:

1. "Close" communion is not "closed" communion. It is rather, carefully supervised communion. By contrast, "open" communion is available to all, each on his own responsibility.

2. The Biblical motive for "close" communion resides in the Church's, that is to say the eldership's, responsibility for each person under her jurisdiction. The Church understands the Lord's warning to Ezekiel as directed to all His ministry: "Son of man, I have made you a watchman for the house of Israel..," and of those who sin without the watchman's warning, the Lord declares, "His blood will I require at your hand" (Ezek. 3:17-18; 20). If communion, then, is served without warning to those who discern not the body and blood of the Lord, judgment falls also upon the Church.

3. Methods of exercising responsibility for "close" communion vary.

a. All members in good standing are warned against unworthy eating and drinking, and invited to partake — the responsibility falls, then, upon the believer. In some churches, consciousness of sin prevents some members from partaking. With these troubled souls the eldership should be much concerned, reminding them that coming to the Supper is not a testimony to a perfect life.

b. Members under discipline are presumed not to discern properly the body and the blood, and are not permitted to partake.

c. Visitors who belong to other congregations find differing practices prevailing:

1) Some congregations require that the visitor identify himself to an elder or minister before the service to assure the office-bearer of his proper understanding of the Supper, and of his membership in the Church of Christ. We lean toward this sign of deep respect for the Supper.

2) Some congregations issue both a warning against unworthy partaking, and an invitation to all who can discern the body and blood, from the pulpit, and consider this sufficient fulfillment of responsibility. We judge that this indicates an individualistic and comparatively low view of the sacrament.

3) Whatever is your congregation's practice, what is most important is that the eldership knows *why* it regulates the Supper as it does, lest the curse of Ezekiel fall upon their heads.

4) We cannot in any way endorse wide open communion, in which everyone is able to participate without warning, without supervision, and at will. This certainly involves the eldership in responsibility for abuse of the Supper.

THE AGED AND THE ILL

Communion is carried to those who are unable to share it in the congregation. This is the work of the ministry and the eldership. It should follow immediately upon celebration of the sacrament by the congregation, and if possible should be accompanied by a tape recording of the whole service for the shutin later to enjoy.

Do not let this service become perfunctory and routine. Your mission is to handle, in symbolic form, the body and blood of the Lord Jesus Christ. Take time to surround your visit with reading from the Word and prayer.

UNCONTROLLED COMMUNION

It is a growing practice to "celebrate" communion at retreats, at conferences, in house-church groups, and at other gatherings. No doubt there is an emotional "high" for participants, but from all that has been said above, it is evident that we cannot endorse such unregulated use of the sacred elements. Not only is there an absence of the sermon, at least a sermon preached under elders' supervision, but there is likely to be little if any supervision, warning of abuse, and restriction to membership in the Body of Christ by public confession. The ultimate consequence of such "communion" is devaluation of the sacrament into an emotional experience, if not an emotional binge.

PERSISTENT NEGLECT

Members who display persistent indifference to the celebration of the sacrament call for counseling and, if that fails, discipline.

Be sure that your pulpit holds before the congregation, especially in sermons accompanying celebration of the sacrament, the meaning and importance of sharing in the communion supper. Not only is the believer fed by the Lord's holy meal, but in partaking he testifies to his faith and love, and proclaims his membership in the Body of the King.

We commend the words of a traditional Reformed formulary: "For as out of many grains one meal is ground and one bread baked, and out of many berries, pressed together, one wine flows and is mixed together, so shall we all who by true faith are incorporated in Christ be all together one body, through brotherly love, for Christ our dear Savior's sake, who before has so exceedingly loved us, and show this towards one another, not only in words but also in deeds."

PART B. HOLY BAPTISM

The Lord's parting command to His disciples, as representatives of His Church, was this: "Go, therefore, and make disciples of all nations, baptizing them in the name of the Father and of the Son and of the Holy Spirit..." (Matt. 28:19).

While there has been less dispute in the Church over baptism than over the sacrament of the Supper, nonetheless divisive differences remain over this sacrament in the Body to this day. The elder must acquaint himself not only with the position of his congregation and denomination, but also with its theological foundation. And the eldership must strive to keep congregational practice from becoming a divisive bone of contention.

THEOLOGY

Baptism signifies the washing away of guilt and sin. It thus symbolizes the forgiveness and reconciliation won for the believer by his Lord's sacrifice of Himself on the cross. What circumcision was to the Old Testament Church, in the form of Israel, baptism is to the New Testament Church — the symbol of membership in the Body.

Those who practice infant baptism draw on the parallel they believe exists between baptism and circumcision to require the baptizing of

171

babies born to member families of the congregation. From another point of view, those who practice infant baptism speak of the covenant as holding between God and the faithful, including their children. We are persuaded that the promise made to Abraham as father of all the faithful obtains today and always: "I will establish my covenant between Me and thee and thy seed after thee throughout their generations for an everlasting covenant, to be a God unto thee and to thy seed after thee" (Gen. 17:7). But we recognize that the Lord's Great Commission, quoted from Matthew above, assumed ability to believe before baptism, and we know that many Christians hold that baptism must be the consequence of mature decision for Christ and membership in His body. We simply urge that the elder be fully persuaded in his own mind, as governed by his confessions and understanding of Scripture, as to the practice of his communion.

TIME OF BAPTISM

Whether, then, baptism be administered to infants as well as to confessing adults, or only to confessing adults, will depend upon denominational or congregational decision. Know why, and participate in teaching others so.

FORM OF BAPTISM

Those who administer baptism to infants employ sprinkling with water to signify baptism, and carry this form over into the baptism of adults.

Some of those who administer baptism only to adults use immersion to signify the full cleansing implied by the sacrament.

Usually some statement of confession is required of adults submitting to baptism, in a form adopted by the denomination or by the local congregation or minister. A statement is also required by the parents of baptized infants. These statements include not only a confession of faith in Jesus Christ, but also adherence to the confessional bases of the congregation.

The elder must be sure that the adult, or parent, fully understands what he accepts for himself or for his child in the confession he has made, and what commitments are promised by him to the Church and her Lord.

Standing as we do in the Reformed tradition, we believe that sprinkling with water *is* the sacrament of baptism as required by the Lord of the Church. But we recognize that the Scripture is open to other interpretations and fully respect these.

UNUSUAL SITUATIONS

Unusual situations which may arise in the administration of the sacrament of baptism are these:

1. The baptism of adopted children: it is to be assumed that by coming into a believing family, the child enters the scope of the covenant and is entitled to baptism — wherever infant baptism is practiced.

2. The child born to a single parent: if the child is born outside wedlock, the mother should — if she is a member of the congregation — present the child for baptism as soon as she herself has, by due repentance, been reconciled to the Church. In the case of the member mother who is unrepentant, the elder should use the covenant status of the child as argument for her reconciliation and the child's baptism.

3. The child born into a family where only one parent is member of the Church: in this case that parent presents the child for baptism. This will be added opportunity for the elder to urge upon the non-member the obligations of full participation in Christ's body for the sake of the other member and of the child.

CONCLUSION

The sacraments are auxiliary to the preaching of the Word. So long as they are viewed thus, controversy over them is unlikely, and division over them hardly possible. Let there be, rather, a variety of opinions as to how the sacraments best serve the primacy of the Word. Recognition of this primacy will draw together those who have differences over the symbols which visualize it.

Chapter 14.

TRAINING THE YOUTH

Your congregation may have a youth program, perhaps even a minister of youth and education. If so, the eldership should be fully aware of what that program is, and fully responsible for the activities of the youth minister.

Or, your congregation may count ministry to youth simply a part of total ministry to the whole Body. One of the elders' important responsibilities, then, is that the youth be among the primary concerns of the Church.

OBJECTIVES

The Church has two goals in her youth ministry:

1. *To teach knowledge of the Word and of her confessions.*

Here the Church, and therefore the eldership, must keep priorities in order. It is the Word of God which guides and directs life in its proper course: "Thy Word is a lamp to my feet and a light to my path" (Ps. 119:105). Again: "How can a young man keep his way pure? By guarding it according to Thy Word" (Ps. 119:9). No amount of other youth activity can compensate for leaving the young in ignorance of the Scriptures and their summaries in the creeds and confessions. Mastery of the Bible, acquaintance with its many stories, knowledge of its many characters, comes most easily to the young. Be sure that there is constant effort, on all fronts to *teach the Bible!* Stress memorization of texts and confessions. Store pliable minds with rich resources of Truth. These will stand against the days of temptation. The only abiding power which the Church has to share is that of the Word of God.

2. *To teach how the Word is to be understood, namely through obedience.*

Learning is never, in the Church, an end in itself. The child memorizes, and comes to know the Truth as guide to behavior. Let it be clearly understood that the child who would have Jesus as elder brother must obey Jesus' commands, and for this reason listens to His inspired Word: "For whoever does the will of My Father in heaven is My brother, and sister..." (Matt. 12:50).

Governed by these two objectives, the elder is able to evaluate and promote the youth goals of the Church. Not every bustle and hustle develops Christian character, but only those things commanded by the Lord. Beware of attempts to create immature child evangelists, who are sent out to "share" truths they have hardly mastered. Let growth be normal, progress steady, and the aim an alert and knowledgable Christian youth.

MEANS

Your congregation may already be using a variety of programs to school the young. Among them should be such as these:

1. The pulpit. Sermons should be aimed to include the young. Let them always be addressed as living parts of the whole, especially willing to hear the vivid stories of the Bible.

2. Youth church, for which children up to a certain age will leave the worship service at a given point, has both its advocates and its critics. The elder will have to judge, in terms of his own congregation, how wise such a program is, or might be. We lean to keeping the children in the regular worship service at as early an age as their conduct and natural restlessness permit.

3. Sunday or Church school is the ideal place for letting children live through the many stories of the Bible. Aided by pictures, slides, and sound films, children here acquire a knowledge of the Bible as living history, and of Biblical characters as real people. Let the stories make their own impression unburdened by theology. No one, said the Brooklyn preacher, Henry Ward Beecher, needs ask a child to listen to a story. Sunday/Church school is the opportunity to capitalize on that.

4. Catechism or religious education classes invest the child with the intellectual backbone of the Church's confessions. Here he acquires the ever important habit of looking at life and its myriad forms in terms of the basic questions answered by the creeds. Once acquired, this habit endures. Children with a basic education in Christian doctrine are prepared to meet alien ideas and to master them. We

cannot stress enough the importance of regular instruction, in Christian doctrine, to be required of all youth from, say, fifth grade level through high school graduation.

5. Do not be misled by modern indifference to memorization. Do not accept "discussion" as a substitute for memory work. To discuss without knowledge is to make bricks without straw. There is more than enough of uninformed talk loose in the world; do not let your Church's youth classes add to the confusion. Remember that what youth loses by skipping memorization of Scripture and doctrine at a time when memory is most perceptive can never be regained. That loss will be laid at your door!

6. Activity groups for youth will vary from place to place. Focus at least some of them on service to the aged, the needy, the handicapped. Give your young people early the thrill of giving as well as of receiving. Reach out into the congregation and the community with good works by your youth. See to it that their efforts are noticed and and duly acknowledged in the congregation and when possible, in the community. The Church thus makes her witness visible.

7. Encourage special classes and lectures on problems encountered by older youth as they move out into their world: smoking, alcohol, drugs, sex, violence, forms of entertainment, education, politics, employment, and the like. Pay attention to the views promoted by these talks, and give time to relate these to sound Christian doctrine if the speaker neglects this.

YOUR ROLE

1. The elder should participate in teaching classes in Christian doctrine. One learns by teaching, and in addition gets an insight into the mind of the congregation's youth.

2. Be sure that instructional materials are made available, that classroom space is open, and any financial responsibilities are met.

3. Be alert to ways employed by other congregations to reach and raise the young. Be imaginative yourself. Keep up with new educational materials.

GROWING UP TODAY

We have observed in discussion of "The Family" that today's young people are bombarded with temptations to waywardness. Be informed. Know what goes on. Not so much to criticize, nor to pine for the good old days, as to know how to help and what to expect.

1. Find out about drugs, including alcohol, as used among teens in your community. You will probably discover that adolescent experimentation begins with beer or wine, goes on to hard liquor. From cigarettes the teenager will be tempted to try marijuana. From there the invitation will be to pills, tranquilizers, amphetamines and barbiturates. The few who go into the drug culture will try L.S.D. and the most dangerous drug of all, heroin. By this time there may be troubles with the law and signs of physical effect.

2. You will try:

    a. To steer your youth away from the drug scene altogether, or failing that,

    b. To turn them back as soon as possible, or failing that,

    c. To steer them into professional help.

3. Meanwhile, do not give up on even the seemingly most hopeless cases. The deeper the drift, the greater the need for the steady, loving arm of the Church — through you. Stand with the parents, suffer with them, and leave judgmentalism at home. Enlist every energy you can tap in the congregation, and in the community, to reduce traffic in drugs and to reveal the awful emptiness of the drug world to those who are tempted by its allure.

4. Sex is the other most common form of temptation lurking in the path of the young. Encourage parents to deal frankly with sex as soon as their children are ready for it. Have the pulpit stimulate an open and trusting relationship between parents and children so that youth turns to the home for advice and support. Take note of the attitudes toward what is called "love" in the pop music which blares at the young from everywhere. You will often find the words suggestive, the thoughts immoral, and physical intercourse taken for granted. It is against this pervasive mentality that you are working with the Word and the Holy Spirit.

5. Oppose the "sex culture" on these fronts:

    a. Be sure that the pulpit and your Church youth programs stress the sanctity of marriage and the sin of fornication.

    b. Stress that there is no "safe" way to violate God's law, even if physical risks can be minimized.

    c. Acknowledge the pressures of peers, the power of sex drives, the absence of moral standards among many — and challenge Christian youth to avoid behavior they will one day regret.

    d. Substitute programs of self-sacrifice for the modern "me" mood, and the satisfactions of doing good for others instead of the passing enslavement to physical drives.

e. Be prepared to deal in love with those who went along with the crowd. Point them to the liberation of repentance, and the renewal of life and challenge that follows upon recommitment to the Lord. Let heaven rejoice in the recovery of the lost (Luke 15:7) through the Spirit's use of your refusal to give up.

PRACTICAL SUGGESTIONS

1. Keep a record of the babies born into your district. Pray for them by name from the beginning. Very soon they will be youngsters, and not so long after that they will be adolescents and young men and women. Go with them in your thoughts and interest and prayers all the way, whether by then you are in the active eldership or not.

2. Know all the children and young people of your district by name, and greet them so at worship services.

3. Try to be informed about special occasions affecting the lives of young people in your district: graduations, awards, accidents, sports, jobs, and the like. Give them a call, drop them a note or card, pay a visit. Let them *know* that the Church, through you, has them at heart.

4. Visit the youth programs from time to time. Share when you can in their services to the elderly and needy. Lend a hand in paper drives, car washes, etc.

5. Attend their sporting events, and at least know where they go for amusement. Don't try to play the "good old boy," nor be the prude; just try to share, even if from a distance, their experiences in growing up in today's world.

6. Train yourself to befriend those in special need, especially those from homes broken by death or divorce or marital troubles. Sit down for a coke or coffee and be a willing ear. Once you secure their trust, you may hear much that is helpful and instructive in giving guidance to youth.

7. Count young people in on visiting the home. If they are absent, make it a point to follow up with seeing them separately. Let them know they were missed, and you count them as your own "kids". See our suggestions on home visitation, Chapter 7.

8. If your congregation has a minister of youth and education, or an education committee, integrate your efforts with theirs, but don't be put off by hints that professionals can do your job better. Only love

can do the job well, and the upshot of our advice is that you must focus all the love you can upon a troubled and torn and greatly tempted generation.

SPECIAL PROBLEMS

You may encounter young people who were once with the Church but now are living together without marriage, and probably have dropped out of the Body. Your effort to show interest may be rebuffed as intrusion. Assume, however, that this is self-defense against what is supposed will be your judgmental condemnation of the sinful arrangement. And you do, indeed, plan to bring this couple to marriage or to separation. But consider carefully how you can go about retrieving them, with God's help, for His Church. We suggest:

1. Deal first with yourself. Be prepared to accept, at first, what is going on, not to endorse it but to gain a hearing. You come in love. You come openly. Your goal is their ultimate good.

2. You may even have to enlist yourself temporarily in trying to help solve the problems of this foolish arrangement, in order to secure — and deserve — their trust. Right now, what bothers them is not the seventh commandment — at least not in the forefront of their minds. To get at that hidden counterforce, gnawing (whether they admit it or not) in their conscience, you may have to begin by being helpful. Be prepared to go that far, never losing sight of your goal. Even be prepared to be "taken in" by these young people, who may turn you out when you try to revise their attitudes and behavior.

3. Always bear in mind this sober truth: God's commandments are intended solely for man's good. Persistent violation of any commandment promises only heartache, if not perdition, in the long run. Knowing this, you intend to work this truth slowly but surely into their consciousness. You will use problems they encounter, misunderstandings that arise, tensions that develop, subtly to point out the lack of future in their arrangement. No stability. No promise of tomorrow. No security against illness, depression, let alone children.

4. If you are able to meet such a couple where they are, to go along as far as you must, and never to lose sight of your ultimate goal, the Spirit may find you useful in bringing back these straying sheep to the fold. Pray for it. Have the eldership pray for it. Enlist members of the congregation who are able to use your approach. And rely on the Savior who said: "What do you think? If a man has a hundred sheep,

and one of them has gone astray, does he not leave the ninety-nine on the hills and go in search of the one that went astray? And if he finds it, truly, I say to you, he rejoices over it more than over the ninety-nine that never went astray. So it is not the will of my Father who is in heaven that one of these little ones should perish" (Matt. 18:12-14).

THE HOMOSEXUAL

The "gay" community emerges more and more openly, and claims its "rights" to establish homosexual "families" and live in openly homosexual relationships. You may discover that, probably not openly, there are homosexuals in your district, or that parents of some Church families have homosexual children now no longer living at home.

If this occurs, we suggest:

1. You deal, once more, first of all with yourself. The emotional reaction to what you instinctively take to be a perverse, if not "dirty," relationship will be natural, but cannot be the point from which you begin your effort to relate the Church to this problem. Remember that sin is always ugly, but normally we encounter it under polite, or commonplace, forms. Here you encounter sin in more obvious hues. Just look it in the eye before you move at all.

2. Seek professional advice from a Christian counselor, or from one of the many books now available on the subject. Discover, for instance, that students of homosexuality are not agreed as to whether it is of the nature of an illness or a deliberate misbehavior. In either case, your goal is the same: to turn the victim away from the grip of his perversion.

3. If you decide to treat homosexuality as an inborn tendency, your object will be to encourage the person, or his parents, against homosexual practice. It is then simply a very strong desire that must be countered, with God's help, by an even stronger refusal to yield.

4. If you decide to treat homosexuality as evidence of badly focused sexual appetite, your aim will be to encourage the person, or his parents, against homosexual practice. And you will strive to encourage the victory over homosexual desires.

5. In no case can the Church join the "gay liberation," or accept the normalization of homosexual "marriages". The command given long ago has not been changed: "You shall not lie with a male as with a woman; it is an abomination" (Lev. 18:22). Again, "If a man lies with a

male as with a woman, both of them have committed an abomination; they shall be put to death, their blood is upon them" (Lev. 20:13). What is said of the male applies as well to the female. It is obvious, then, that whether homosexuality be accounted simply a perverse desire or an inborn disposition, the Lord assumes that the victim is able to control acting out his passion. For this degree of self-control, the Church must seek by suasion, through prayer, and in understanding (but firm) love. And so it must advise the parents of homosexual children.

Chapter 15.

CARING AND COMFORTING

PART A. THE AGED, SHUTIN, RETIREE

Age slowly transforms those who once were pillars of the Church into those who lean upon the Body. The aged saint has progressed from the childish into the childlike, and now is threatened by senility with childishness once more. You as elder have a special reponsibility to the aged in your district.

Why You Must Visit the Aged:

1. To give visible expression, through your visit, of the spiritual unity of the Body of Christ. Your visit incarnates the Church's love.

2. You may find that the elderly are the forgotten members of the communion. Yet their spiritual needs may be among the most urgent. Tucked away in rest homes, or elsewhere, the aged are easily forgotten. They are rarely seen, and all too commonly neglected.

3. There may be needs which you as elder can meet through the resources of the Church: lack of funds, transportation, communication, reading material, tracing of relatives, etc.

4. The proportion of the aged in our population is growing. Your own efforts to visit the elderly may fall short of their needs, and you should enlist the attention of other members of the Body to this growing challenge. Perhaps your congregation should appoint deaconesses for regular visiting.

Before Your Visit

Well-planned is, as always, half done. Consider things like these:

1. Expect, usually, to go alone. This makes your visit more a personal than an "official" one. You may decide, of course, to be accompanied by your wife who may minister very effectively to the oldster's needs.

2. Consider, in advance, the differences between your way of life and that of the elderly. You freely come and go; you have your job to give meaning to life; you plan for the future. The older person may be bound, most of the time, by four walls; he or she may find the rest home unpleasant; anticipation of the future confronts the fact of death. You must strive to enter into the mind and feelings of the aged, and to see things from his limited perspective. Try to understand in advance what you may find of discouragement, frustration, apathy, or anxiety. It may be profitable to discuss at elders' meetings what the "mind" of the aged is apt to be.

3. Know, if you can, something about the person you are going to visit, if this be the first time: previous occupation, family, children near or far, even financial circumstances and physical condition.

4. Learn from the experience of others that certain problems and concerns are common to the elderly, and consider your response to these, like:

a) The gnawing loneliness. Often a spouse has passed away; friends are dead or too old to visit; children may not be coming very often; Sunday services can no longer be attended (try to arrange for regular delivery of tapes of these, and for equipment to play them). The pastor probably does find time to visit, but not often enough to please the aged member. You can help the elderly to understand the busy-ness of others, and to avoid crabbing at the children when they do drop by. Point to the presence of Christ in the Word, and to His always hearing prayer.

b) Doubts and fears. Age does not always bring tranquillity. The elderly are often plagued by doubts and fears. There may be some ground for this, in a sense of wasted years, missed opportunities, disobedience. Listening renders a real service in these circumstances; let the older person talk it out. Be patient. Decline giving glib answers. Meet doubt with promises out of the Word. Do not expect that problems reaching back into youthful indiscretions will readily be brushed aside. Expect to hear the same catalog of concerns on many visits; and each time respond from the Scriptures. Try to lead the thoughts from self to God, from unhappy past to glorious future. Assure the doubtful that heaven awaits upon faith, not works, and that the Christ died to liberate us from the curse and burden of all sins.

c) Expect to encounter the physical disabilities of age: failing vision, poor memory, bad hearing, and even embarrassing physical handicaps. Overlook these.

d) Think over the doctrinal problems which seem to trouble many of the elderly; draw answers from Word and confession. Problems like these:

(1) Will we know each other in heaven? (No doubt we will)

(2) Why must the believer still undergo physical death? (The last remnant of Adam's sin, used by God as gateway to His presence)

(3) Will Christians be judged for their works? (Yes, but in terms of Christ's forgiving love, and the believer's will to do His will — even now in declining years)

(4) Why are my prayers unanswered, perhaps for wayward children or grandchildren? (God has His own mysterious ways; but He lays upon us the duty to pray without ceasing, and He will do what is best)

(5) Why does the Lord keep me here with my ailments and in my loneliness? (He has His appointed time, and until then calls upon each of us to serve Him in our circumstances, with prayer and praise and in faith)

(6) Why do I live on while another is snatched away, perhaps in accidental death? (No one is the Lord's counselor, or knows the secrets of His hidden will, but He does all things well, as one day we will all understand)

(7) Will God forgive sins like...? (God forgives all sins confessed and repented of, and eagerly awaits such turning to Him)

(8) Could I be guilty of the sin against the Holy Spirit, which is not forgiven? (Not so long as you are concerned that you might be)

(9) How can I warn my child, or someone else, against my mistakes? (Write. Call. But most of all use your free time to pray)

The answers suggested above are simply points of view from which to develop your own responses to these, and like, questions. We list some texts at the end of this book to assist you further. Discussion of these and similar questions in elders' meetings is helpful and important.

Select a Bible passage for reading and application before you leave for your visit.

During the Visit

1. Be on time. Despite the time on their hands, the elderly expect others to be punctual; they have little to do but watch the clock.

2. The purpose of your visit is spiritual, but don't slight the social aspects of life. Be willing to hear, perhaps for the so-manyeth time, the

same stories, and to laugh at the same jokes. Listen with interest to stories of the past, no matter how often repeated.

3. Remember that the Word of the Lord has power to give peace, and will linger on long after your words have been forgotten. So keep that Word foremost on your lips, as opportunity affords. Apply Scripture as frequently and naturally as you can.

4. Try making appropriate application of the Bible passage you selected, and have brought your own Bible to read. You could compare the green pastures of Psalm 23 with the eventide of life, a time of security because the Good Shepherd is always at hand. Psalm 139 points to the never-failing presence of God. John 14 speaks of the many mansions that await us. John 15 stresses the unity of Christ and His children.

5. Remember that the elderly need a listener more than they need a talker, most of the time. Your listening is their therapy. They seek someone to talk *to*, often, more than to talk *with*. Be that someone.

6. Take the problems told you seriously, while yet aware that they may be complaints made to everyone. But offer to help with unpleasant living conditions, changes required in nutrition or medication, indifferent children, etc., to the extent that you can. Do not promise correction. There probably are circumstances which account for situations complained of. But do what you can.

7. Let your parting prayer indicate that you have indeed heard the words spoken to you, and care about the problems raised.

8. Despite entreaties, do not overstay. The oldster who urges you to stay overtime may, when you are gone, complain that you tired him out too much. Just as he may spoil his childrens' visits by saying that they never visit him.

9. Promise another visit. Soon, if you can, or can get another to share visiting duties with you. Having something to look forward to means much to the elderly.

After the Visit

1. Find time to pray God's blessing on the results of your visit.

2. Remember the elderly in your district and congregation in your daily prayers.

3. Reflect on what you yourself learned from the Word spoken to the older one. It speaks to you also. Old age is the future of most of us. Remembering that will help you cope with the tasks of visiting the elderly now.

4. Carry through on promises you made, and problems you think should be corrected. Contact wayward or thoughtless children. Help them arm themselves against recrimination when they do visit. Alert deacons to financial problems.

5. Be prepared to discover that you heard complaints made to every visitor, and long since as nearly met as possible. Do not feel taken in; this is what age does to all of us.

6. Always seek out, by reflection, what was effective and what was not in your approach to these visits. Stress the one; drop the latter.

7. Acquaint yourself with studies on the nature of aging; there are many of them.

8. Keep a notepad close as you read the Bible for your own devotions, and jot down passages of especial import for your next visit. You will develop your own effectiveness, and have a treasure to pass on to another elder later.

A Program for the Elderly

Many of the elderly are not confined to their rooms, and have a store of talents for the Church to put to use. The eldership should have a committee to facilitate such use. Be sure some of your retirees serve on the committee to represent their age group. There will be things like these for the committee to plan and implement:

1. Prayer chains among the elderly to make regular intercession for congregational needs. Keep the chain informed of special problems like illnesses, surgeries, accidents, troubles, and the myriad other matters which touch people's lives.

2. Card and letter chains: furnished stationary and postage, the elderly can correspond with missionaries, others who no longer get about, and those suffering special needs or celebrating special events.

3. Skill chains: with materials provided, the elderly can knit, sew, mend, paint, carve, repair, etc. This may be done not only for members of the Body, but in the name of the Body for others in the community.

4. Influence chains: the elderly can be encouraged to keep their places of influence in society by writing letters to public officials, to local newspapers and radio/television stations, and wherever a voice for righteousness might be heard.

5. Many other tasks could be planned for putting the talents of the active elderly to use in and for the Church, like:

    a. Duty in the Church library.

    b. Assistance in keeping the building neat and clean.

    c. Work in yard and flower garden.

    d. Painting and decorating.

    e. Keeping records of various kinds.

    f. Helping with outreach programs for the distribution of goods and clothing to the needy.

    g. Teaching the youth, and working with them in various projects.

Putting talent to use results from being aware of needs and fitting the skills others have overlooked to meeting them. You can do that if you try.

PART B. THE SICK

"I was sick and you visited Me" (Matt. 25:36).

"Is any among you sick? Let him call for the elders of the church, and let them pray over him, anointing him with oil in the name of the Lord" (Jas. 5:14).

Illness respects no one.

Just as shadows are better perceived in sunshine, so sickness is better prepared for in health. Such preparation is the task of the pulpit. The elders' care of the sick must be facilitated by the minister's instruction of the well.

God does not explain in detail why He visits some with illness. It is not for man to make God's explanations for Him. But illness is not desertion. It is, rather, one form of God's dealing with His children. This the congregation must clearly understand, and of it they must constantly be reminded. Elders who encourage such instruction from their pulpit will find their effort amply rewarded in their own ministrations to the ill. Both patient and elder will start from a common understanding and shared faith in the fatherly goodness of God.

The Bible bears ample testimony to chastisement by illness, and otherwise, as testimony to God's love:

"Behold, happy is the man whom God reproves; therefore despise not the chastening of the Almighty. For He wounds, but He binds up; He smites, but His hands heal" (Job 5:17-18).

"My son, do not despise the Lord's discipline or be weary of His reproof, for the Lord reproves him whom He loves, as a father the son in whom he delights" (Prov. 3:11-12, quoted also in Hebrews 12:5-6).

The writer to the Hebrews adds: "It is for discipline that you have to endure. God is treating you as sons; for what son is there whom his father does not discipline?" (Heb. 12:7).

Illness is no doubt one of the dark fruits of Adam's fall, and may itself be the mischief of the devil. But in His controlling providence, God uses illness for purposes of His own with the believer. The congregation must frequently be reminded of this in good health and bad.

Physical illness illustrates spiritual sickness — not just in the patient but in us all. Attention readily focuses on the material goods of life, often to the neglect of the soul. We strive for comfort, security, wealth in things rather than in God. Illness, our own or that of others, can alert us to this grave imbalance by reminding us that health is always precarious, and the material affords no lasting habitation. Illness is a reminder of that, "You cannot serve God and mammon" (Matt. 6:24).

The attention given physical illness highlights by contrast the little attention commonly given things of the spirit. The state of the body and its symptoms crowds out concern with the state of the soul.

The minister who instructs his people in these and like lessons to be learned from the ill prepares the way in advance for the elders' ministry to the sick.

We make these suggestions regarding visiting the sick:

Why Visit the Sick?

1. Because the Lord wills to be found in them: "I was sick and you visited Me" (Matt. 25:36). Ministry to the sick is ministry to Him. He waits on the sickbed and in the hospital.

2. Because the Lord's Body, the Church, thus extends its loving concern to those unable by reason of illness to come to her. Thus the arms of communion of saints embrace the physically separated one, to unite together in visible concern and love.

3. To assist the patient to set this trial in Biblical perspective, as suggested above (and in many other appropriate texts), and thus cooperate with the Holy Spirit in reaping fruit out of adversity: "Out of the eater came something to eat. Out of the strong came something sweet" (Judg. 14:14).

4. To permit the patient to give expression to fears, resentments, questions in the context of loving and understanding concern.

5. To share with the patient in prayer and the reading of the Word.

6. To ascertain if there are needs of patient or family that are not

189

known or being met. To relieve his mind of worry over these, and to
alert the diaconate if necessary.

Before the Visit:

1. Plan carefully. Know the illness, but do not intend to play
amateur physician. Know his condition. What hospital, or whether at
home, and when is suitable visiting time. Anticipate problems, like
concern over job, or family, or future.

2. Select Scripture passages in advance. Bring your own Bible.
Come to comfort through the Word and prayer, not as professional
counselor.

3. Reflect on what you will say in prayer. Don't plan on lecturing
the patient, or God. Learn, and plead on, the promises: "I will never
fail you nor forsake you" (Heb. 13:5), and the like.

4. Pray for the "success" of the visit, for a right spirit in yourself
and the patient, for the right words and responses. Commit the
outcome to the Lord, and go in His strength.

During the Visit:

1. If you are new to the office of elder, go with your minister or an
experienced elder or deacon. Observe and learn from them, and let the
patient benefit from their greater wisdom.

2. Once the visit becomes necessary, *do* it! Don't procrastinate,
tempting as that will be.

3. If you need to make a visit in an intensive care unit, explain your
mission at the desk and they will give you proper instruction. Obey
especially time limits and avoid taxing the patient's strength.

4. Do not sit on the bed.

5. If the patient cannot speak, ask him to squeeze your hand if he
can hear and understand.

6. Use Biblical passages to bring the conversation to spiritual
things. Invite reaction from the patient. Refer to sermonic instruction
regarding illness. Be prepared to receive instruction from the patient,
who may see things from his perspective more profoundly than do you.
Avoid matters of controversy or dispute. There are better times for
these.

7. Address the patient by name. Try to use names of family and
near relatives if appropriate. Show thus a familiarity with the patient's
circle.

8. Sometimes you may want to include the roommate in
conversation and your prayer.

9. Keep the visit short. Leave with your welcome still warm.

After the Visit:

1. Pray for God's blessing upon it.

2. Reflect on what went well, what went poorly, what can be better done next time and what will be generally useful.

3. Decide if another visit is desirable, and if so when and by whom.

4. Alert fellow elders or the deacons to needs discovered by the visit.

5. Compare notes with the eldership as to how these difficult visits can be made ever greater blessing for patient and Church.

6. Reflect, for your own encouragement, that you have done the Lord's work, both in extending the love of His Body to the sick and in serving Him through serving the sick. Retire this evening in peace.

The handling of illness, both by patient and by the Church, becomes God's opportunity for schooling His children. Do it that way.

PART C. THE CRITICALLY ILL

You may very well shrink from the idea of visiting the critically ill or the dying in your capacity as elder. After all, you are not a pastor, and you feel ill-prepared to extend pastoral care in such situations. Your fears are real. Prepare to defeat them now, when no such calls may be pending. Consider that the pastor may not always be available, or the congregation may be without one for a time. Then the needs of the patient, and of his family must overshadow your own timidity. Moreover, even under ordinary circumstances, a member of the Church does have a right to the care and prayer of the elder.

Before the Visit

1. Prepare yourself for what you are likely to encounter. The patient may well be tired, in pain, confused, or unable to communicate. You will need to be brief, to make the most of the time by putting the Word of God foremost, and prayer next to it. Consider texts suitable to the needs you anticipate.

2. Remember that members of the patient's family are apt to be on hand, also seeking strength and comfort. Be prepared to minister to their needs, also from the Word and in prayer.

3. Do not anticipate dramatic events, nor hold yourself responsible if there are none, like: ringing testimonies of faith, deathbed conversions or confessions, last memorable words.

4. Try to take a realistic view of death. It is indeed, "the last enemy," as St. Paul calls it (I Cor. 15:26). But it is an enemy already defeated in our Lord's glorious resurrection (consider carefully all of I Cor. 15). Now it is possible to say "blessed are those who die in the Lord" (Rev. 14:13). "Death is swallowed up in victory" (I Cor. 15:54). Difficult as it may be, death for the Christian can be met with the triumphant cry, "O grave, where is thy victory? O death, where is thy sting?" (I Cor. 15:55). The awesome fact of the body's dissolution cannot be ignored or glossed over, but underneath your sympathy must be your conviction that death is not the end but the beginning of life for those who love the Lord. Try to let this perspective master your soul as you approach the sickroom if death seems likely there.

During the Visit

1. On arrival at the home or hospital, find out whether the patient is able to communicate with you. If he is in a coma, or otherwise unable to appreciate your presence, your concern goes out at once to the relatives and friends present. Minister comfort in the Lord, and from His Word, to them. Perhaps you can find a quiet room in the hospital to meet a few moments with those concerned about the patient.

2. If the patient is able to communicate, even only through the clasp of a hand, request from others present that you be left with him alone for a few moments. It is very difficult to have a meaningful visit unless you are able to concentrate all attention upon the patient.

3. Avoid playing doctor. Even if the patient appears to have but a short time to live, you do not know this and must not suggest it. How frank you can be will depend upon what you know of the patient, upon previous experience, and always upon prudent and cautious judgment. Death need not be imminent to be mentioned in the context of illness and viewed as under the providence of God: "Yea, though I walk through the valley of the shadow of death, I fear no evil, for Thou art with me" (Ps. 23:4) is always appropriate if you express it as a solemn joy, and not as a prediction.

4. Try to respond honestly to the patient's concerns, be it fear, doubt, lack of trust, gloomy expectation, concern for spouse and family, and the like. Lean on the Word. Promise to convey messages, get help, etc. to the degree that you actually can deliver.

5. Try to lead the patient to a declaration of his own faith, prodding him with the promises and knowledge that the Lord is ever near. If he has difficulty, draw out if you can the root of that difficulty so that you

may encounter it with the Word if possible.

6. Have your Bible with you. Let the patient suggest passages he treasures, or subjects he would like to hear the Word speak of: "In the few minutes we have together shall we read of God's presence, forgiveness, love?" (for example).

7. Be prepared to make a quick summary of the Gospel if that be called for by the patient's extreme uncertainty. Use a familiar guide like the three parts of the Heidelberg Catechism, or Question/Answer 1 of that Catechism; or the Apostles Creed; or your own summary of guilt/grace/gratitude.

8. Avoid argument. Meet doubt with Scripture. Reckon that the Devil is very busy aggravating fear and uncertainty. Defeat him with the Word and its boundless promises.

9. If the patient wants to talk about his illness, hear him out but not too long.

10. Do not overstay. Ten to fifteen minutes is usually long enough.

After the Visit

1. Pray earnestly for the patient and all others involved and for blessing on your visit.

2. Learn from each visit how to do the next one better for patient, for Church, and for the Lord.

3. Carry out any promises made or report to relatives why you cannot do so.

Conclusion

"It is appointed unto men once to die, but after this the judgment" (Heb. 9:27). But a little experience at the side of the deathbed will convince you that this judgment falls not only upon the one dead. It falls also upon:

1. You. How much ministry has this person enjoyed from you as an elder? How much warning of that impending judgment? How much encouragement in well-doing? How well did you know the patient's circumstances, his inner life, before this last visit so that you could minister best? Your eldership comes, too, under judgment.

2. The Pastor. How pastoral has he been over this member of the flock?

3. The eldership. How much instruction has the congregation received, from the pulpit and by other means, in the reality of death and judgment? How aware is the congregation that the Lord Himself speaks most often of hell and final judgment? that the death and

resurrection of Jesus point those who believe toward the strait gate and narrow way rather than excuse living like everybody else?

4. The Church as communion of saints. How well does the Body extend its arms around the bereaved family? meet its needs? give peace of mind to the dying that this will be so?

All this comes to judgment in the death of a member of the congregation. Take sober note of that. Prepare against it by diligence in your duties as elder: "And that servant, who knew his lord's will, and prepared not himself, neither did according to his will, shall be beaten with many stripes" (Luke 12:47), "for you know that we who teach shall be judged with greater strictness" (Jas. 3:1).

Much of life and "culture" is a conspiracy against facing the ultimate reality of death. But you as an elder cannot lightly push aside the responsibilities which come to the surface when the death of a member of the congregation has to be faced. Let this sober experience stimulate you to greater diligence in doing your duties toward the living while "it is yet today" (Heb. 3:13).

PART D. THE BEREAVED

"Naked came I from my mother's womb, and naked shall I return; the Lord gave, and the Lord has taken away; blessed be the name of the Lord" (Job 1:21).

In this age of comfort, security, insurance, pension, promise, mobility, and freedom, at least in the Western world, the Church desperately needs instruction in Providence and God's pedagogy. For life is not, in fact, unblemished by sorrow and concern, but the mood of the times ill prepares even the believer to surmount them when they strike.

The elders' ministry of comfort begins, once again, with obligations laid upon the pulpit. The Bible is full of instruction regarding God's sovereign disposition of men's lives and fortunes, and the believer must be prepared, by preaching, to stand where Job stood: "The Lord gave, and the Lord has taken away; blessed be the name of the Lord" (Job 1:21). "Am I not allowed to do what I choose with what belongs to me?" asks the Master in Jesus' parable (Matt. 20:15).

The congregation must be given a living perspective on loss, sorrow, fear, insecurity, anxiety, concern. Life must be understood as divine pedagogy, God's education of His children through means He chooses as best adapted to the believer's growth toward full maturity: "The

Lord disciplines him whom He loves and chastises every son whom He receives" (Heb. 12:6, quoting Proverbs 3:12). The writer adds: "It is for discipline that you have to endure. God is treating you as sons; for what son is there whom his father does not discipline?" (Heb. 12:7). This teaching prepares the congregation to accept God's disposition of their lives in the spirit of Job. It is antidote to cynicism and despair. When well and persistently done, the elder will find his own burden in communicating comfort to those in need of it greatly relieved.

A fine line must be drawn, however, between appropriate instruction in God's pedagogy and sentimentality. God is not praised for suffering, loneliness, and sorrow in themselves; all these are fruits of man's fall. Christians do not seek out hardship or loss; even the Lord Himself sought, if possible, to avoid the cross: "My Father, if it be possible, let this cup pass from Me; nevertheless, not as I will, but as Thou wilt" (Matt. 26:39). Christ's suffering on the cross was sin in its deadliest form. For that He gave no thanks. Nor should we for whatever suffering, pain, anxiety, hardship we must endure as descendants of Adam and candidates for heaven. The believer must learn that out of hurt, loss, anxiety, and sorrow God can bring forth blessing in stronger faith, deeper maturity, larger sympathy for others, more profound trust in Him: "Out of the eater came forth food, and out of the strong came forth sweetness" (Judges 14:14). It is for this overcoming evil with good (Rom. 12:21) that the believer learns to praise God, and in it discovers the reality of the divine promise: "I will never fail you nor forsake you" (Heb. 13:5). And he can comfort others who has learned to say: "It is good that I was afflicted, that I might learn Thy statutes. I know, O Lord, that Thy judgments are right, and that in Thy faithfulness Thou has afflicted me" (Ps. 119:71;75).

The Bible prepares the believer for the results that sin has brought into the world. The Church should be the instrument for diffusing this preparation into the consciousness of the congregation.

VARIETIES OF SORROW

Sharpest grief is occasioned by the loss of a loved one in death. The elder must school himself in the rich promise of the Word if he is to be of any use to the bereaved at this awesome time. But the Church must be sensitive to many other sources of hurt and sadness, not always conspicuous or even known: divorce in the family, the straying away of a child, loss of friendships, loss of job, disappointment of hopes, ending of an active involvement in life, a settled depression, a "what's to live for" attitude. Moreover, grief may be accompanied by some sense of guilt — lack of love for the departed, lack of concern for the errant child, indifference to opportunity. The elder must be aware, too, that some are tempted to dote on their sorrow because it gets them attention not otherwise shown. The antidote to all hardship and grief is the Word. The elder must not be quick to shift the burden of concern to professional counselors as we have observed in chapter 9.

PRACTICAL SUGGESTIONS

1. Strive to put yourself into the frame of mind of the sorrowing one, and be prepared to admit that, most often in the case of death, you cannot wholly succeed. Do not betray your inability by overmuch talk, or superficial suggestions. Death remains, in the Apostle's words, "the last enemy" (I Cor. 15:26), not only of the dying but also of those left behind. Try to enter into that, and recognize how little all words but God's can mean.

2. If death has not taken place, try through the Word to prepare the survivors for its coming. Lay stress here on the promises suggested in the texts at the end of this book. Be sure that you believe them yourself.

3. If you are present when death occurs, or arrive shortly thereafter, extend your sympathy to the family and friends and quickly go to God's Word. Say, perhaps, something like this: "I know that you want to be together as a family and friends, so just allow me to read some words of comfort from the Word of God and to pray with you for God's nearness and blessing." Do so. Then leave. Assure them of your eagerness to be of whatever help you can in the trying days ahead.

4. Remember that when the bustle of the funeral is past, sorrow invades lonely hours. Be on hand with comfort from the Word and indication of the Church's compassion as often as you can and find advisable. Be prepared to meet some anger or hostility, probably in the form of, "Why my spouse, or my son or daughter, while they...live on?" Patience, prayer, love are absolutely essential here.

5. Understand yourself, and try to help the grieving understand, that the Lord uses life itself gradually to heal wounds. Effort must be made to live the day, do the things required, or found, to be done. Living must be in the present. Focus must not be on the seemingly endless hours ahead. Memories of the past may ease the present.

Judge when they overshadow it.

6. Take note of practical needs, and discourage the bereaved from making hasty decisions as to disposal of property, investment, change of residence, etc. Help, or find help, in the matter of wills, debts, doctor and hospital bills, etc. when this seems necessary. Do so without intruding yourself into private affairs, and only when no one else seems available.

7. The bereaved may have to be encouraged to participate in Church or civic affairs not previously done. Funds from the Church itself may have to be used for re-training for employment if the bereaved is young, a widow, and there are children to support. This road is hard, and the elder should keep in touch. Mothers of young children should be kept, and supported, in the home.

8. Beware of problems growing out of loneliness, like drinking, finding bad company, spending too freely, and other efforts to "drown" sorrow in ungodly ways.

9. Do not try to make the funeral home a place for eulogies of the dead, or mistaken efforts to comfort the living by references to "how nice" the body looks, and the like. Be brief, be kind, and promise to keep close to the family and its needs in the days ahead. Better to send a personal note than a printed sympathy card.

11. Surround your visits and your efforts with prayer. The depths of sorrow are accessible to God alone. His Spirit must comfort and heal. You are but His agent, albeit a most important agent nonetheless. Keep this consciousness before you, nourish it by fervent prayer before and after your visits.

12. Always compare notes with fellow elders and your pastor on those who need comfort in the congregation. The believer needs to experience the communion of the saints. You need ever to improve your calling as comforter.

PART E. THE MENTALLY HANDICAPPED

Can the elder, who is untrained and nonprofessional, minister to the mentally ill?

Of course he can! And must!

Only remember that you come to extend the love of Christ, to make real the communion of saints, and to minister from the Word of God. Yours is an errand of fellowship. You come, not as an amateur psychiatrist, but as representative of the Church of Jesus Christ. To this you are called, and for it the Spirit will equip you if you are faithful in living with the Word.

ONE CAUTION

We are naturally impatient and often expect quick results. These impulses you must subdue when dealing with mental problems. A "cure" or even a change may not come quickly. If you expect that, you may become discouraged or delinquent in your visits. Think about the mystery of mental handicap; try to enter somehow into the mood of the "patient," and come simply hoping to let a little light into a dark world. God will bless your efforts in His own way, not only to those you visit but also to you.

PARENTS OF THE HANDICAPPED

We divide this section into two parts: dealing with the parents of handicapped children, and dealing with the handicapped themselves.

As to the parents:

1. The first problem these parents must face is acceptance of the trial God lays upon them. The birth of a retarded child, or the loss of normalcy in a seemingly fully healthy child, can be a severe blow to the parent. There may be:

    a. Feelings of rebellion: why does God do this to us? how can we still love Him?

    b. Feelings of guilt: what did we do to bring this upon us? how did we go astray? were we poor parents (if it is a changed older child)? were we lacking in preparation for parenthood (if it is a child born abnormal)?

    c. Feelings of withdrawal: how can we face our friends after this? how can we be seen with the child? everyone will be staring at us!

    d. Feelings of resentment toward the child: if only...?

2. Do not suppose that by the quotation of a few texts you will drive these and similar reactions away. People are in fact cruel. They do assess blame. They will stare at the abnormal child, and their eyes or faces will reveal distaste or pity or indictment. Yours is the task, as part of the Body of Christ, to help parents live through these experiences, to regain or retain their faith that "in everything God works for good with those who love Him" (Rom. 8:28) — a conviction that may be long in coming. Keep them close to the Church, regular in

attendance upon its services; and keep the Body close to the family, in prayer, by word and deed, by card and by call. Plan on taking months, if necessary, to bring about the parents' understanding that God indeed holds all things in His hand.

3. Although, therefore, you must not expect — as pointed out above — that your quotation of a few Biblical texts will produce instant results, in the long run it is only by constant, and patient, and understanding application of the Word that you may hope to be of lasting service here. Persevere!

4. Parents of handicapped children may be slow to seek your assistance, for some of the reasons listed under point 1 above. They may fear that you will come on with blame or accusation, or that you will expect their "confession" of fault. You may have to seek them out, therefore, and by your conduct indicate how baseless such fears were. Let them make their confessions, if they have any, to God, while you bring Word of His love and that of the congregation.

5. If such a situation does indeed arise in your district, try to familiarize yourself with the experience of other parents of handicapped children. There are published stories of how families overcame this trial. You can read them and, at the right time, recommend them to the parents to whom you are ministering. No doubt there are families in your community who have had to overcome this experience, and you can learn from them. Public service agencies probably could put you in touch with such cases. You will find that parents of handicapped children draw naturally together, and you may be able to help bring this about. This, too, is the communion of the saints.

6. As the handicapped child grows older, or if such illness overtakes an older child, there may be major expenses involved in care, cure, or lodging in an institution, or for special education. Tactfully find out if the family needs the concern of the deacons, and if so then enlist them in your service to this home. Discover, too, if local civic groups have programs to aid both the child and his parents. You will find many more open doors than you might at first suspect existed, if you take seriously your responsibility for both parents and child.

7. Remember also that the handicapped child affects other children in the same family. They too may find him hard to accept, an embarrassment before their friends. They may come to resent the extra care he requires and extra attention he may receive. Help the parents meet these difficulties as best you can.

8. Finally, both as individual elder and as council or session draw on the resources of professionals in the mental health field. Get their advice. Draw on their assistance. But remember that yours is the unique role of representing the Body of Christ to these afflicted parents and children.

THE MENTALLY HANDICAPPED THEMSELVES

There will be those in your congregation who experience "mental illness" in one form or another. Try to understand enough of the symptoms of such illness to know when professional or institutional assistance is mandatory, and then seek it for the person involved.

These suggestions may be useful:

1. If the handicapped is a child, like those considered above, treat him with love, care, and without reflection upon his deficiencies. Be "normal" in your relationship so far as possible.

2. If the mental problem strikes an older child or adult, avoid trying to "joke" them out of it, or giving lectures on "backbone". The need is for the hand and voice of love, not the rod of discipline. Don't play detective as to why and how "this" happened. Listen. Love. Speak the Word. Pray. And be very, very patient. Remember that often feelings are simply out of control, and no amount of lecturing from you will restore the victim's power over himself. Let God do this via His Word.

3. Remember that modern medicine now scores many victories over depression and other forms of mental disturbance. Point the person to help, and see that he gets it. But be sure that it is genuine help, and not endless "counseling," to which you direct him, help such as is offered by Christian institutions and professionals.

4. If the patient is admitted to a mental hospital, remember several things:

a. Your visits, and those of others, will threaten to taper off as the months go by. Don't let that happen to you.

b. Other expressions of sympathy and concern also dwindle. Try to keep cards and calls coming from within the congregation.

c. Make visits as natural as you can, and don't play professional.

d. Have church bulletins and announcements and news letters mailed regularly to the patient. Check on this from time to time to make sure it has not been dropped. Send the church magazine at diaconal expense. Be sure that the minister regularly calls.

5. When the patient returns home, give him a warm welcome. Don't

exaggerate this first meeting, and plan on regular visits for a while. Encourage those of others. Always treat the patient as normally as possible, and keep eyes looking up and ahead in hope.

6. Understand, and be sure that the congregation understands, that it may be difficult for someone recently released from a mental hospital to resume regular church attendance at once. Express pleasure, but not surprise, when the patient is able to attend. This should be the mood of the whole congregation, and perhaps the minister needs to make clear how Christians should treat such fellow members, from time to time as part of his regular preaching (not, of course, with specific reference to anyone).

IN SUMMARY

Ministry to the parents of handicapped children, and to such children, and to those caught in the toils of mental problems and illness will tax your patience, exceed your competence sometimes, and yet will be a source of growth for yourself and of great blessing to those to whom you minister. As always, turn to the Word (for which purpose we list some useful passages — add to them your own) and to prayer. Keep the eldership informed of these families and persons; they need the concern of the whole Church.

PART V

THE ELDER AND THE CHURCH

PART V

"WHICH HE WON BY HIS OWN BLOOD"

A brief summary of what the Bible, the Apostles Creed, and the Reformation confessions teach concerning the Church in which the elder serves, and her exercise of the keys of the kingdom of heaven. The priesthood of all believers seen as the self-sacrificial way of life taught in the Church and lived by the congregation under the elders' oversight. A "who are you?" historical introduction to the office of elder today.

Chapter 16.

THE CHURCH

The elder holds an office he does not create in a Body not his own. The office is prescribed by Christ. The Body is Christ's Church. Your Master is this Christ. Your guide is His inspired Word. Your model is this Lord who "loved the Church and gave himself up for her" (Eph. 5:25).

Love the Church, after the model of her Lord and Head.

Serve the Church in ruling over her, after the model of her Lord and Savior.

Take with utter seriousness the Church and your role in her obedience. To do so, what must the elder know about the Church?

At least, these things:

WHAT THE BIBLE SAYS

The Bible teaches that the foundation of the Church is God's election: "...even as He chose us in Him before the foundation of the world, that we should be holy and blameless before Him" (Eph. 1:4).

Through the Word preached, as applied to human hearts by the Holy Spirit, God calls out and assembles His people. The Greek term for such a calling-to-assemble is *ekklesia,* commonly translated "Church". It is the *ekklesia*, the people of God, whom the elder serves through ruling according to God's Word.

There is something to be learned from the terms used in the Bible to describe the Church. Savor and meditate on these; they will add dimension to your work; the Church is referred to as: the saints (I Cor. 1:2), the elect (II Tim. 2:10), disciples (Acts 11:26), servants or slaves (I Pet. 2:16), a family or household (I Tim. 3:15), a body (Col. 1:22). Discover other names given the Church by the Spirit in the Scriptures. They enable the elder better to understand what God expects the

Church to be, and what, therefore, He expects the elder to seek for his own congregation.

Two Biblical descriptions of the Church are especially useful in helping the elder master a conception of his high calling; they are:

1. The Church is the Body of Christ (Eph. 1:23). She is the means through whom the risen and ascended Lord, the Head of the Church, now acts among men. What the Church is to say and to do is revealed to her in the Scriptures. Her doing is to be His doing, and two aspects of His work on earth stand out:

a. Jesus tells Pontius Pilate what He came to do: "For this was I born, and for this I have come into the world, to bear witness to the truth. Every one who is of the truth hears my voice" (Jn. 18:37).

As the Head, so the Body. The Church's primary calling is to bear continual witness to the truth. To what truth? Only to that deposited in the Holy Scriptures, the inspired Word of God. The Church bears such witness through courageous preaching of the Word. She exists, first of all, to provide and sustain and fill pulpits for such preaching. So important is this calling, and the elder's oversight of it, that we have devoted Chapter 12 to preaching.

b. Christ also "went about doing good" (Acts 10:38). This was not random charity. The Lord did good for a purpose: "If I am not doing the works of My Father, then do not believe Me," He said; "but if I do them, even though you do not believe Me, believe the works, that you may know and understand that the Father is in Me and I am in the Father" (Jn. 10:37-38).

Today the Church must validate her claim to speak for Christ by doing the good which Christ did. The Church herself is called to proclaim that, "Faith by itself, if it have no works, is dead" (Jas. 2:17). She must apply that test to herself first of all. Through her deacons the Church does the good she preaches. The power of her preaching will depend upon the power of her witness through doing good: "So then," the Apostle says, "as we have opportunity, let us do good to all men, and especially to those who are of the household of faith" (Gal. 6:10). The Church's saying, like her Lord's, must be validated by her doing: "Not everyone who says to Me, 'Lord, Lord,' shall enter the kingdom of heaven, but he who does the will of My Father who is in heaven" (Matt. 7:21). As the deacon does good for the congregation as a whole, so the individual believer is to do good in witness to the reality of his own faith. (So important is the work of the diaconate in validating the witness of the Church to the truth, that we intend to devote a separate volume to this office). Meanwhile, it is of crucial importance that the elder concern himself with the Church's witness to the authenticity of her preaching by the range and extent of her doing good in God's world.

2. The Church is also described as Christ's Bride, whom He intends to present "to Himself in splendor, without spot or wrinkle or any such thing, that she may be holy and without blemish" (Eph. 5:27). As the Lord's Bride, who is also His handiwork, the Church is called the "New Jerusalem" (Rev. 21:2). She is a community made into a communion of saints through the love of one member to another. It becomes the elders' concern, day in and day out, that love as defined by God's Word be exercised by the members one with another. Only thus is Christ's work done, that the Church may aspire to become "without blemish" of anyone's sin against another. How the elder goes about realizing this ideal is what much of this manual is about.

WHAT THE CREED TEACHES

The Christian faith is most succinctly summarized in the Apostles Creed. This familiar confession does not in fact date back to Christ's Apostles, but it is one of the oldest and most commonly accepted compendiums of Christian doctrine.

What does the Apostles Creed teach us about the Church?

Two things; don't confuse them with each other:

1. The Creed first states the attributes, or characteristics, of the Church: "I believe a holy, catholic Church." Take note of each adjective; it points to one aspect of the Church which the elder must bear in mind:

a. I believe "a" — or "one" — Church. The Body of Christ is one in its essence, its reality, though since the Reformation the Church appears in a variety of denominational forms. Being the victims of sin and depravity, even as believers, Christians do not agree on various doctrines revealed in the Bible. This is not surprising. It will no doubt be so until the end of time, and of sin, and of depravity. But beneath the differences there is "a" Church: "For there is one God, and there is one mediator between God and men, the man Jesus Christ, who gave Himself a ransom for all" (I Tim. 2:5). And there is, therefore, "One body and one Spirit, just as you were called to the one hope that belongs to your call, one Lord, one faith, one baptism, one God and Father of us all, who is above all and through all and in all" (Eph. 4:4-6).

Without sacrificing doctrinal integrity, the elder must recognize the oneness of the Church, believing that the closer Christians draw to their Head, the closer they will be drawn together. Doctrinally, this unity comes to best expression in the Apostles Creed, no doubt the most widely accepted of all Christian confessions.

b. I believe a "holy" Church. This points to the calling-out of the Church for special service to her Lord. The "holy" is the separated, the set aside for unique purpose. The Church is chosen for doing her Head's work in the world, as noted above. The better she does that work, the more "holy" she becomes. A "holy" congregation is the elders' ideal. By that ideal is your work defined.

c. I believe a "catholic" Church. The term points to the universality of the Body. There are no geographical, racial, language, or other boundaries which really divide the Body. Its oneness extends 'round the world. Always, at some place and in every moment, the Church is in prayer, in praise, at service. And we are a part of that universal Body on which the sun never sets, and against whom "the gates of hell shall not prevail" (Matt. 16:18). Take courage from the catholicity of the Church; walk head high, and with firm step. Yours is an office in the greatest international Body the world knows.

d. Other ancient creeds name also the "apostolic" character of the Church, meaning that she stands today as successor to the Apostles appointed by her Lord to do His bidding on earth.

Let the elders reflect together on these attributes of the Church they are called to serve through oversight. They give scope to your calling, and remind you that the Body in which you hold office endures across the centuries and around the world.

2. The Apostles Creed also characterizes the Church as "the communion of saints". This is not simply restating in other words what is meant by "a holy catholic Church". The communion of saints is the creation of the Church through the Word by the Spirit. It is the universal fellowship which all Christians should enjoy with each other, a fellowship sought through Word preached, sacraments administered, and discipline done. In this communion there need be no denominational barriers. Members of various denominations can discover a communion by working, praying, praising together, despite theological differences — and without blunting or sacrificing these differences at all. The more clearly beliefs are held, the more readily Christians of different persuasions find integrity in each other. The denominationalized Church may never find ecclesiastical unity, but

Christians find that along different denominational routes they arrive at communion with one another, and can together strive to do the Lord's will in the world.

The elder can, therefore, stand firmly for denominational doctrinal loyalty while at the same time promoting common Christian effort on many fronts. And all the while, the communion of the saints must be sought in and among the membership of the local congregation as well.

WHAT THE REFORMATION CONFESSIONS PROCLAIM

Having been separated from the Church of Rome, the Reformers were obliged to seek in the Scriptures for those marks by which the true Church is to be known. Commonly they found three such marks:

1. First of all, and most important, where the Word of God is purely preached according to the Scriptures, there is the true Church of Jesus Christ. This means that the true Church is visible, and found in the local congregation. Such a congregation as meets where yours does, gathered by, and for, the true preaching of the divine Word — the power used by the Spirit to call out God's people into the communion of saints. Christ's Body *is* where the preaching goes on. The true Church is a living and active entity, always able thus to be abreast of the times, to be running with the Spirit on Christ's errands in history. Where true, active, inspiring, commanding preaching occurs, here *is* Christ's Body, throbbing with life, trembling with vitality, under the watchful and obedient oversight of the eldership.

2. God makes His Word "visible" in the sacraments of baptism and the Lord's Supper. By these the Christ "preaches" His vivifying Word through senses other than hearing — sight, touch, taste, even smell. A correlative mark of the true Church, then, is where the sacraments are administered according to the inspired instruction of God's Word.

3. The Word preached and made visible is not truly heard until it is believed, and not truly believed until it is obeyed. Once again, the witness to the truth emerges in the witness of obedient deeds. The true Church, therefore, must be solicitous of her members' obedience. This concern is revealed in the exercise of discipline, and this becomes the third mark of the true Church. The Church is identified through discipline conscientiously carried out by the eldership according to the Scriptures.

Elders are obliged by the Lord of the Church to require that their congregation display, ever more prominently, these three indubitable marks of the true Church: the Word courageously preached; the sacraments obediently administered; discipline appropriately exercised.

THE CHURCH AND ECUMENICITY

The division of the Church into denominations need not fracture the communion of the saints, but it is evidence that the Church lacks a perfection she is bound to seek. That is, the perfection of a visible unity.

Ecumenicity is the name given to efforts made to overcome denominational separatism. We believe that these efforts best go into practice of the communion of saints, Christians working, praying, praising, obeying together regardless of denominational loyalty. But strenuous efforts have been made in this century to unite denominations through various councils, associations, and the like. Such efforts have produced the World Council of Churches, various national Councils, and other Alliances, Synods, and Conferences.

In order to unify themselves into a Council, denominations have been obliged to surrender most of what makes each one doctrinally distinctive. What remains, as a doctrinal basis for unity, is so bland as to be almost meaningless. It exercises essentially no control over statements made in the name of the various Councils, and these have come to represent the ruling bureaucracy rather than the member denominations — and carry, accordingly, little weight anywhere. The ecumenical movement, as represented in the creation of Councils, has passed its peak.

Remaining to be taken seriously is the ecumenicity represented in the active and obedient communion of saints. Christians find that in obedience to their own doctrinal convictions they are drawn into mutual efforts to get God's work done on earth. They enjoy the strength of communion in the integrity of denominational commitment.

We predict that this will be the ecumenicity of the future, one to which the loyal elder can be wholly committed.

THE CHURCH AND THE KEYS

The awesome responsibility laid upon the eldership comes to sharpest expression in the doctrine of the keys to the kingdom of heaven.

Speaking to His Apostles as founders of the New Testament Church, Christ says: "I will give you the keys of the kingdom of heaven, and whatever you bind on earth shall be bound in heaven, and whatever you loose on earth shall be loosed in heaven" (Matt. 16:19). This promise, spoken before His death and resurrection, is confirmed by the risen Lord: "He breathed on them, and said to them, 'Receive the Holy Spirit. If you forgive the sins of any, they are forgiven; if you retain the sins of any, they are retained' " (Jn. 20:22-23). Clearly, the power of the keys is the power to bind or loose for eternity; and that power has to do with the remission or retention of sins. Such is the power entrusted by the Head of the Church to His Body, and is exercised by that Body through the eldership.

This awesome authority is frequently forgotten, often ignored. In an age of wholesale "evangelism," with "free" salvation divorced from repentance and service, the church's control of the keys is commonly obscured. But there is no evidence in the Scriptures that the Christ has removed the keys from the hands of the visible Church. Be they ignored, or be they forgotten in the tumult of competing evangelists, the keys to the kingdom reside still in your hands as an eldership. What you bind will be bound; what you loose will be loosed; and the power you forget to excercise will be charged to your account against the Judgment Day.

The Church did not seek the power of the keys. That power was alloted her by the Christ. He will hold her responsible for how that power is employed. His purpose is obvious: to secure proper respect and awe for the Church and her eldership. And to alert the Church and eldership to the full extent of their responsibilities for the eternal destinies of men.

The gates to the Kingdom are opened by the preaching of the Word, confirmed by the administration of the sacraments — when all is done according to the Scriptures. This is the first of the elders' responsibilities as regards the keys. The gates to the kingdom are closed by discipline when it comes to excommunication. All is under the oversight of the eldership. At stake is the destiny of each soul drawn into the congregation.

Be not misled by the world with its indifference to Church and keys. Be not misled, either, by indifference to the doctrines of the keys within the Church and among Para-Church groups. The Body of Christ remains His appointed means for pointing men's footsteps toward heaven and guiding them there. And yours, as elder, is the appointed

213

task to oversee the Church's doing of God's revealed will.
These things, then, you should know about the Church.

Chapter 17

THE PRIESTHOOD OF ALL BELIEVERS

St. Paul exhorts all believers to present their bodies, that is their every act, "as a living sacrifice" to God (Rom. 12:1). This, he adds, is the "spiritual worship" required of the Christian.

The writer to the Hebrews speaks of doing good and sharing what we have as "sacrifices pleasing to God" (Heb. 13:16), and urges us to "continually offer up a sacrifice of praise to God" (Heb. 13:15).

SACRIFICE IN THE OLD TESTAMENT

Sacrifice is an Old Testament religious rite. Sacrifice is associated, first, with the heads of families, like the Patriarchs Abraham, Isaac, and Jacob. Soon sacrifices for the sins of the people became the task of the priesthood, drawn from the tribe of Levi (Deut. 33:8-11). Living creatures, lambs, bullocks, birds, were killed and burned upon the altar to acknowledge, and atone for, the sins of the people. The ceremony of sacrifice prefigured the shedding of Christ's blood upon Calvary for the sin of the world (Jn. 1:29; I Pet. 2:24). The writer of Hebrews pictures Jesus as the great High Priest whose self-sacrifice on the cross fulfilled the Old Testament figure and annulled its ceremonies. The sacrifice of animals by a Levitical priesthood is required no longer of the Church.

SACRIFICE IN THE NEW TESTAMENT

A New Testament priesthood replaces that of the Old Testament. It is now a priesthood still realized in sacrifice. It is a priesthood required, now, of all believers. It is a priesthood called to the continual sacrifice of self, after the pattern of Jesus Christ the great High Priest. The believer is called by his Lord to take up the cross of obedience, and in so doing to sacrifice his will and his ways to God's will and God's law.

Already in the Old Testament the ritual of sacrifice was compared to obedience. Samuel tells a rebellious King Saul that "to obey is better than sacrifice" (I Sam. 15:22), and the Psalmist declares that God prefers those who delight to do His will in preference to sacrifice (Ps. 40:6), while the prophet Hosea testifies that God desires "stedfast love and not sacrifice" (6:6). All these point through, and beyond, the ceremonial priesthood which acts for the believer to the priesthood of the believer himself.

The time of that universal priesthood was ushered in by Calvary. There the shedding of blood for the forgiveness of sins reached its ultimate reality. The blood of the sinless One atoned for the sins of all who believed, and they no longer shed blood but sacrifice themselves. The believer, in the words of Paul already quoted, presents himself as a living sacrifice to God. In this universal priesthood God is now worshipped. Twice Peter refers to the Church as priesthood of believers (I Pet. 2:4,9), while St. John describes the Church as a "kingdom of priests" (Rev. 1:6).

Rediscovered by the Reformation, the universal priesthood of all believers implies the self-sacrifice to God's law which the Bible calls "love".

NOT A SOURCE OF AUTHORITY

The universal priesthood is an office in the Church. Every believer is a priest because every believer is required to sacrifice himself. But this office is one of obligation, not one of authority.

Luther at one time taught that the priesthood of all believers endowed everyone with authority in the Church, an authority which was then delegated at will to elders and pastors who served at the good pleasure of the people. Others have held the same view, especially among the sectarians. It is natural that this view should appeal to Christians living in a democracy like the United States where political power resides in the people.

But it is clearly not so in the Church, where Jesus Christ is Lord and King, and God's revealed will establishes laws of behavior. Luther later understood the Scriptures in this way, and the early Synods of the Reformed churches in France affirmed it against the teaching of one, Jean Moreley.

216

PRIESTHOOD AND THE ELDER

The call to self-sacrificing priesthood laid upon all believers by God is not the source of authority in the Church, but it is the foundation of the elder's claim upon the congregation's respect. The elder is appointed by God, through election by the congregation, to oversee the "spiritual worship" of God through self-sacrifice in obedience to God's Word. Because believers are required to be priests, the elders have the right—and the duty—by divine calling to encourage each believer in obedience, and to admonish in the name of the Lord those who fail faithfully to perform their priestly sacrifices.

PRIESTHOOD AND PASTOR

The priesthood of all believers also establishes the role of the Word preached in the Church. Sacrifice requires an instrument, a weapon, a sword. Spiritual sacrifice requires a spiritual implement. And the sword of the Spirit "is the Word of God" (Eph. 6:17). This is why the Church gathers, and is gathered, where the Word of God is preached. For here the sword is applied to the self-sacrifice which is the believer's reasonable service.

The Reformation, therefore, identified the true Church of Jesus Christ primarily where the Word of God is truly preached, that is where the sword of the Spirit is fearlessly supplied for purposes of self-sacrifice. That Word is made visible in the Sacraments. And the believer's progress in the priesthood is disciplined by the eldership, called to follow the sword of the Spirit to its appointed goal of creating a "holy priesthood" of all believers.

PRIESTHOOD AS A WAY OF LIFE

The believer enters upon the priesthood by faith. This is not the end but rather the beginning of the journey of obedience. It is to be a strenuous journey. Paul says: "Therefore, beloved, as you have always obeyed, so now, not only as in my presence but much more in my absence, work out your own salvation with fear and trembling; for God is at work in you, both to will and to work for His good pleasure" (Phil. 2:12-13). Paul here echoes the Lord's warning: "For the way is hard, that leads to life . . ." (Matt. 7:14).

Paul elsewhere compares the self-sacrificial life required of the believer to the training required by participation in the Olympics: "Do you not know that in a race all the runners compete, but only one receives the prize? So run that you may obtain it! Every athlete exercises self-control in all things. They do it to receive a perishable wreath, but we an imperishable. Well, I do not run aimlessly, I do not box as one beating the air; but I pommel my body and subdue it, lest after preaching to others, I myself should be disqualified" (I Cor. 9:24-27). And to Timothy the Apostle says, "An athlete is not crowned unless he competes according to the rules" (II Tim. 2:5). It is to the laying down of these rules, as revealed in the Scriptures, that the pulpit is called. And it is to the supervision of that pulpit's own obedience, in both word and life, and the obedience of the priesthood of believers that the eldership is ordained.

The utter seriousness of it all is reflected in Paul's own confession: "Not that I have already obtained . . . or am already perfect; but I press on to make it my own, because Christ Jesus has made me His own. Brethren, I do not consider that I have made it my own; but one thing I do, forgetting what lies behind and straining forward to what lies ahead, I press on toward the goal for the prize of the upward call of God in Christ Jesus. Let those of us who are mature be this minded" (Phil. 3:12-15).

Birth *through* faith must develop into mature priesthood *by* faith, under the preaching of the Word and discipline of the eldership: "For I am not ashamed of the gospel: for it is the power of God for salvation to everyone that has faith . . . For in it the righteousness of God is revealed through faith for faith; as it is written, 'He who through faith is righteous shall live'" (Rom. 1:16-17). The faith which receives the priestly life in Christ becomes the faith which reaches out to ever richer priesthood through obedience.

MOTHER OF BELIEVERS

Calvin writes of the Church, "Let us learn from the single title 'mother' how useful, indeed how necessary, it is that we should know her. For there is no other way to enter into life unless this mother conceive us in her womb, give us birth, nourish us at her breast, and lastly, unless she keep us under her care and guidance until, putting off mortal flesh, we become like the angels" (*Inst.* IV. I.4). He adds, "Our weakness does not allow us to be dismissed from her school until we have been pupils all our lives. Furthermore, away from her bosom one cannot hope for any forgiveness of sins or any salvation, as Isaiah (37:32) and Joel (2:32) testify. Ezekiel agrees with them when he declares that those whom God rejects from heavenly life will not be enrolled among God's people (13:9). On the other hand, those who turn to the cultivation of true godliness are said to inscribe their names among the citizens of Jerusalem (Is. 56:5; Ps. 87:6)" (Ib. IV.I.4).

It is evident that the believer's estimate of the strenuousness of the priesthood to which he is called will govern his estimation of the Church, and of the necessity of his enrolling himself among her faithful members. If the priestly, self-sacrificial life is easy, and if salvation is to be had for the asking, then membership in the Church is almost optional. But if, as the Scripture repeatedly teaches, the prize of eternal life awaits only those who train in godliness as the athlete trains for the Olympics, then membership in the Church, under the guidance of her officers, is indispensable for salvation.

The believer understands that the Christ builds His Church, *not* so much *of* those who have in passive faith come to the gospel, as *for* and *by* those who, having found themselves called by Christ, seek the means He has established for enrollment in the membership of His true and obedient, priestly Body. The true believer seeks out the Church, into which he has been born, as the infant seeks its mother — for survival, and growth toward maturity.

MODELS OF BEHAVIOR

Revelation sets forth two models for human behavior, two modes of possibility open to mankind: 1) the model of the first Adam, whose behavior witnesses to the maxim: 'Not God's, but my, will be done' (Gen. 3:1-13); and, 2) the model of the second Adam, whose word and behavior witness to the maxim: "Not My will, but Thine, be done" (Luke 22:42). All history divides, finally, between the two "ways" modeled in the first, or second, Man.

To all who choose as model the first Adam, there opens the broad way of self-affirmation, a way which leads, finally, to dissolution. It is on this way that the Church is called to preach judgment, in obedience to its witness to Truth as Word. And it is in reaction to such witness that the Church suffers persecution at the hands of a world running pell-mell down the broad way: "Indeed, all who desire to live a godly life in Christ Jesus will be persecuted, while evil men and impostors will go on from bad to worse, deceivers and deceived" (II Tim. 3:12-13).

Says the Lord of the Church to His Body in history: "If they persecuted Me, they will persecute you; if they kept My word, they will keep yours also...Indeed, the hour is coming when whoever kills you will think he is offering service to God" (Jn. 15:20; 16:2). Popularity is, obviously, not one of the marks of the true Church.

To all who choose the model of the second Adam, there opens through the Church the narrow way of self-denial, the way which leads, finally, to eternal life in the Church triumphant. It is into this model that the Church, as mother of believers, bends every effort to lead her children. And it is for such education into godliness that Christ builds His Church and ordains precisely the offices the Church enjoys.

The narrow road is not an easy road. Some who enter upon it in joy and enthusiasm fall away. In the parable of the sower, the Lord specifies those who hear the Word, passively, with enthusiasm, and then, "when tribulation or persecution arises," or "the cares of the world and the delight of riches choke the Word," fall away and are of the true Church no more (Matt. 13:21-22).

There are ups and downs for the believer who strives to remain an obedient servant of the Truth. Paul speaks of him: "I do not understand my own actions, for I do not do what I want, but I do the very thing I hate" (Rom. 7:15). Thus burdened, the priest flees ever and again to the comfort of the Mother, who as in possession of the keys may bear witness to *this* Word: "There is now, therefore, no condemnation to them which are in Christ Jesus, who walk not after the flesh, but after the Spirit" (Rom. 8:1). What a liberation, then, for the priestly believer to know that of the Church it is said: "Whatever you loose on earth shall be loosed in heaven" (Matt. 18:18).

In their struggle to sacrifice self, all believers enjoy an equality in the eye of the Mother. The commandments to love God above all, and the other as the self, apply equally to all. Neither the learned nor the unlearned, neither the rich nor the poor, neither the gifted nor the untalented has any priority in capacity for obedience. The Word is spoken to all. Differences among those who hear are not in comprehension but in intensity of obedience: "Other seeds fell on good soil and brought forth grain, some a hundredfold, some sixty, some thirty. He who has ears, let him hear" (Matt. 13:8-9). It is to this equality of priesthood in sacrifice of self that Paul has reference: "There is neither Jew nor Greek, there is neither slave nor free, there is neither male nor female; for you are all one in Christ Jesus" (Gal. 3:28).

The offices of the Church function, then, to this end: "That He who began a good work in you will bring it to completion at the day of Jesus Christ" (Phil. 1:6).

To this end the Word is preached by those ordained to the office of the ministry. To this end the Body is served in its needs, and seeks to serve the world in its needs, by those appointed to the diaconate. To this end all is administered by overseers, appointed as ruling elders in each congregation.

The renewal of the Church so urgently required by our times will take its impetus from a renewal of the office of the ruling elder.

We therefore go on, now, to deal specifically with this office as specified by the Word of God.

Chapter 18.

THE ELDERSHIP IN PERSPECTIVE

Who is the "elder"?

The term is, first, both ancient and honorable. Not only do the "elders" have a leadership role very early in the history of Israel, but all civilizations seem to have had councils of elders.

The term "elder" has, secondly, obvious reference to age. The "eldest" is at opposite pole, chronologically, from the "youngest".

But, thirdly, it is not the calendar alone which has made of the name "elder" a badge of respect. Age of and by itself is simply...age. There is no fool like an old fool.

The term "elder" has acquired its universal respect from the fact that knowledge must be tempered by experience to become wisdom. And experience takes time. Wisdom is born of time, time lived in obedience to divine law, as that is written on the human conscience and in the inspired Scriptures. Those who reap a harvest of wisdom across the field of time become "elders" in the traditional and venerated sense of the term. And across the centuries men have turned to their "elders" for guidance and advice in good times and, especially, in bad.

THE ELDER AND THE EXPERT

The "elder" is at odds with the "expert". This is a distinction often ignored by the young and impatient.

The expert deals in information, made more and more abundant by science. The elder deals in wisdom, acquired only through long and patient obedience to law and ideal. The elder is the product of time, the expert the product of training. The elder is reflective, the expert is impulsive. The elder is sensitive to human frailty, especially his own; the expert is cocksure. The elder tends to listen, the expert to assertion. The expert may indeed impress the naive by overwhelming the wise with the quantity of his information — but a Church or a culture which cannot distinguish between the quantitative and the qualitative — between knowledge and wisdom — has not long to flourish.

In the Church the theological expert assumes that redemptive knowledge can be extracted from the Scriptures by the science of hermeneutics, exactly as the knowledge necessary to landing men on the moon can be extracted from nature by scientific techniques. The Bible is thus mistakenly treated like any other object, and wisdom like any other knowledge — both accessible by mere study to anyone schooled in the techniques of investigation.

By such confusion of knowledge and wisdom, the expert can appear vastly superior to the elder, and the elder may modestly hold his peace while the expert leads many astray. For yesterday's expert is often tomorrow's dunce, and today's theory is the next day's blunder.

It is of crucial importance to the Church, now, whether the elder reassumes his Biblical status of wise leadership or whether the Church follows further after an expertise which shifts with the fads from one speculation to another.

THE ELDER IN THE OLD TESTAMENT

The first reference to elders — always, it appears, to councils of elders — in the Old Testament is from the lips of God. Speaking to Moses from out of the burning bush, God directs Moses to return to Egypt and to assemble together the elders of enslaved Israel: "Go, and gather the elders of Israel together, and say to them, 'The Lord God of your fathers, the God of Abraham, of Isaac, and of Jacob'..." (Ex. 3:16). And in Exodus 4:29 it is recorded that Moses, accompanied by Aaron, did as commanded.

How the eldership of Israel originated and how men were chosen to occupy this office is nowhere recorded. Significant it is, however, that God couples the names of the Patriarchs — Abraham, Isaac, and Jacob, also esteemed for their venerable wisdom — with reference to the elders who apparently acted for, and guided, the people. And so accustomed are we to the natural precedence of age and experience that God's instruction to Moses to assemble the elders (not the young, or the expert, or the 'underground') does not impress us at all as unusual.

The elders figure again and again in the life of Israel, as the people leave Egypt, dwell in the wilderness, and come at last to occupy the Promised Land. In Deuteronomy the elders are assigned specific responsibilities for both civil and religious behavior (19:12; 21:19-20; 22:15-18; 25:7-9; 31:9-13), and they are present with Moses when Aaron and his sons assume the priesthood (Lev. 9:1). The unity of the people comes to visible expression in the council, or college as it is sometimes called, of elders. Through the elders God extends to the people instructions given to Moses and Joshua, and from the elders these leaders received support, assistance, and accounting.

In the period of the Judges, before Israel had her first king, councils of elders exercised political, military, and judicial authority in cities and districts of Israel. It is by decision of the elders that the ark is brought into battle against the Philistines (I Sam. 4:3). The elders represent the people in asking of God and Samuel a king (I Sam. 8:4-5), and by a treaty with the elders David assumes the throne (II Sam. 3:17). The elders appear in the consecration of Solomon's temple (I Kings 8:1-3), and suffer loss of prestige only as Solomon becomes more and more an absolute monarch.

In the Exile, the elders return to leadership both among those who remain in Palestine and those who are taken to foreign lands.

In summary, the thread of the eldership rises in the mists of Israel's beginnings as a people of God, passes through the historical books and those of the Prophets, and weaves an unmistakable pattern of leadership and supervision in the Old Testament Church.

THE ELDER IN THE NEW TESTAMENT

By the time of Jesus, the eldership had been institutionalized in the ruling Sanhedrin while councils of elders governed the synagogues. Besides the elders, who were the lay membership of the Sanhedrin, this body was composed of Scribes (the scholars) and Priests (at Jesus' time largely Sadduces).

The councils of elders responsible for the synagogues exercised authority over the worship and teaching done there, and watched over the behavior of those who attended the services. It is this synagogue administration which becomes a model for the early Christian congregations.

The council of Christian elders first mentioned in Acts 11:30 as receiving gifts for the Jerusalem poor appears on the scene as naturally as did the council of elders to whom Moses was sent long before. This elders' council sits with the Apostles to decide whether circumcision was to be required of all believers (Acts 15), and Paul reports to both elders and Apostles meeting together on the fruits of his missionary travels (Acts 21:15-26).

Paul and Barnabas appointed elders in the congregations newly formed by their missionary labors (Acts 14:23), thus setting a pattern for the organization of Christian congregations — and setting these congregations on the foundations long established in the history of the Old Testament Church.

The Church now receives inspired instruction concerning the office of the elder. In both his First Letter to Timothy (3:2-7) and in his letter to Titus (1:5-9) Paul spells out the tasks and qualifications for eldership, while in his farewell address to the Elders of Ephesus (Acts 20:28-31) he establishes their authority and responsibilities — a pattern upon which this book is based.

The New Testament thus assigns to the office of the elder the following functions: 1) to rule the household of God (I Tim. 3:4-5; 5:17); 2) to teach (I Tim. 3:17); 3) to protect sound doctrine from perversion and to guard against the intrusion of error (Titus 1:9); 4) to oversee the Lord's flock as representative of the Lord Himself (Jn. 21:16; Heb. 13:7; I Pet. 5:2).

First chosen by the Apostles (probably with consent of the Church) and now by election of the congregation, the elder has his office by gift of the Holy Spirit (Acts 20:28).

THE ELDER IN THE PRE-REFORMATION CHURCH

By the second century after Christ, the New Testament Church began the transformation which resulted in the priestly hierarchy still characteristic of Roman Catholicism. The terms "presbyter" and "episcopos" which Paul uses interchangably in the letter to Titus come to designate the regular priesthood over which Bishops, appointed by the Pope, exercise jurdisdiction. The priest celebrates the Mass, primary channel of grace in the Roman Church, and Bishops ordain the priests, while the role of the laity in congregational administration falls away. By the fourth century the division between clergy and laity was absolute, and the eldership was no longer a ruling office.

Preaching declined in both quantity and quality as the centuries passed. In reaction to the Reformation, the Catholic Council of Trent (1545-1563) essentially re-affirmed the hierarchical system which had developed: the Church's offices are those of bishop, priest, deacon; appointment to office is the prerogative of the Pope, delegated by him to the Bishops in the case of priest and deacon. The office of elder has disappeared.

THE ELDER AND THE REFORMATION

Luther's rupture of the hierarchical structure did not immediately restore the elder to his New Testament role in the Church. The Lutheran Church retained the administrative role of bishops (superintendents) with some exceptions appearing in the nineteenth century. The Reformation in England retained the bishop's (episcopal) role.

It was in the Genevan Reformed Church, under the leadership of John Calvin, that the New Testament office of the elder was once again given its administrative role. And it is in the Reformed (Presbyterian) tradition that the eldership, with its corporate form as council or consistory, is once again introduced as lay administration of the Church.

Calvin distinguished, on the basis of I Timothy 5:17, between the ordained ministry (sometimes called the teaching elder) and the lay (or ruling) elder. He understood the terms bishop and presbyter both to refer to the office of elder, both of equal status in the Church.

Parallels to Calvin's effort to restore the New Testament office to the Church were those of Bucer in Strassburg, and of John Knox in Scotland. In France the eldership was confirmed by the first Reformed Synod, held in secret in 1559. The office of elder is re-affirmed in the latest French Reformed Church Order, that of 1938.

In the Netherlands, the eldership appears in the Church Order adopted by the first Reformed synod, held at Embden in 1571. In 1560 the Reformed Church of Scotland adopted a Church Order providing for the eldership.

Throughout the Reformation churches, under a number of different titles, the office of the elder as ruling layman appears. Among the Reformed and Presbyterian churches the term commonly used for the office we are discussing is that of "elder," though the terms "trustee" and "presbyter" are also found. Congregational churches use the term "elder" for ruling laymen, while Baptist churches may use it to designate the pastor or even an itinerant evangelist. Among Methodists the term "elder" also appears, although in the Methodist Episcopal communion the ruling office is commonly designated "superintendent".

A MATTER OF TERMINOLOGY

Two Greek terms are used in the New Testament to designate the office of the elder. They are *presbyteros* and *episcopos*. You will observe that each term appears, now, in a denominational name: Presbyterian and Episcopal. *Presbyteros* points to wisdom and spiritual maturity, often the fruits of age; *episcopos* points to oversight, authority, and responsibility.

The Roman Catholic, Greek Orthodox, and Episcopal churches derive their episcopal structure from *episcopos,* translated as "bishop". The Bishop is the ruling authority in the Church, and appoints the priests who carry out that authority.

Churches in the Reformed tradition, including the Presbyterian and Congregational, combine in the eldership the significance of both presbyter and bishop, according to St. Paul's own usage. Paul instructs Titus to "appoint elders in every town as I directed you," and then he goes on to say, "For a bishop, as God's steward, must be blameless" (Titus 1:5,7). He here uses both "elder" and "bishop" to designate the same person and the same office. Churches in the Reformed and Presbyterian traditions have, therefore, declined to consider bishops as holding higher authority in the Church than that of the elder. Lutherans have, on the other hand, tended to follow the Episcopal pattern in their administrative structure.

RULING AND PREACHING ELDERS

In his first letter to Timothy, St. Paul writes: "Let the elder who rules well be considered worthy of double honor, especially those who labor in teaching and preaching" (I Tim. 5:17). Elders must take note of what the Apostle is here teaching, as follows:

1. Note that Paul classes all those to whom ruling authority in the Church is given under the general title of "elders". Among them there is no priority of status or authority. Each elder is the equal of each other elder, whatever his function in the Church. None is "more equal" than others, and the vote and voice of all are of equal weight.

2. Note further that Paul then points to some ruling elders whose special function is teaching and preaching. Today we call these elders "ministers" or "pastors". Reformed and Presbyterian churches commonly authorize their ministers to preach by the rite of ordination, while they "install" or "induct" into office those called to the ruling eldership. Ordination is for life. In the Reformed churches installation in the eldership is for a stipulated term of office, though in some Presbyterian churches election to the eldership is also for life even when the elder is not on active duty.

3. Ordination to the teaching and preaching function does not confer a superior authority or status. It rather obliges the ministry to undertake the awesome task of courageously and faithfully proclaiming the inspired Word of God with a confident, "Thus saith the Lord!" In this responsibility the ordained ministry requires the ardent support of the eldership, for it is a witness-bearing that cost our Lord and many of his faithful mouthpieces their lives. It could be so again, even in free countries, and is so already in totalitarian states. The ruling elders' oversight of the preaching of the Word includes their encouragement of the ministry to proclaim "the whole counsel of God" (Acts 20:27) without fear or favor.

3. In this manual we refer to the ruling elder by the term "elder," and to the ruling elder who is also ordained to preach the Word as the "minister". This is in accord with common parlance in the Reformed, and generally in the Presbyterian, churches. Members of other communions who may also find this manual useful can make the necessary adaptation of terminology. We consider that the "elder" and the "minister" are, according to the Scriptures, of equal status and authority while differing in the function to which each is called. We recognize that the minister, by virtue of training and occupation and community recognition, may seem to exercise a higher authority in affairs of the Church than does the elder. But this seeming superiority has no foundation in the Bible. In this same sense, we believe that the Episcopal structure, according central authority to the Bishop, is a misunderstanding of the Scriptures — though not one that keeps us from recognizing in such churches fellow members of the communion of saints.

IN SUMMARY

The elder has ruled the Church, as God's representative, since the earliest history of Israel. It is an office of awesome responsibility. If you and countless other elders, across the churches, will rise to take hold of your appointed calling with a new spirit, fresh hope, and eager anticipation, there may well be a renewal of the Church of Christ which will foretell a new day for Western civilization.

And if you who are not now elders, into whose hands this book may come, will join countless other laypersons in demanding that *elders be elders* (!), the outcome will be the same creative impulse. Demand a living eldership! — Now!!

PART VI

AN EYE ON TOMORROW

PART VI

"SAVAGE WOLVES
WILL COME IN AMONG YOU,
THEREFORE BE ALERT."

The elders' role in overseeing the Church as discipling agent under the Lord's Great Commission. Defense against the intrusion of deviations in doctrine or life from without and from within. A brief catalog for alerting the elder to the doctrines and practices of contemporary sects and cults.

Chapter 19

THE GREAT COMMISSION

> "All authority in heaven and on earth has been given
> to Me. Go therefore and make disciples of all nations,
> baptizing them in the name of the Father and of the
> Son and of the Holy Spirit, teaching them to observe
> all that I have commanded you; and lo, I am with you
> always, to the close of the age" (Matt. 28:18-20).

These words spoken by Jesus to His disciples just before His
ascension are commonly called the Great Commission.

The disciples to whom this Commission is given represent the New
Testament Church, the very Church in which you, as elder, now hold
important office. The Church's responsibility for discipling now rests
upon your shoulders. How shall you do your part in fulfilling it?

THE TASK

Notice first what the Lord asks the Church to do.

She is to make disciples.

This is your key to evaluating the countless forms of "evangelism"
being promoted today. Judge each carefully. Endorse for your congregation only those which seek to gain *disciples* for the Lord. Ask: is
that the aim? how well is the aim accomplished?

Separate this one aim from other attractive alternatives or sub-
stitutes: the Lord simply said, "make disciples"!

DISCIPLE

What is a disciple?

A disciple is a follower. A disciple is a chosen follower. All of the
Lord's disciples were called into His service by name: "Follow Me,"

He said.

Notice that disciples follow according to the Master's purpose, not according to their own.

The Lord makes clear, in the Commission, what He wants His disciples to be, namely baptized ones. What does this mean?

Baptism means that the disciple acknowledges who Jesus Christ is: He is the one to whom has been given "all authority in heaven and on earth".

Baptism means that the disciple is cleansed of all guilt inherited from Adam, and of all sin committed in serving another authority, like that of the Devil or himself.

Baptism means that the disciple is liberated from the burden and the bondage of sin and death. Like Israel passing through the Red Sea (by which baptism was foretold), the disciple is freed in baptism from the threat of bondage to another lord.

And baptism means that the disciple liberated from the servitude now commits himself to the service which truly frees.

And the Lord defines exactly what this service requires: "Teaching them to observe all that I have commanded you."

A disciple, then, in terms of the Great Commission is one who is enlisted by the Church in the life of obedience to Jesus Christ. Just as Israel, once delivered from Egypt entered the service of God as defined by the Commandments given from Sinai.

The elder who keeps this in view will have no great difficulty in discriminating appropriate evangelistic methods from inappropriate ones. The test: making disciples, that is those committed to learning the will of Jesus and doing it.

THE COMMANDS

What are "all that I have commanded you"?

The eldership which takes the Great Commission seriously — and you should! — must come to grips with this question: what does the Lord command?

Begin with the Gospels, and sort out His commands. You will fill several pages with them, among the hardest being His requirements laid down in the Sermon on the Mount (Matt. 5-7, and parallel passages). How will the Church teach disciples to do what their Lord commands?

The answer to this question defines the Church. She teaches

through the Word preached, and taught; and through the Word made visible in the Sacraments. And the Church surrounds her teaching with the encouragement and admonition of discipline. Together these three — preaching, sacraments, discipline — are the marks of the true Church, assumed by the Great Commission.

But the Church preaches more than the Gospels. Yes, the entire Word of God is His Word — for Jesus is God. To teach *all* that He has commanded, then, is to teach all the commands of the Scriptures, summed up in the Decalog, which in turn is summarized in the two great commandments: to love God above all, and the neighbor as oneself (Matt. 22:34-40).

The Church fulfills the Great Commission by being truly herself.

The elder fulfills his role in the Great Commission by striving to make the Church the Body she ought to be.

TACTICS

If the above outlines the strategy of the Great Commission, what about the tactics? How will the elder choose among evangelistic methods?

The aim of evangelism is, obviously, to make disciples. The method is by bringing those who are presently outside the Church into the Church, where they can come under the power of the Word preached and taught. Only in and by the Church can the disciple become the kind of servant the Lord seeks.

Notice that Christ calls disciples to follow Him into obedience. He does not hold out promise of ease, or bliss, or even heaven: "Then Jesus told His disciples, 'If any man would come after Me, let him deny himself and take up his cross and follow Me. For whoever would save his life will lose it, but whoever loses his life for My sake will find it' " (Matt. 16:24-25).

Do not permit your congregation to be misled into using the Christ as their servant, as their guarantee of bliss. His call is *for* servants, who will take up the cross of obedience to His commands.

Never be anxious about evangelism. Never succumb to the "numbers" game of seeing how many "commitments" your congregation can boast of. Your task is to keep your congregation faithfully the Church. And, while you will eagerly extend the influence of the Church over as many lives as you can, be assured that the Lord knows His own, and none will be lost who is His: "My sheep hear My voice, and I know them, and they follow me; and I give them eternal life, and they shall never perish, and no one shall snatch them out of my hand. My Father, who has given them to me, is greater than all, and no one is able to snatch them out of the Father's hand" (Jn. 10:27-29).

We make the following tactical suggestions for carrying out the Great Commission:

1. Evangelism is the Church's business; the Commission was given to the disciples who laid the foundations of the New Testament Church.

2. This means that evangelism must be done under the supervision of the eldership, by means and through persons approved by them, according to the Word.

3. The preaching and doing of the Word are the calling of the Church, and are, therefore, her primary means of evangelizing.

4. Preaching is the Church's special mark and prerogative; doing is the congregation's special task and obligation. Combined, these draw others into the Body of Christ.

5. The order laid down in the Commission is normative: preaching the gospel of liberation from sin and self; baptism upon repentance and confession of faith in the exalted Lord; then training in good works and obedience. See to it that this is the order of priorities under your administration. Good works flow from sound doctrine. Sound doctrine flows from a pulpit which preaches the Truth of the Word.

6. Overwhelming stress is laid upon the life of discipleship, the life of obedience, in the Scriptures: "Let your light so shine before men, that they may see your good works and give glory to your Father who is in heaven" (Matt. 5:16). To the disciple whose heart is aflame to do Him service, the Lord declares: "No one after lighting a lamp puts it in a cellar or under a bushel, but on a stand, that those who enter may see the light" (Luke 11:33) — and the light of which He speaks is that shed abroad by the good works of obedience.

IN PRACTICE

Not only must each disciple witness by his good works, but your congregation must do so as well. We make these suggestions:

1. Aid to the poor and needy. The Church, through her deacons, should ever be on the alert to demonstrate Christ's love to those in need. This task begins with those within the body who suffer want, and extends to the whole community: "So then, as we have

opportunity, let us do good to all men, and especially to those who are of the household of faith" (Gal. 6:10). The Lord's command is stringent: "Lend, expecting no return" (Luke 6:35). Give, even at the risk of being "taken in," just as the Lord healed ten lepers, knowing that of these only one would return thanks to Him (Luke 17:11-19).

2. Community services: set up, if you can, counseling services, using the talents of the congregation. Be helpful, have the church door open. Extend a hand to victims of alcohol, of drugs, of their sex drives. Let the public know that the Church serves her Lord by being willing to serve others in these ways.

3. Legal and business advice: using members of the congregation, offer legal and business services to those without means otherwise to afford them. The ignorant are easily cheated by the unscrupulous, and the poor know little about the business of handling money. Help them! Let the city know that your congregation holds out the hand of love!

4. Invite the community to share in the organizations of the Church: discussion groups, Bible study, youth activities. Pay attention to the kinds of outside influence brought to bear upon the congregation in these ways, and be prepared to step in and prevent the spread of bad habits.

5. Consider hot lunch programs for the children of the poor, and warm meal programs for the elderly shut-ins.

Spend time in eldership meetings on other means, perhaps more suitable to your situation, of letting the light of love shine brightly in the place where the Lord has placed you. Not as social-gospel do-goodism, but as sober and obedient witness to the Lord of the Great Commission: "But if anyone has the world's goods and sees his brother in need, yet closes his heart against him, how does God's love abide in him?" (I Jn. 3:17). What is true for the disciple is equally true for the Church: "Little children, let us not love in word or speech but in deed and in truth" (I Jn. 3:18).

SUMMARY

The Great Commission is the Church's charter for enlisting disciples in the service of the Lord to whom all authority has been given. The Church does so by being the Church, preaching and practising the inspired Word of God. To oversee this witness of Word and work is the elder's grave responsibility toward his Lord's Commission.

Chapter 20.

SAVAGE WOLVES

If the wolves of whom St. Paul speaks really looked like wolves there would be little trouble in spotting them. The threat of theological wolves lies in their appearing in sheep's attire. Just as the Devil may either play dead (though he never is!) or don the garb of "an angel of light" (II Cor. 11:14).

Therefore, the Apostle admonishes elders to be always on guard against enemies of the Church, from without and especially those from within.

Doctrinal deviation, and open attack upon doctrinal standards take too many forms for a complete listing and discussion here. We will, rather, suggest indications of departure from the truth to which the elder must be alert. It will be your responsibility to investigate signs of defection and to bring about correction or discipline.

THE POWER IS IN THE TRUTH

Never lose sight of one fundamental principle: error is overcome only by truth. What the true Church stands *for* remains her strongest bulwark against doctrinal deviation. Keep before yourselves as elders, and before the congregation through sound preaching and instruction, the fundamentals summarized in your creeds and confessions. These are the foundation stones of a strong and healthy congregation, and the touchstones of departure from orthodoxy. Examine "new" doctrines, and different emphases, in the light of your doctrinal standards — and the wolves will not escape detection for very long. The Church falls prey to heresy only after she has first dulled her sensitivity to the truth of her confessions. A creed or confession gathering dust on the shelf, or glass-enclosed in the Church's trophy case, threatens no wolves. You must be determined and persistent in creating a high degree of doctrinal awareness in your congregation. This will ever be the strongest antidote against infection by theological error.

Wolves invade the Church, or arise within her, on two fronts: in doctrine and in life. What is believed may be corrupted, or what is done may be perverted. Against both — and they are intimately related — the eldership must be on guard.

CORRUPTION OF DOCTRINE

1. The error that concerns St. Paul most of all in his two letters to Timothy is speculation and idle disputation. These are carried on, of course, under the guise of "understanding" the truth. They may be detected for the wolves they are by contrast with the very practical character of Biblical truth. The Bible is not given to fuel gossip, inspire speculation, or stimulate talk. The inspired Word is given, Paul reminds Timothy, to this end: "...that the man of God may be complete, equipped for every good work" (II Tim. 3:17). This is not a passing conclusion of Paul's. It is echoed by St. James: "But be doers of the Word, and not hearers only, deceiving yourselves" (Jas. 1:22). A deception practised by speculators and idle talkers not only upon the Church but upon themselves. And both Paul and James echo their Lord's teaching, for He embraces "doers" of His Word as "wise" (Matt. 7:24) not only, but as His very own "brother, and sister, and mother" (Matt. 12:50). And in this very practical emphasis the Christ only repeats the teaching of His great prophets and of the Law which God Himself wrote with His own fingers on tablets of stone (Ex. 31:18).

Be alert, then to the dangers inherent in talk which only issues in more talk. Suspect theological ideas which are simply entertained as interesting possibilities. Discourage theories unrelated to Christian behavior. All these fall under Paul's condemnation of "forever learning and never coming to a knowledge of the truth" (II Tim. 3:7), that is talk which never issues in obedient behavior. Worst of all, speculation presumes itself to be high service of God and the Church. Discourage it.

It is, moreover, of the nature of speculation never to reach certainty. It thus always impedes action for God in the world. One problem seemingly resolved opens upon two or more problems yet to be tackled, a fact which shows God's own abhorrence of the idle speculation which Paul condemns — and so must you!

Your test of idle speculation is quite simple: "Show us what difference your theorizing makes in obedient behavior!" Or again: "Show us in your own life how your speculation will stimulate the congregation's 'doing' of the will of God." Then test the result on your fingertips. Decline to be put off by theological jargon or high-sounding phrases. The witness of deed must bear out the fidelity of witness in word.

Bear always in mind that a true understanding of God's will emerges from striving to do God's Word, not merely talking about it.

The elder will find speculation in the Church's schools, in her classrooms in the local congregation, on retreats, in various study groups. It becomes your difficult task to point all these to words that become works, lest doctrine be corrupted by idle speculation.

2. The source of both sound doctrine and of true, living obedience is the Bible. Quite naturally, the wolves will be gnawing away at its content and authority.

Acquaint yourself thoroughly with what your doctrinal standards teach about the Bible. Insist upon allegiance to that teaching, from the pulpit and in all the Church's classrooms and study groups. Be alert for the intrusion of mistaken views of the Scriptures garbed as "scholarship" or "research" or "criticism".

Can the elder really match wits with the "learned" over the Bible? Yes, you can! How? By grasping, and then always applying, the Reformation principle of *"Sola Scriptura"*! Translated, this Latin phrase means "only Scripture". It was once the Reformer's stoutest weapon against a priestly hierarchy in the Roman Catholic Church. It is now the elders' stoutest weapon against the self-appointed "priesthood" of scholarship — no less a threat to freedom of listening to the Bible.

Sola Scriptura means that Scripture alone truly expounds Scripture. Now, you take sober note of that and never let it go! Scripture interprets Scripture — not "research," nor language study, nor "criticism," nor monstrous theological treatises. Not at all! Scripture interprets Scripture — and that means that you have as much right to work out the meaning of a text as anyone else who loves and reads the Word. Texts and passages difficult to interpret are illumined, according to *Sola Scriptura*, by texts and passages you already do understand. Let the Word explain the Word; there is no other inspired commentary!

Aware of this long established principle, the one for which and on which much of the Reformation was fought, the layman finds himself on an equal footing with the professor. In fact, it will be the more saintly of the two whose life of obedience fills him with the more wisdom in understanding the Word. And it is for such wisdom that elders are chosen.

Test by the Word what is said about the Word. Insist that conclusions about the meaning of Biblical passages which are derived from history or criticism bow humbly before what both you and the critic can — if he will — hear the Bible saying for itself.

Sola Scriptura! Beware of him who denies or belittles it!

3. Be on guard, also, for those who play the Holy Spirit off against the Scriptures, claiming that they have private and personal "revelations" of "new truths". Christ teaches the disciples that the Holy Spirit "will not speak on His own authority, but whatever He hears He will speak" (Jn. 16:13). It is with the revealed Word that the Spirit works, and all who claim special revelation through the Spirit must submit that to the test of the Scriptures. The Bible ends with St. John's curse upon any who add to, or take from, his prophecy (Rev. 22:18-19), and this meant for the Church that the age of new revelation was over. Sufficient for what Christians must believe and how Christians must live is contained in the Bible. New revelations are neither needed nor to be anticipated. Always insist, therefore, that claims to "new" revelation from the Spirit be tested by the Bible. Then go on to insist that such claims themselves have no footing in Scripture, and must be repented of. For, unless restrained, illusions of special favors of the Holy Spirit soon introduce division into the congregation between the "more holy" haves and the ordinary have-nots.

4. Remember as you encounter signs of doctrinal deviation that errors are rarely if ever brand new. We may think so, and usually the victim of the error is certain, but in fact what we take to be new has already been met and exposed in the history of the Church. We are taken in because we know too little of Church history. The conscientious elder will do reading in the history of the Church — in books from his church library or a religious bookstore. The Devil has assaulted the Church across the centuries, and the forms of his attack may be novel but are rarely new. Find out how what you encounter today was treated maybe ten centuries ago. It will give you a poise and confidence as you deal with error.

5. In another area, take note of how doctrinal shortcoming creeps into the Church under the guise of evangelism.

Evangelism is the Church's business. But it is a mistake to say that "the Church is mission". The Church is, as we have seen in Chapter 16, a Body called to do her Lord's work in the world, namely bearing witness to the truth in word and deed. Mission and evangelism simply enlist outsiders into joining the Church in its witnessing.

Seen from this point of view, evangelism is far from pressuring a "prospect" into some easy "commitment" in exchange for the promise of heaven. The Church indeed has possession of the keys to the kingdom, but these are by no means committed to self-appointed evangelists. For the keys are preaching, done under the supervison of the eldership, and discipline done by the eldership.

Crusade evangelism has, in these days, become big and profitable business. Profitable even if the evangelist turns little of the income to personal use; his organization grows, his staff enlarges, and the number of those who feed on the stream of gifts increases. And to keep the money rolling in, the "evangelists" must multiply their claims to "success" — always measured in numbers of "commitments to Christ". Studies have shown that a pitifully tiny number of those making commitments do in fact join and remain in the Church. But the claims go on, the "numbers game" becomes competitive, and the Church is readily tempted to join in. Beware of that!

There is a marked difference between the evangelism of Jesus and of St. Paul and the wholesale offer of "salvation" in crusade "evangelism" today. Jesus and Paul begin by requiring repentance: "From that time Jesus began to preach, saying, 'Repent, for the kingdom of heaven is at hand' " (Matt. 4:17). And St. Paul testifies before Festus and Agrippa: "I was not disobedient to the heavenly vision, but declared first to those at Damascus, then at Jerusalem and throughout all the country of Judea, and also to the Gentiles, that they should repent and turn to God..." (Acts 26:19-20).

What was this "repent"? It was the requirement that, to enter the kingdom, the disciple must forsake his previous way of life, give up his idols of power, success, wealth, and self-interest, and as Paul goes on to say: "perform deeds worthy of their repentance" (Acts 26:20). That is, witness to the truth of their word-repentance by deed. Christ makes this sequence clear in His "great commission" by requiring of the Church, through the Apostles, that she preach, baptize, and then teach "them to observe all that I have commanded you" (Matt. 28:20). And the Lord makes clear in His parable of the Last Judgment (Matt. 25:31-46) that He will Himself sit as a Judge as to how well the would-be disciple did indeed do what He commands.

Entrance into the Church involves self-denial and cross-bearing: "If any man would come after Me, let him deny himself and take up his cross and follow Me" (Matt. 16:24). And Christ makes no pretence of offering an easy route to heaven: "Enter by the narrow gate; for the gate is wide, and the way is easy, that leads to destruction, and those who enter by it are many. For the gate is narrow and the way is hard, that leads to life, and those who find it are few" (Matt. 7:13-14). No "numbers game" here!

The Church offers salvation those who will take up the cross of self-denial, and the yoke of obedience (Matt. 11:29-30). The Church schools such converts under her preaching and her discipline — and these are the keys she places in their hands en route to the kingdom. There need be no challenges to "accept Christ". Christ's challenge is to take up a cross! There need be no special "evangelistic" services. The pulpit is always engaged in maturing disciples for service through self-denial and obedience to the commandments. The convert may come in under the Church's wing at any time, and go on from there. Heaven is not handed out some Sunday evening. Heaven is the reward to those who devote their lives to hearing and doing the Word: "To those who by patience in well-doing seek for glory and honor and immortality, He will give eternal life" (Rom. 2:7). And they will naturally join themselves to His Body: "All that the Father gives Me," Jesus says, "will come to Me" (Jn. 6:37). And again, "My sheep hear My voice, and I know them, and they follow Me; and I give them eternal life, and they shall never perish, and no one shall snatch them out of My hand" (Jn. 10:27-28). The elder need never fear that one of the elect shall be lost. Your concern is that the Church be faithful in her exercise of the keys, and diligent in inviting all who will to come under the preaching and discipline. This is true evangelism.

DEVIATIONS IN LIFE

Our concern with deviations in life, in this Chapter, is not with the discipline of these. This is dealt with in Chapters 9 and 10.

Important here is the fact that the Church herself may be corrupted by the subtle intrusion of false lifestyles, leading inevitably to tensions in the Body and dilution of doctrinal stability.

The Christian life flows from sound belief. So we have been pointing out.

But sound belief may be attacked by way of deviations from Christian conduct.

Introduction of the commune, for example, may lead to devaluation of the so-called "nuclear" (that is regular) family. And the Church's pattern for ideal family life, for the rearing of children, even for monogamous relationships may all come under indirect, but damaging, critique by the adoption of communal lifestyle by some members. This would bear close observation by the eldership.

The Church teaches respect for, and obedience to, the state. St. Paul requires, for example, that "every person be subject to the governing authorities. For there is no authority except from God, and those that exist have been instituted by God. Therefore he who resists the authorities resists what God has appointed, and those who resist will incur judgment" (Rom. 13:1-2). There is room in the democratic state for protest by word and deed, but when non-violent demonstration breaks the law, such protest becomes rebellion. Not the less so when the protest is done by members of the Church. But unless such action is disciplined by the eldership, it lets into the Church a subtle devaluation of the Bible's teaching on obedience to the state.

Youth, and adults also, are urged to "witness" for Christ. But some forms of witness depend upon assumptions, like Arminianism, which depreciate doctrinal positions held by the congregation. Error may thus invade the Body under the guise of highly laudable endeavor.

The elder must constantly be on the alert for the wolves which invade the flock in the form of deviant behavior — even when that lifestyle has the approbation of the spirits of the age and may be widely popular.

Remember that conduct always embodies belief. The conduct which the Bible approves is that which gives form and content to Biblical beliefs. Other conduct, if permitted without censure, will quietly undermine what the Church stands for and should be. Let the elder always be aware of this danger.

Chapter 21.

SECTS AND CULTS

"For the time is coming," the inspired Apostle Paul writes, "when people will not endure sound teaching, but having itching ears they will accumulate for themselves teachers to suit their own likings, and will turn away from listening to the truth and wander into myths" (II Tim. 4:3-4).

Such a time is at hand.

To understand, and try to counter, the sects and cults, the elder must reflect upon the full import of what the Spirit is here revealing through St. Paul. The sects and the cults do not seduce people from true religion; they are raised up by people who desire escape from the Christ and His gospel. The followers create the false leader. He comes in answer to their call. Thus the sectarian and the cultist is at the opposite pole from the true believer, who is raised from the dead by his Lord's call: "He who enters by the door is the shepherd of the sheep...the sheep hear His voice, and He calls His own sheep by name and leads them out...I am the good shepherd" (Jn. 10:2,3,11).

Only if you can make this crucial contrast clear to the cultist or sectarian can you hope to offset the temptation of the false religion. And only as this truth is kept before the congregation will sects and cults have a hard time making progress among your people. Those who are misled want to be misled. To escape being further misled they must first understand their predicament. The sect or the cult is the answer to their own call; their only hope, by contrast, is to hear and respond to the Lord's call as heard in His Word and from your pulpit.

The answer to the cults and sects, then, roots in resounding affirmation in the Church, and by the Church, of Christ's call to repent and believe: "Now after John was arrested, Jesus came into Galilee, preaching the gospel of God, and saying, 'The time is fulfilled, and the kingdom of God is at hand; repent, and believe in the gospel' " (Mk.

1:14-15). The cultist must choose between adapting religion to his own demands, and adapting himself to the demand of Christ: "And He said to all, 'If any man would come after Me, let him deny himself and take up his cross daily and follow Me' " (Luke 9:23).

We draw no firm line of distinction between "sects" and "cults". The sect is often viewed as arising within established religion, and withdrawing from its communion. The cult is often associated with some charismatic leader who sometimes develops an independent body of beliefs. But lines cross, and we shall hereafter use the terms interchangeably.

Summarized below are the basic tenets, along with other useful information, associated with the more prominent sects of our time. We have included the conception of God and of Christ held by the sect, and concluded with a selection of Biblical texts for comparison with the cultic views. The varieties among the sectarians, and even within given sects, are large. The elder should, if a given cult arises in his area, take time to acquaint himself with its beliefs and prepare himself to answer them from Scripture.

EASTERN RELIGIONS

Religions from the Orient seep into the Western world in a number of forms, among them these three:

Hare Krishna - a cult founded by the Swami Prabhupada

Transcendental Meditation - a cult founded by the Maharishi Mahesh Yogi

Zen - a variety of Buddhism

Doctrines: are rooted in Eastern and Hindu philosophy, which holds that all existence constitutes a single reality, impersonal, and destined to evolve into pure being, that is a union with the divine in which all individuality is lost.

Worship: consists in meditation, in chanting the secret and sometimes meaningless word called a "mantra". Through this self-hypnosis the soul loses its personality and achieves oneness with what may be variously called the cosmic spirit, pure awareness, or pure being, or "god". Steps along the road are concentration, contemplation, and meditation, combined with physical exercise like deep breathing. A moral lifestyle is commended, but there are no specific moral demands.

JEHOVAH'S WITNESSES

History: developed in the USA by its first three presidents, who assumed office on dates indicated:

Charles Taze Russell (early called Russellites) 1884

Joseph Franklin Rutherford 1917

Nathan Home Knorr 1942

Doctrines: rejection of the Trinity as a false doctrine designed by Satan to defame the name of Jehovah.

Jehovah has the attributes of power, justice, love, and wisdom. He established, on earth, a righteous kingdom in 1914; and all history will find its meaning in the great battle of Armageddon when Jehovah will vindicate His kingdom against Satan and all his hosts. This victory is more important than the salvation of men.

Jesus was the first and finest creation of Jehovah, but was not divine. He was put to death and resurrected only as a spirit, and now reigns from heaven as spirit.

The holy spirit is an invisible, active force of the Almighty which moves Jehovah's servants to do his will. The spirit is neither deity nor person.

Witnessing is the way of salvation; the harder the witness works now, the more prominent will be his role in the earthly paradise promised Jehovah's faithful.

JW alone are Jehovah's true people; all others are followers of the devil, who are annihilated at death.

The devil's organization is both visible and invisible:

Visible: all political organizations of the world

all religious systems except Watchtower Society

Invisible: demons

Characteristics: members meet in Kingdom Halls, and ring doorbells.

Some of their common views:

Opposition to blood transfusions

Refusal to salute any flag, to vote, to hold public office

Emphasis on prophecy

Identification of the USA as the beast of Revelation 13

Among the Witnesses is an elite class of 144,000 who are Jehovah's channel of enlightenment of all people on earth.

Publications: there is no official statement of belief.

New World Translation of the Holy Scriptures, in which anonymous translators impose their system on the Bible.

Two bi-weekly magazines are published in 25 languages:

Awake

Watchtower Announcing Jehovah's Kingdom

MORMONISM

History: begun by Joseph Smith, to whom the angel Maroni revealed the location of buried golden plates from which he translated the *Book of Mormon*.

Continued after Smith's murder by Brigham Young, who led the Mormons from Illinois to Salt Lake Valley, Utah, in 1847.

Doctrines: God is one of thousands of gods who exist in the universe.

God has progressed from having been a man to being a god, and such progress will continue. Mormons receive ongoing revelation.

God lives in heaven with a plurality of wives, procreating spirit children, who are then born into the bodies of earthly children.

Jesus Christ: is the first-born of pre-existent spirits.

is not unique, neither in divinity nor incarnation.

is the product of a physical union between God and Mary.

had many wives and natural children.

Mankind: existed as spirits in a pre-mortal period of probation, progression, and schooling.

Life on earth is probationary period of preparation to meet God again.

Only Mormons in good standing can prepare themselves for highest heaven, called the Celestial Kingdom, through tithing, doing temple duties, following prescribed moral regulations.

Baptism is performed for the dead in the temples on proxies who represent ancestors who died without knowledge of the gospel restored by Joseph Smith.

Celestial marriage, which seals a union for eternity, is performed in the Mormon temples.

Organization: stakes, wards, branches

Ruled by a President and Council of Twelve Apostles

Publications: *Book of Mormon,* 1830 (seems to contradict some Mormon doctrines)

Book of Commandments, 1833.

Doctrine and Covenants, 1835.

Pearl of Great Price, 1830.

Amended version of the Bible.

THE UNIFICATION CHURCH (MOONIES)

Otherwise called: Holy Spirit Association for Unification of World Christianity.

History: founded in 1954 by Korean, excommunicated Presbyterian minister, Sun Myung Moon, who received a vision of the divine principle of the universe, and wrote *The Divine Principle,* basic text for the movement.

Doctrines: Moon is called the Master, or Father, and considers himself greater than any past prophets or leaders of the Church, and greater than Jesus as well. Moon and his wife are the true Parents Come to Save; he is true savior, the living God.

God is single, not triune. The Holy Spirit is female, the true spiritual Mother of Mankind. Jesus established a divine salvation, but was crucified before He could marry and produce sinless children.

Man has fallen, spiritually by not keeping faith with God, and physically by yielding to seduction by Satan.

Aim is to establish the kingdom of God by fund raising, by renovation of old buildings, by recruiting new members, by marrying to produce sinless children. Control of property is in hands of Moon.

Converts allowed to manipulate people, to practice "heavenly deception" to obtain goods and money.

Stand is anti-communist, on ground that Christ brought about democracy to provide best social order.

THE WAY INTERNATIONAL

History: founded by Victor Paul Wierville in 1968.

Wierville is graduate of Mission House College and Seminary, and has master's degree from Princeton in practical theology. Claims that his insights surpass all others since first century. Makes his own translation of of Scriptures for Bible study courses.

Doctrines: everyone is to speak in tongues, aloud and to self; this is true worship of God.

Stress on personal witnessing, door-to-door, seeking converts and funds — with 15-20% given to the Way.

Christ is a son of God, the revealed Word of God, but not God.

Holy spirit is but another name for God.

The holy spirit (not capitalized) refers to gifts from God of spiritual talents, and not to a person; there are nine kinds of such gifts.

The Old Testament is rejected as invalid for Christians.

Practice: the convert is rigidly controlled, is required to keep a a diary of every hour from 5 in the morning to midnight, and to do daily physical exercise.

Training is done at the Way Corps, a school in Emporia, Kansas, where converts receive insufficient nourishment, are allowed but little sleep, and are kept to a rigorous program of study and activity.

Structure; the Way Tree: roots, trunk, limbs, branches, twigs. The twig is the local fellowship, not considered a church.

Publication: Wierville's *Power For Abundant Living*

CONCLUSION

Why should the elder arm himself and his congregation against intrusion by the cults? Don't they do some good, despite their strange doctrines?

The answer to that question cries out from the nature of the cults and sects themselves: they enslave their believers. Seeking independence and freedom, or escape from what they think oppressive in Christianity, the converts fall into bondage to cultist doctrines and leaders.

Set against the claims and perversions of the cults the sound teaching of the Word: "If you continue in My word, you are truly My disciples, and you will know the truth, and the truth will make you free" (Jn. 8:31-32).

There is but one source of true liberty: "So if the Son makes you free, you will be free indeed" (Jn. 8:36).

How can you permit anyone, unwarned, to neglect this true freedom and follow after the enslavement of the cults?

APPENDIX

To overcome the seductions of the sects and cults, the elder must do battle with "the sword of the Spirit, which is the word of God" (Eph. 6:17). To assist in that battle, we offer the following selection of texts dealing with truths most often questioned by the cultists:

On Jesus Christ

Matt. 16:16 - You are the Christ, the Son of the living God.

Jn. 17:3 - And this is eternal life, that they know Thee the only true God, and Jesus Christ whom Thou hast sent.

Acts 2:36 - Let all the house of Israel therefore assuredly know that God has made Him both Lord and Christ, this Jesus whom you crucified.

Acts 18:28 - For he powerfully confuted the Jews in public, showing by the Scriptures that the Christ was Jesus.

I Cor. 1:30 - He is the source of your life in Christ Jesus, whom God made our wisdom, our righteousness and sanctification and redemption.

Eph. 2:19-22 - So then you are no longer strangers and sojourners, but you are fellow citizens with the saints and members of the household of God, built upon the foundation of the apostles and prophets, Christ Jesus Himself the cornerstone, in whom the whole structure is joined together and grows into a holy temple in the Lord, in whom you also are built into it for a dwelling place of God in the Spirit.

Phil. 2:9-11 - Therefore God has highly exalted Him and bestowed on Him the name which is above every name, that at the name of Jesus every knee should bow, in heaven and on earth and under the earth, and every tongue confess that Jesus Christ is Lord, to the glory of God the Father.

I Tim. 1:15 - The saying is sure and worthy of full acceptance, that Christ Jesus came into the world to save sinners.

I Tim. 2:5 - For there is one God, and there is one mediator between God and men, the man Christ Jesus.

I Jn. 5:20 - And we know that the Son of God has come and has given us understanding, to know Him who is true; and we are in Him who is true, in His Son Jesus Christ.

On the Holy Spirit:

Luke 11:13 - If you then, who are evil, know how to give good gifts to your children, how much more will the heavenly Father give the Holy Spirit to those who ask Him!

Rom. 5:5 - And hope does not disappoint us, because God's love has been poured into our hearts through the Holy Spirit which has been given us.

Rom. 8:9 - But you are not in the flesh, you are in the Spirit, if the Spirit of God really dwells in you. Any one who does not have the Spirit of Christ does not belong to Him.

Rom. 8:11 - If the Spirit of Him who raised Jesus from the dead dwells in you, He who raised Christ Jesus from the dead will give life to your mortal bodies also through His Spirit which dwells in you.

Rom. 8:16-17 - When we cry, "Abba, Father!" it is the Spirit Himself bearing witness with our spirit that we are children of God, and if children, then heirs, heirs of God and fellow heirs with Christ.

Rom. 8:26-27 - Likewise the Spirit helps us in our weakness; for we do not know how to pray as we ought, but the Spirit Himself intercedes for us with sighs too deep for words. And He who searches the hearts of men knows what is the mind of the Spirit, because the Spirit intercedes for the saints according to the will of God.

I Cor. 2:10 - For the Spirit searches everything, even the depths of God.

I Cor. 2:11-13 - So also no one comprehends the thoughts of God except the Spirit of God. Now we have received not the spirit of the world, but the Spirit which is from God, that we might understand the gifts bestowed on us by God. And we impart this in words not taught by human wisdom but taught by the Spirit, interpreting spiritual truths to those who possess the Spirit.

I Cor. 6:19 - Do you not know that your body is a temple of the Holy Spirit within you, which you have from God?

I Cor. 12:3 - Therefore I want you to understand that no one speaking by the Spirit of God ever says "Jesus be cursed!" and no one can say "Jesus is Lord" except by the Holy Spirit.

II Cor. 3:17 - Now the Lord is the Spirit, and where the Spirit of the Lord is, there is freedom.

Col. 2:8 - See that no one makes a prey of you by philosophy and empty deceit, according to human tradition, according to the elemental spirits of the universe, and not according to Christ.

I Jn. 4:2-3 - By this you know the Spirit of God: every spirit which confesses that Jesus Christ has come in the flesh is of God, and every spirit which does not confess Jesus is not of God.

I Jn. 5:7 - And the Spirit is the witness, because the Spirit is the truth.

On the Holy Scripture:

Jn. 2:22 - When therefore He was raised from the dead, His disciples remembered that He had said this; and they believed the Scripture and the word which Jesus had spoken.

Jn. 5:39-40 - You search the Scriptures, because you think that in them you have eternal life; and it is they that bear witness to Me; yet you refuse to come to Me that you may have life.

Jn. 7:38 - He who believes in Me, as the Scripture has said, "Out of his heart shall flow rivers of living water."

Rom. 15:4 - For whatever was written in former days was written for our instruction, that by steadfastness and by the encouragement of the Scriptures we might have hope.

Rom. 16:26-27 - Now to Him who is able to strengthen you according to my gospel and the preaching of Jesus Christ, according to the revelation of the mystery which was kept secret for long ages but is now disclosed and through the prophetic writings is made known to all nations, according to the command of the eternal God, to bring about the obedience of faith — to the only wise God be glory for evermore through Jesus Christ.

257

II Tim. 3:16-17 - All Scripture is inspired by God and is profitable for teaching, for reproof, for correction, and for training in righteousness, that the man of God may be complete, equipped for every good work.

II Pet. 1:20-21 - First of all you must understand this, that no prophecy of Scripture is a matter of one's own interpretation, because no prophecy ever came by the impulse of man, but men moved by the Holy Spirit spoke from God.

EPILOGUE

These, then, are the challenges and the opportunities and the obligations laid by God, in Christ, upon His appointed elders.

Well may you ask, with St. Paul, "But who is sufficient for these things?" (II Cor. 2:16).

All by himself, no one is.

But you as elder do not stand alone. There are, first of all, your colleagues in the eldership. There is, next, the whole Body of the Lord whom you must draw more and more into His service. And there is, above all, the Lord of abundant promise. As the same St. Paul says, "But thanks be to God, who in Christ always leads us in triumph, and through us spreads the fragrance of the knowledge of Him everywhere" (II Cor. 2:14). "And I am sure," the Apostle writes elsewhere, "that He who began a good work in you will bring it to completion at the day of Jesus Christ" (Phil. 1:6).

Let it be your desire faithfully to perform your high calling, your goal being set by the faithful Apostle, "Moreover, it is required of stewards that they be found trustworthy" (I Cor. 4:2), and with God be the rest.

> *"Now to Him who by the power at work within us is able to do far more abundantly than all that we ask or think, to Him be glory in the church and in Christ Jesus to all generations, for ever and ever. Amen" (Eph. 3:20-21).*

A CATALOG OF USEFUL TEXTS

AFFLICTED, OUR DUTY TOWARD:

1. To bear them in mind: Heb. 13:3 - Remember those who are in prison, as though in prison with them; and those who are ill-treated, since you also are in the body.

2. To comfort them: Job. 16:5 - I could strengthen you with my mouth, and the solace of my lips would assuage your pain.

Job. 29:25 - I chose their way, and sat as chief, and I dwelt like a king among his troops, like one who comforts mourners.

II Cor. 1:4 - (God) who comforts us in all our afflictions, so that we may be able to comfort those who are in any affliction, with the comfort with which we ourselves are comforted by God.

I Thess. 4:18 - Therefore comfort one another with these words.

3. To pity them: Job 6:14 - He who withholds kindness from a friend forsakes the fear of the Almighty.

4. To pray for them: Acts 12:5 - So Peter was kept in prison; but earnest prayer for him was made to God by the church.

Jas. 5:14-15 - Is any among you sick? Let him call for the elders of the church, and let them pray over him, anointing him with oil in the name of the Lord; and the prayer of faith will save the sick man, and the Lord will raise him up; and if has committed sins, he will be forgiven.

5. To protect them: Psalm 82:3 - Give justice to the weak and the fatherless; maintain the right of the afflicted and the destitute.

Prov. 22:22-23 - Do not rob the poor, because he is poor, or crush the afflicted at the gate; for the Lord will plead their cause and despoil of life those who despoil them.

6. To relieve them: Job 31:16-17; 19; 22 - If I have withheld anything that the poor desired, or have caused the eyes of the widow to fail, or have eaten my morsel alone, and the fatherless has not eaten of it...If I have seen any one perish for lack of clothing, or a poor man without covering...then let my shoulder blade fall from my shoulder, and let my arm be broken from its socket.

Is. 58:10 - If you pour yourself out for the hungry, and satisfy the desire of the afflicted, then shall your light rise in the darkness and your gloom be as the noonday.

Phil. 4:14 - Yet it was kind of you to share my trouble.

I Tim. 5:10 - And she must be well attested for her good deeds, as one who has brought up children, shown hospitality, washed the feet of the saints, relieved the afflicted, and devoted herself to doing good in every way.

7. To sympathize with them: Rom. 12:15 - Rejoice with those who rejoice, weep with those who weep.

Gal. 6:2 - Bear one another's burdens, and so fulfil the law of Christ.

8. To visit them: Jas. 1:27 - Religion that is pure and undefiled before God and the Father is this: to visit orphans and widows in their affliction, and to keep oneself unstained from the world.

AFFLICTIONS, MADE BENEFICIAL:

1. Convincing of sin: Job 36:8-9 - And if they are bound in fetters and caught in the cords of affliction, then He declares to them their work and their transgressions, that they are behaving arrogantly.

Ps. 119:67 - Before I was afflicted I went astray; but now I keep thy word.

Luke 15:17-18 - But when he came to himself he said, "How many of my father's hired servants have bread enough and to spare, but I perish here with hunger! I will arise and go to my father, and I will say to him, 'Father I have sinned against heaven and before you....' "

2. Further the Gospel: Acts. 8:3-4 - But Saul laid waste the church, and entering house after house, he dragged off men and women and commited them to prison. Now those who were scattered went about preaching the word.

Acts 11:19-21 - Now those who were scattered because of the persecution that arose over Stephen traveled as far as Phoenicia and Cyprus and Antioch, speaking the word to none except Jews. But there were some of them, men of Cyprus and Cyrene, who on coming to Antioch spoke to the Greeks also, preaching the Lord Jesus. And the hand of the Lord was with them, and a great number that believed turned to the Lord.

Phil. 1:12 - I want you to know, brethren, that what has happened to me has really served to advance the gospel....

II Tim. 2:9-10 - the gospel for which I am suffering and wearing fetters like a criminal. But the word of God is not fettered. Therefore I endure everything for the sake of the elect, that they also may obtain the salvation which in Christ Jesus goes with eternal glory.

II Tim. 4:16-17 - At my first defense no one took my part; all deserted me. May it not be charged against them! But the Lord stood by me and gave me strength to proclaim the word fully, that all the Gentiles might hear it.

3. **Promoting the glory of God:** Jn. 9:1-3 - As He passed by, He saw a man blind from his birth. And His disciples asked Him, "Rabbi, who sinned, this man or his parents, that he was born blind?" Jesus answered, "It was not that this man sinned, or his parents, but that the works of God might be made manifest in him."

Jn. 11:3-4 - So the sisters sent to Him, saying, "Lord, he whom you love is ill." But when Jesus heard it He said, "This illness is not unto death; it is for the glory of God, so that the Son of God may be glorified by means of it."

Jn. 21:18-19 - "Truly, truly, I say to you, when you were young, you girded yourself and walked where you would; but when you are old, you will stretch out your hands, and another will gird you and carry you where you do not wish to go." (This He said to show by what death he was to glorify God.) And after this He said to him, "Follow me."

4. **Returning us to God:** Judg. 4:3 - Then the people of Israel cried to the Lord for help; for he had nine hundred chariots of iron, and oppressed the people of Israel cruelly for twenty years.

Job 34:31-32 - For has any one said to God, "I have borne chastisement; I will not offend any more; teach me what I do not see; if I have done iniquity, I will do it no more"?

Is. 10:20 - In that day the remnant of Israel and the survivors of the house of Jacob will no more lean upon him that smote them, but will lean upon the Lord, the Holy One of Israel, in truth.

Jer. 31:18 - I have heard Ephraim bemoaning, "Thou has chastened me, and I was chastened, like an untrained calf; bring me back that I may be restored, for thou art the Lord my God."

Lam. 2:18-19 - Cry aloud to the Lord! O daughter of Zion! Let tears stream down like a torrent day and night! Give yourself no rest, your eyes no respite! Arise, cry out in the night, at the beginning of the watches! Pour out your heart like water before the presence of the Lord! Lift your hands to Him for the lives of your children, who faint for hunger at the head of every street.

Ezek. 14:10-11 - And they shall bear their punishment—the punishment of the prophet and the punishment of the inquirer shall be alike—that the house of Israel may go no more astray from me, nor defile themselves any more with all their transgressions, but that they may be my people and I may be their God, says the Lord God.

Hos. 5:14-15 - For I will be like a lion to Ephraim, and like a young lion to the house of Judah. I even I, will rend and go away, I will carry off, and none shall rescue.

Jonah 2:1 - Then Jonah prayed to the Lord his God from the belly of the fish. . . .

5. Teaching us the will of God: Ps. 119:71 - It is good for me that I was afflicted, that I might learn thy statutes.

Is. 26:9 - My soul yearns for thee in the night, my spirit within me earnestly seeks thee. For when thy judgments are in the earth, the inhabitants of the world learn righteousness.

Mic. 6:9 - The voice of the Lord cries to the city—and it is sound wisdom to fear thy name.

6. Testing our faith and obedience: Gen. 22:1 - After these things God tested Abraham, and said to him, "Abraham!" And he said, "Here am I."

Ex. 15:23-25 - When they came to Marah, they could not drink the water of Marah because it was bitter; therefore it was named Marah. And the people murmured against Moses saying, "What shall we drink?" And he cried to the Lord; and the Lord showed him a tree, and he threw it into the water, and the water became sweet.

Deut. 8:12, 16 - And you shall remember all the way which the Lord your God has led you these forty years in the wilderness, that He might humble you, testing you to know what was in your heart, whether you would keep His commandments, or not.

Heb. 11:17 - By faith Abraham, when he was tested, offered up Isaac, and he who had received the promises was ready to offer up his only son. . . .

I Pet. 1:7 - So that the genuineness of your faith, more precious than gold which though perishable is tested by fire, may redound to praise and glory and honor at the revelation of Jesus Christ.

Rev. 2:10 - Do not fear what you are about to suffer. Behold, the devil is about to throw some of you into prison, that you may be tested, and for ten days you will have tribulation. Be faithful unto death, and I will give you the crown of life.

7. **Turning us to God**: Deut. 4:30-31 - When you are in tribulation, and all these things come upon you in the latter days, you will return to the Lord your God and obey His voice, for the Lord your God is a merciful God; He will not fail you or destroy you or forget the covenant with your fathers which He swore to them.

Neh. 1:8-9 - Remember the word which thou didst command thy servant Moses, saying, "If you are unfaithful, I will scatter you among the peoples; but if you return to Me and keep My commandments to do them, though your dispersed be under the farthest skies, I will gather them thence and bring them to the place which I have chosen, to make My name dwell there."

Ps. 78:34 - When He slew them, they sought for Him; they repented and sought God earnestly.

Is. 10:21 - A remnant will return, the remnant of Jacob, to the mighty God.

Hos. 2:6-7 - Therefore I will hedge up her way with thorns; and I will build a wall against her, so that she cannot find her paths. She shall pursue her lovers, but not overtake them; and she shall seek them, but shall not find them. Then she shall say, "I will go and return to my first husband, for it was better with me then than now."

ASSURANCE:

1. **Attain and maintain**: Heb. 2:14-15, 18 - Since therefore the children share in flesh and blood, He himself likewise partook of the same nature, that through death He might destroy him who has the power of death, that is, the devil, and deliver all those who through fear of death were subject to lifelong bondage . . . .For because He himself has suffered and been tempted, He is able to help those who are tempted.

II Pet. 1:10 - Therefore, brethren, be the more zealous to confirm your call and election, for if you do this you will never fall....

2. Produced by faith: Eph. 3:12 - In whom (Christ) we have boldness and confidence of access through our faith in Him.

II Tim. 1:12 - And therefore I suffer as I do. But I am not ashamed, for I know whom I have believed and I am sure that He is able to guard until that Day what has been entrusted to me.

Heb. 10:22 - Let us draw near with a true heart in full assurance of faith, with our hearts sprinkled clean from an evil conscience and our bodies washed with pure water.

3. Through obedience: Ps. 103:17-18 - But the stedfast love of the Lord is from everlasting to everlasting upon those who fear Him, and His righteousness to children's chilren, to those who keep His covenant and remember to do His commandments.

Ps. 119:2, 4-6 - Blessed are those who keep His testimonies, who seek Him with their whole heart. . . .Thou hast commanded thy precepts to be kept diligently. O that my ways be steadfast in keeping thy statutes! Then I shall not be put to shame, having my eyes fixed on all thy commandments.

Is. 1:19 - If you are willing and obedient, you shall eat the good of the land. . . .

Matt. 12:50 - For whoever does the will of My Father in heaven is my brother, and sister, and mother.

Luke 8:21 - But He said to them, "My mother and my brothers are those who hear the word of God and do it."

Jn. 8:51 - Truly, truly, I say to you, if anyone keeps my word, he will never see death.

BACKSLIDING:

1. Avoid: II Cor. 11:3 - But I am afraid that as the serpent deceived Eve by his cunning, your thoughts will be led astray from a sincere and pure devotion to Christ.

Gal. 5:4, 7 - You are severed from Christ, you who would be justified by the law; you have fallen away from grace. . . .You were running well; who hindered you from obeying the truth?

2. Consequences of: Num. 14:43 - For there the Amalekites and the Canaanites are before you, and you shall fall by the sword; because you have turned back from following the Lord, the Lord will not be with you.

Ps. 125:5 - But those who turn aside upon their crooked ways the Lord will lead away with evil-doers!

Is. 59:2 - But your iniquities have made a separation between you and your God, and your sins have hid His face from you so that He does not hear.

Jer. 5:6 - Therefore a lion from the forest shall slay them, a wolf from the desert shall destroy them. A leopard is watching against their cities, everyone who goes out of them shall be torn in pieces; because their transgressions are many, their apostasies are great.

Jer. 15:6 - You have rejected me, says the Lord, you keep going backwards; so I have stretched out My hand against you and destroyed you—I am weary of relenting.

Luke 9:62 - Jesus said to him, "No one who puts his hand to the plough and looks back is fit for the kingdom of God."

3. **Return from:** II Chron. 30:6 - So couriers went throughout all Israel and Judah with letters from the king and his princes, as the king had commanded, saying, "O people of Israel, return to the Lord, the God of Abraham, Isaac, and Israel, that He may turn again to the remnant of you who have escaped from the hand of the kings of Assyria...."

Is. 31:6 - Turn to Him from whom you have deeply revolted, O people of Israel.

Jer. 3:12 - Go, and proclaim these words toward the north, and say, "Return, faithless Israel, says the Lord. I will not look on you in anger, for I am merciful, says the Lord; I will not be angry forever...."

Jer. 14:22 - Are there any among the false gods of the nations that can bring rain? Or can the heavens give showers? Art thou not He, O Lord our God? We set our hope on thee.

Hos. 6:1 - Come let us return to the Lord; for He has torn, that He may heal us; He is stricken, and He will bind us up.

Gal. 6:1 - Brethren, if a man is overtaken in any trespass, you who are spiritual should restore him in a spirit of gentleness. Look to yourself, lest you too be tempted.

Jas. 5:10, 20 - As an example of suffering and patience, brethren, take the prophets who spoke in the name of the Lord. . . .Let him know that whoever brings back a sinner from the error of his way will save his soul from death and will cover a multitude of sins.

CHILDREN:

1. To glorify God: Ps. 8:2 - By the mouth of babes and infants, thou has founded a bulwark because of they foes, to still the enemy and the avenger.

Ps. 148:12-13 - Young men and maidens together, old men and children! Let them praise the name of the Lord, for His name alone is exalted; His glory is above earth and heaven.

Matt. 21:15-16 - But when the chief priests and the scribes saw the wonderful things that He did, and the children crying out in the temple, "Hosanna to the Son of David!" they were indignant; and they said to Him, "Do you hear what these are saying?" And Jesus said to them, "Yes; have you never read, 'Out of the mouths of babes and sucklings thou has brought perfect praise'?"

2. Gift of God: Gen. 33:5 - And when Esau raised his eyes and saw the women and the children, he said, "Who are these with you?" Jacob said, "The children whom God has graciously given your servant."

Ps. 113:9 - He gives the barren woman a home, making her the joyous mother of children. Praise the Lord!

Ps. 127:3 - Lo, sons are a heritage from the Lord, the fruit of the womb a reward.

3. Christian nurture: Deut. 6:6-9 - And these words which I command you this day shall be upon your heart; and you shall teach them diligently to your children, and shall talk of them when you sit in your house, and when you walk by the way, and when you lie down, and when you rise. And you shall bind them as a sign upon your hand, and they shall be as frontlets between your eyes. And you shall write them on the doorposts of your house and on your gates.

Ps. 119:9-11 - How can a young man keep his way pure? By guarding it according to thy word. With my whole heart I seek thee; let me not wander from thy commandments! I have laid up thy word in my heart, that I might not sin against Thee.

Prov. 3:1 - My son, do not forget my teaching, but let your heart keep my commandments. . . .

Eccl. 12:1 - Remember also your Creator in the days of your youth, before the evil days come, and the years draw nigh, when you will say, "I have no pleasure in them."

I Tim. 4:12 - Let no one despise your youth, but set the believers an example in speech and conduct, in love, in faith, in purity.

4. Discipline: Gen. 18:19 - For I have chosen him, that he may charge his children and his household after him to keep the way of the Lord by doing righteousness and justice; so that the Lord may bring to Abraham what He has promised him.

Deut. 8:5 - Know then in your heart that, as a man disciplines his son, the Lord your God disciplines you.

Prov. 3:11-12 - My son, do not despise the Lord's discipline or be weary of His reproof, for the Lord reproves him whom He loves, as a father the son in whom He delights.

Prov. 13:24 - He who spares the rod hates his son, but he who loves him is diligent to discipline him.

Prov. 19:18 - Discipline your son while there is hope; do not set your heart on his destruction.

Prov. 22:6 - Train up a child in the way he should go, and when he is old he will not depart from it.

Heb. 12:7 - It is for discipline that you have to endure. God is treating you as sons; for what son is there whom his father does not discipline?

5. Temptations: Prov. 1:10 - My son, if sinners entice you, do not consent.

Prov. 3:31-32 - Do not envy a man of violence and do not choose any of his ways; for the perverse man is an abomination to the Lord, but the upright are in His confidence.

Prov. 4:24-25 - Put away from you crooked speech, and put devious talk far from you. Let your eyes look directly forward, and your gaze be straight before you.

Prov. 5:20-21 - Why should you be infatuated, my son, with a loose woman and embrace the bosom of an adventuress? For a man's ways are before the eyes of the Lord, and He watches all his paths.

Prov. 6:10-11 - A little sleep, a little slumber, a little folding of the hands to rest, and poverty will come upon you like a vagabond, and want like an armed man.

CHURCH:

1. Belongs to God: I Tim. 3:15 - If I am delayed, you may know how one ought to behave in the household of God, which is the Church of the living God, the pillar and bulwork of the truth.

2. Body of Christ: Eph. 1:23 - (the Church) which is His body, the fulness of Him who fills all in all.

Eph. 5:23 - For the husband is the head of the wife as Christ is the head of the Church, His body, and is Himself its Savior.

3. Christ the Foundation: I Cor. 3:11 - For no other foundation can anyone lay than that which is laid, which is Jesus Christ.

Eph. 2:20 - (the household of God) built upon the foundation of the apostles and prophets, Christ Jesus Himself being the chief cornerstone . . . . .

4. Christ the Head: Eph. 1:22 - And He has put all things under His feet and has made Him the head over all things for the Church....

Eph. 5:23 - For the husband is the head of the wife as Christ is the head of the Church, His body, and is Himself its Savior.

5. Purchased by Christ: Acts 20:28 - Take heed to yourselves and to all the flock, in which the Holy Spirit has made you guardians, to feed the Church of the Lord which He obtained with His own blood.

Eph. 5:25 - Husbands, love your wives, as Christ loved the Church and gave Himself up for her.....

Heb. 9:12 - He entered once for all into the Holy Place, taking not the blood of goats and calves but His own blood, thus securing an eternal redemption.

6. Subject to Christ: Rom. 7:4 - Likewise, my brethren, you have died to the law through the body of Christ, so that you may belong to another, to Him who has been raised from the dead in order that we may bear fruit for God.

Eph. 5:24 - As the Church is subject to Christ, so let wives also be subject in everything to their husbands.

CONSECRATION:

1. Not your own: I Cor. 6:19-20 - Do you not know that your body is a temple of the Holy Spirit within you, which you have from God? You are not your own; you were bought with a price. So glorify God in your body.

2. Be intent: II Tim. 4:2 - Preach the word, be urgent in season and out of season, convince, rebuke, and exhort, be unfailing in patience and in teaching.

3. **Witness:** Is. 43:10 - "You are My witnesses," says the Lord, "and My servant whom I have chosen, that you may know and believe Me and understand that I am He."

DEATH:

1. **Comfort:** Ps. 23:4 - Yea, though I walk through the valley of the shadow of death, I fear no evil; for Thou art with me; Thy rod and Thy staff, they comfort me.

2. **And eternal life:** Jn. 10:28-29 - And I give them (My sheep) eternal life, and they shall never perish, and no one shall snatch them out of My hand. My Father, who has given them to Me, is greater than all, and no one is able to snatch them out of the Father's hand.

Jn. 11:25-26 - Jesus said to her, "I am the resurrection and the life; he who believes in Me, though he die, yet shall he live, and whoever lives and believes in Me shall never die. Do you believe this?"

Jn. 14:1-3 - Let not your hearts be troubled; believe in God, believe also in Me. In My Father's house are many rooms; if it were not so, would I have told you that I go to prepare a place for you? And when I go and prepare a place for you, I will come again and will take you to Myself, that where I am you may be also.

3. **Risen in Christ:** Rom. 6:4 - We were buried therefore with Him by baptism into death, so that as Christ was raised from the dead by the glory of the Father, we too might walk in newness of life.

I Cor. 15:20 - But in fact Christ has been raised from the dead, the first fruits of those who have fallen asleep.

4. **Promise of eternal life:** II Pet. 3:13 - But according to His promise we wait for new heavens and a new earth in which righteousness dwells.

I Jn. 2:25 - And this is what He has promised us, eternal life.

Rev. 21:3-4 - And I heard a great voice from the throne, saying, "Behold, the dwelling of God is with men. He will dwell with them, and they shall be His people, and God Himself will be with them; He will wipe away every tear from their eyes, and death shall be no more, neither shall there be mourning nor crying nor pain any more, for the former things have passed away."

5. Victory in Christ: I Cor. 15:54-57 - When the perishable puts on the imperishable, and the mortal puts on immortality, then shall come to pass the saying that is written: "Death is swallowed up in victory." "O death, where is thy victory? O death, where is thy sting?" The sting of death is sin, and the power of sin is the law. But thanks be to God, who gives us the victory through our Lord Jesus Christ.

DISCIPLINE IN THE CHURCH:

Job 36:10 - He opens their ears to discipline and commands that they return from iniquity.

Matt. 18:17 - If he refuses to listen to them, tell it to the church, and if he refuses even to listen to the church, let him be to you as a Gentile and a tax collector.

I Cor. 4:14 - I do not write this to make you ashamed, but to warn you as beloved children.

I Cor. 5:11-12 - But I rather wrote to you not to associate with any one who bears the name of brother if he is guilty of immorality or greed, or is an idolater, reviler, drunkard, or robber — not even to eat with such a one....Is it not those inside the church whom you are to judge?

I Cor. 5:13 - Drive out the wicked person from among you.

II Cor. 2:5-8 - But if any one has caused pain, he has caused it not to me, but in some measure — not to put it too severely — to you all. For such a one this punishment by the majority is enough; so you should rather turn to forgive and comfort him, or he may be overwhelmed by excessive sorrow. So I beg you to reaffirm your love for him.

Gal. 1:7-9 - Not that there is another gospel, but there are some who trouble you and want to pervert the gospel of Christ. But even if we, or an angel from heaven should preach to you a gospel contrary to that which we preached to you, let him be accursed. As we have said before, so now I say again, If any one is preaching to you a gospel contrary to that which to you received, let him be accursed!

Gal. 6:1 - Brethren, if a man is overtaken in any trespass, you who are spiritual should restore him in a spirit of gentleness. Look to yourself, lest you too be tempted.

I Thess. 5:14 - And we exhort you, brethren, warn the idle.

II Thess. 3:14-15 - If any one refuse to obey..., do not

270

look on him as an enemy, but warn him as a brother.

I Tim. 1:20 - Whom I have delivered to Satan, that they may learn not to blaspheme.

I Tim. 5:20 - As for those who persist in sin, rebuke them in the presence of all, so that the rest may stand in fear.

Titus 1:13 - Therefore rebuke them sharply, that they may be sound in the faith.

Titus 3:10-11 - As for the man who is factious, after admonishing him once or twice, have nothing more to do with him, knowing that such a person is perverted and sinful, he is self-condemned.

DUTIES:

1. To love and obey: Deut. 10:12-13 - And now, Israel, what does the Lord your God require of you, but to fear the Lord your God, to walk in all His ways, to love Him, to serve the Lord your God with all your heart and with all your soul, and to keep the commandments and the statutes of the Lord, which I command you this day for your good?

2. Justice: Mic. 6:8 - He has showed you, O man, what is good; and what does the Lord require of you but to do justice, and to love kindness, and to walk humbly with your God?

3. Let light shine: Matt. 5:16 - Let your light so shine before men, that they may see your good works and give glory to your Father who is in heaven.

4. Living sacrifice: Rom. 12:1 - I appeal to you, therefore, brethren, by the mercies of God, to present your bodies as a living sacrifice, holy and acceptable to God, which is your spiritual worship.

5. Work out salvation: Phil. 2:12-13 - Therefore, my beloved, as you have always obeyed, so now, not only as in my presence but much more in my absence, work out your own salvation with fear and trembling; for God is at work in you, both to will and to work for His good pleasure.

6. Press forward: Phil. 3:13-14 - Brethren, I do not consider that I have made it my own; but one thing I do, forgetting what lies behind and straining forward to what lies ahead, I press on toward the goal for the prize of the upward call of God in Christ Jesus.

7. Run the race: Heb. 12:1-2 - Therefore, since we are surrounded by so great a cloud of witnesses, let us also lay aside every weight, and sin which clings so closely, and let us run with perseverance the race that is set before us, looking to Jesus the pioneer and perfecter of our faith, who for the joy that was set before Him endured the cross, despising the shame, and is seated at the right hand of the throne of God.

ELDERS:

1. In the Old Testament: Gen. 50:7 - So Joseph went up to bury his father; and with him went up all the servants of Pharaoh, the elders of his household, and all the elders of Egypt....

Num. 22:4 - And Moab said to the elders of Midian....

Josh. 9:11 - And our elders and all the inhabitants of our country said to us....

2. With heads of tribes: Deut. 5:23 - And when you heard the voice out of the midst of the darkness, while the mountain was burning with fire, you came near to me, all the heads of your tribes, and your elders....

3. Ordained in every church: Acts 14:23 - And when they had appointed elders for them in every church, with prayer and fasting, they committed them to the Lord in whom they believed.

Tit. 1:5 - This is why I left you in Crete, that you might amend what was defective, and appoint elders in every town as I directed you.

4. Responsibilities: Acts 15:6 - The apostles and the elders were gathered together to consider this matter (circumcision of believers).

Acts 20:28 - Take heed to yourselves and to all the flock, in which the Holy Spirit has made you guardians, to feed the Church of the Lord which He obtained with His own blood.

I Tim. 5:17 - Let the elders who rule well be considered worthy of double honor, especially those who labor in preaching and teaching.

Jas. 5:14 - Is any among you sick? Let him call for the elders of the Church, and let them pray over him, anointing him with oil in the name of the Lord....

I Pet. 5:1-5 - So I exhort the elders among you, as a fellow elder and a witness of the sufferings of Christ as well as a partaker in the glory that is to be revealed. Tend the flock of God that is your charge, not by constraint but willingly, not for shameful gain but eagerly, not as domineering over those in your charge but being examples to the flock. And when the chief Shepherd is manifested you will obtain the unfading crown of glory. Likewise you that are younger be subject to the elders. Clothe yourselves, all of you, with humility toward one another, for "God opposes the proud, but gives grace to the humble."

5. To be honored: I Tim. 5:17 - Let the elders who rule well be considered worthy of double honor, especially those who labor in preaching and teaching....

Heb. 13:17 - Obey your leaders and submit to them; for they are keeping watch over your souls, as men who will have to give account. Let them do this joyfully, and not sadly, for that would be of no advantage to you.

6. Qualifications: I Tim. 3:1-7 - The saying is sure: If any one aspires to the office of bishop, he desires a noble task. Now a bishop must be above reproach, the husband of one wife, temperate, sensible, dignified, hospitable, an apt teacher, no drunkard, not violent but gentle, not quarrelsome, and no lover of money. He must manage his own household well, keeping his children submissive and respectful in every way; for if a man does not know how to manage his own household, how can he care for God's church? He must not be a recent convert, or he may be puffed up with conceit and fall into the condemnation of the devil; moreover he must be well thought of by outsiders, or he may fall into reproach and the snare of the devil.

Tit. 1:5-9 - This is why I left you in Crete, that you might amend what was defective, and appoint elders in every town as I directed you, if any man is blameless, the husband of one wife, and his children are believers and not open to the charge of being profligate or insubordinate. For a bishop, as God's steward, must be blameless; he must not be arrogant or quick-tempered or a drunkard or violent or greedy for gain, but hospitable, a lover of goodness, master of himself, upright, holy, and self-controlled; he must hold firm to the sure word as taught, so that he may be able to give instruction in sound doctrine and also to confute those who contradict it.

FINANCIAL STEWARDSHIP:

1. Liberality: Ps. 41:1 - Blessed is he who considers the poor! The Lord delivers him in the day of trouble.

Ps. 112:9 - He has distributed freely, he has given to

the poor; his righteousness endures for ever; his horn is exalted in honor.

Prov. 11:25 - A liberal man will be enriched, and one who waters will himself be watered.

Matt. 5:42 - Give to him who begs from you, and do not refuse him who would borrow from you.

Matt. 19:21 - Jesus said to him, "If you would be perfect, go, sell what you possess and give to the poor, and you will have treasure in heaven; and come, follow Me."

Luke 3:11 - He who has two coats, let him share with him who has none; and he who has food, let him do likewise.

I Cor. 16:1-2 - Now concerning the contribution for the saints: as I directed the churches of Galatia, so you also are to do. On the first day of every week, each of you is to put something aside and store it up, as he may prosper....

I Tim. 6:18 - They are to do good, to be rich in good deeds, liberal and generous....

Heb. 13:16 - Do not neglect to do good and to share what you have, for such sacrifices are pleasing to God.

Jas. 2:15-16 - If a brother or sister is ill-clad and in lack of daily food, and one of you says to them, "Go in peace, be warmed and filled," without giving them the things needed for the body, what does it profit?

I Jn. 3:17 - But if any one has the world's goods and sees his brother in need, yet closes his heart against him, how does God's love abide in him?

2. **Tithing:** Lev. 27:30 - All the tithe of the land, whether of the seed of the land or of the fruit of the trees, is the Lord's, it is holy to the Lord.

Deut. 14:22 - You shall tithe all the yield of your seed, which comes forth from the field year by year.

HELL

Matt. 7:13-14 - Enter by the narrow gate; for the gate is wide and the way is easy, that leads to destruction, and those who enter by it are many. For the gate is narrow and the way is hard, that leads to life, and those who find it are few.

Matt. 13:41-42 - The Son of Man will send His angels, and they will gather out of His kingdom all causes of sin and all evildoers, and throw them into the furnace of fire; there men will weep and gnash their teeth.

Matt. 22:13 - Then the king said to the attendants, "Bind him hand and foot, and cast him into the outer darkness; there men will weep and gnash their teeth."

Matt. 25:41, 46 - Then He will say to those at His left hand, "Depart from Me, you cursed, into the eternal fire prepared for the devil and his angels".....And they will go away into eternal punishment, but the righteous into eternal life.

I Cor. 6:9-10 - Do you not know that the unrighteous will not inherit the kingdom of God? Do not be deceived; neither the immoral, nor idolaters, nor adulterers, nor homosexuals, nor thieves, nor the greedy, nor drunkards, nor revilers, nor robbers will inherit the kingdom of God.

JUDGMENT:

1. By our works: Eccl. 12:14 - For God will bring every deed into judgment, with every secret thing, whether good or evil.

2. Day appointed: Acts 17:31 - Because He has fixed a day on which He will judge the world in righteousness by a man whom He has appointed, and of this He has given assurance to all men by raising Him from the dead.

3. All will be judged: Rom. 14:10-11 - Why do you pass judgment on your brother? Or you, why do you despise your brother? For we shall all stand before the judgment seat of God; for it is written, "As I live, says the Lord, every knee shall bow to Me, and every tongue shall give praise to God."

4. After death: Heb. 9:27 - And just as it is appointed for men to die once, and after that comes judgment....

5. Final opening of the books: Rev. 20:12-13 - And I saw the dead, great and small, standing before the throne, and books were opened. Also another book was opened, which is the book of life. And the dead were judged by what was written in the books, by what they had done. And the sea gave up the dead in it, and all were judged by what they had done.

LOSS OF LOVED ONES:

II Sam. 12:23 - But now he (David's son) is dead; why should I fast? Can I bring him back again? I shall go to him, but he will not return to me.

Job. 9:12 - Behold, He snatches away; who can hinder Him? Who will say to Him, What doest Thou?"

Job 14:2 - Man comes forth like a flower, and withers; he flees like a shadow, and continues not.

Ps. 39:5 - Behold, Thou has made my days a few handbreadths, and my lifetime is as nothing in Thy sight.

Ps. 103:15-16 - As for man, his days are like grass; he flourishes like a flower of the field; for the wind passes over it, and it is gone, and its place knows it no more.

OBEDIENCE:

1. **Better than sacrifices:** I Sam. 15:22 - And Samuel said, "Has the Lord as great delight in burnt offerings and sacrifices, as in obeying the voice of the Lord? Behold, to obey is better than sacrifice, and to hearken than the fat of rams."

Ps. 40:6-8 - Sacrifice and offering Thou dost not desire; but Thou hast given me an open ear. Burnt offering and sin offering Thou hast not required. Then I said, "Lo, I come; in the roll of the book it is written of me; I delight to do Thy will, O my God; Thy law is within my heart."

Prov. 21:3 - To do righteousness and justice is more acceptable to the Lord than sacrifice.

Jer. 7:22-23 - For in the day that I brought them out of the land of Egypt, I did not speak to your fathers or command them concerning burnt offerings and sacrifices. But this command I gave them, "Obey My voice, and I will be your God, and you shall be My people; and walk in all the way that I command you, that it may be well with you."

Matt. 9:13 - Go and learn what this means, "I desire mercy and not sacrifice...."

Mk. 12:33 - And to love Him with all the heart, and with all the understanding, and with all the strength, and to love one's neighbor as oneself, is much more than all whose burnt offerings and sacrifices."

2. **As a child:** I Pet. 1:14 - As obedient children, do not be conformed to the passions of your former ignorance....

3. **As slaves:** Rom. 6:16 - Do you not know that if you yield yourselves to any one as obedient slaves, you are slaves of the one

whom you obey, either of sin, which leads to death, or of obedience, which leads to righteousness?

PRAYER:

1. Admonished to: Matt. 26:41 - Watch and pray that you may not enter into temptation; the spirit indeed is willing, but the flesh is weak.

Acts 8:22 - Repent, therefore, of this wickedness of yours, and pray to the Lord that, if possible, the intent of your heart may be forgiven you.

2. What to pray: Matt. 6:7 - And in praying do not heap up empty phrases as the Gentiles do; for they think they will be heard for their many words.

Matt. 21:22 - And whatever you ask in prayer, you will receive, if you have faith.

Mk. 14:35-36 - And going a little farther, He fell on the ground and prayed that, if it were possible, the hour might pass from Him. And He said, "Abba, Father, all things are possible to Thee; remove this cup from Me; yet not what I will, but what Thou wilt."

Luke 11:2-4 - And He said to them, "When you pray, say: 'Father, hallowed be Thy name. Thy kingdom come. Give us each day our daily bread; and forgive us our sins, for we ourselves forgive every one who is indebted to us; and lead us not into temptation.' "

Rom. 8:26 - Likewise the Spirit helps us in our weakness; for we do not know how to pray as we ought, but the Spirit himself intercedes for us with sighs too deep for words.

3. When to pray: Ps. 55:16-17 - But I call upon God; and the Lord will save me. Evening and morning and at noon I utter my complaint and moan, and He will hear my voice.

Luke 18:1 - And He told them a parable, to the effect that they ought always to pray and not lose heart.

Eph. 6:18 - Pray at all times in the Spirit, with all prayer and supplication.

I Thess. 5:17 - Pray constantly.

PROVIDENCE:

1. Preservation: Neh. 9:6 - And Ezra said: "Thou art the Lord, Thou alone; Thou hast made heaven, the heaven of heavens, with all their host, the earth and all that is on it, the seas and all that is in them; and Thou preservest all of them; and the host of heaven worships Thee.

Ps. 36:6 - Thy righteousness is like the mountains of God, Thy judgments are like the great deep; man and beast Thou savest, O Lord.

Col. 1:17 - He is before all things, and in Him all things hold together.

Heb. 1:3 - He reflects the glory of God and bears the very stamp of His nature, upholding the universe by His word of power.

2. Concurrence: Deut. 8:18 - You shall remember the Lord your God, for it is He who gives you power to get wealth; that He may confirm His covenant which He swore to your fathers, as at this day.

Ps. 104:20 - Thou makest darkness, and it is night, when all the beasts of the forest creep forth.

Amos 3:6 - Is a trumpet blown in a city, and the people are not afraid? Does evil befall a city, unless the Lord has done it?

Matt. 5:45 - So that you may be sons of your Father who is in heaven; for He makes His sun rise on the evil and on the good, and sends rain on the just and on the unjust.

Acts 14:17 - Yet He did not leave Himself without witness, for He did good and gave you from heaven rains and fruitful seasons, satisfying your hearts with food and gladness.

Phil. 2:13 - For God is at work in you, both to will and to work for His good pleasure.

3. Believers: Gen. 50:20 - As for you, you meant evil against me; but God meant it for good, to bring it about that many people should be kept alive, as they are today.

Ex. 33:14 - And He said, "My presence will go with you, and I will give you rest."

Ps. 36:7 - How precious is Thy steadfast love, O God! The children of men take refuge in the shadow of Thy wings.

Ps. 91:1-2, 11 - He who dwells in the shelter of the Most High, who abides in the shadow of the Almighty, will say to the Lord, "My refuge and my fortress; my God, in whom I trust." For He will give His angels charge of you to guard you in all your ways.

Rom. 8:28, 38-39 - We know that in everything God works for good with those who love Him, who are called according to

His purpose...For I am sure that neither death, nor life, nor angels, nor principalities, nor things present, nor things to come, nor powers, nor height, nor depth, nor anything else in all creation, will be able to separate us from the love of God in Christ Jesus our Lord.

REPENTANCE:

1. Preached by John the Baptist:

Matt. 3:2, 7-8 - "Repent for the kingdom of heaven is at hand." But when he saw many of the Pharisees and Sadducees coming for baptism, he said to them, "You brood of vipers! Who warned you to flee from the wrath to come? Bear fruit that befits repentance...."

Mk. 1:4 - John the baptizer appeared in the wilderness, preaching a baptism of repentance for the forgiveness of sins.

Luke 3:3 - And he went into all the region about the Jordan, preaching a baptism of repentance for the forgiveness of sins.

2. Preached by Jesus:

Matt. 4:17 - From that time Jesus began to preach, saying, "Repent, for the kingdom of heaven is at hand."

Mk. 1:14-15 - Now after John was arrested, Jesus came into Galilee, preaching the gospel of God, and saying, "The time is fulfilled, and the kingdom of God is at hand; repent, and believe in the gospel."

Luke 5:32 - I have not come to call the righteous, but sinners to repentance.

3. Preached by Peter:

Acts 2:38 - And Peter said to them, "repent, and be baptized every one of you in the name of Jesus Christ for the forgiveness of your sins; and you shall receive the gift of the Holy Spirit...."

Acts 3:19 - Repent therefore, and turn again, that your sins may be blotted out, that times of refreshing may come from the presence of the Lord....

Acts 8:22 - Repent therefore of this wickedness of yours....

4. Preached by Paul: Acts 17:30-31 - The times of ignorance God overlooked, but now He commands all men everywhere to repent, because He has fixed a day on which He will judge the world in

righteousness by a man whom He has appointed, and of this He has given assurance to all men by raising Him from the dead.

Acts 20:21 - Testifying both to Jews and to Greeks of repentance to God and of faith in our Lord Jesus Christ.

Acts 26:20 - But declared first to those at Damascus, then at Jerusalem and throughout all the country of Judea, and also to the Gentiles, that they should repent and turn to God and perform deeds worthy of their repentance.

5. Preached by the Apostles:

Mk. 6:12 - So they went out and preached that men should repent.

6. Required by Christ of all preachers:

Luke 24:45-47 - Then He opened their minds to understand the Scriptures, and said to them, "Thus it is written, that the Christ should suffer and on the third day rise from the dead, and that repentance and forgiveness of sins should be preached in His name to all nations, beginning from Jerusalem...."

7. Brings joy in heaven: Luke 15:7 - Just so, I tell you, there will be more joy in heaven over one sinner who repents than over ninety-nine righteous persons who need no repentance.

8. Precedes forgiveness: Deut. 4:30 - When you are in tribulation, and all these things come upon you in the latter days, you will return to the Lord your God and obey His voice....

Ezek. 18:21-23 - But if a wicked man turns away from all his sins which he has committed and keeps all My statutes and does what is lawful and right, he shall surely live; he shall not die. None of the transgressions which he has committed shall be remembered against him; for the righteousness which he has done he shall live. Have I any pleasure in the death of the wicked, says the Lord God, and not rather that he should turn from his way and live?

Amos 5:4-6 - For thus says the Lord to the house of Israel: "Seek Me and live; but do not seek Bethel, and do not enter into Gilgal or cross over to Veer-sheba; for Gilgal shall surely go into exile, and Bethel shall come to naught. Seek the Lord and live, lest He break out like fire in the house of Joseph, and it devour, with none to quench it for Bethel."

Luke 13:2-3 - Do you think that these Galileans were worse sinners than all the other Galileans, because they suffered thus? No; but unless you repent you will all likewise perish.

SUFFERING:

1. God's testing: Job 2:10 - But he said to her, "You speak as one of the foolish women should speak. Shall we receive good at the hand of God, and shall we not receive evil?" In all this Job did not sin with his lips.

Ps. 66:10 - For Thou, O God, hast tested us; Thou hast tried us as silver is tried.

Ps. 119:71 - It is good for me that I was afflicted, that I might learn Thy statutes.

Rom. 5:3-5 - More than that, we rejoice in our sufferings, knowing that suffering produces endurance, and endurance produces character, and character produces hope, and hope does not disappoint us, because God's love has been poured into our hearts through the Holy Spirit which has been given to us.

Heb. 12:6 - For the Lord disciplines him whom He loves, and chastises every son whom He receives.

I Pet. 1:6-7 - In this we rejoice, though now for a little while you may have to suffer various trials, so that the genuineness of your faith, more precious than gold which though perishable is tested by fire, may redound to praise and glory and honor at the revelation of Jesus Christ.

2. To learn obedience: Ps. 25:16-18 - Turn Thou to me, and be gracious to me; for I am lonely and afflicted. Relieve the troubles of my heart, and bring me out of my distresses. Consider my affliction and my trouble, and forgive all my sins.

Heb. 5:8 - Although He was a Son, He learned obedience through what He suffered....

I Pet. 2:20-21 - For what credit is it, if when you do wrong and are beaten for it you take it patiently? But if when you do right and suffer for it you take it patiently, you have God's approval. For to this you have been called, because Christ also suffered for you, leaving you an example, that you should follow in His steps.

3. Preparation for eternal life:

Rom. 8:18 - I consider that the sufferings of this present time are not worth comparing with the glory that is to be revealed to us.

II Cor. 4:17-18 - For this slight momentary affliction is

preparing for us an eternal weight of glory beyond all comparison, because we look not to the things that are seen but to the things that are unseen; for the things that are seen are transient, but the things that are unseen are eternal.

4. Prolonged suffering: II Cor. 4:8-10 - We are afflicted in every way, but not crushed; perplexed, but not driven to despair; persecuted, but not forsaken; struck down, but not destroyed; always carrying in the body the death of Jesus, so that the life of Jesus may also be manifested in our bodies.

II Cor. 12:7-10 - And to keep me from being too elated by the abundance of revelations, a thorn was given me in the flesh, a messenger of Satan, to harass me, to keep me from being too elated. Three times I besought the Lord about this, that it should leave me; but He said to me, "My grace is sufficient for you, for My power is made perfect in weakness."

I Pet. 4:12-13 - Beloved, do not be surprised at the fiery ordeal which comes upon you to prove you, as though something strange were happening to you. But rejoice in so far as you share Christ's sufferings, that you may also rejoice and be glad when His glory is revealed.

THANKSGIVING:

1. Always with prayer: Neh. 11:17 - ...to being the thanksgiving with prayer...

Phil. 4:6 - Have no anxiety about anything, but in everything by prayer and supplication with thanksgiving let your requests be made known to God.

Col. 4:2 - Continue steadfastly in prayer, being watchful in it with thanksgiving....

2. Before meals: Jn. 6:11 - Jesus then took the loaves, and when He had given thanks, He distributed them to those who were seated; also the fish, as much as they wanted.

Acts 27:35 - And when He had said this, He took bread, and giving thanks to God in the presence of all He broke it and began to eat.

3. Christ's example: Matt. 11:25 - At that time Jesus declared, "I thank Thee, Father, Lord of heaven and earth, that Thou hast hidden these things from the wise and understanding and revealed them to babes....'

Matt. 26:26 - Now as they were eating, Jesus took bread, and blessed, and broke it, and gave it to the disciples....

Jn. 11:41 - So they took away the stone. And Jesus lifted up His eyes and said, "Father, I thank Thee that Thou hast heard Me...."

WORD OF GOD:

1. Book: Neh. 8:3 - And he read from it facing the square before the Water Gate from early morning until midday, in the presence of the men and the women and those who could understand; and the ears of all the people were attentive to the book of the law.

Ps. 40:7 - Then I said, "Lo, I come; in the roll of the book it is written of Me...."

Is. 34:16 - Seek and read from the book of the Lord....

Gal. 3:10 - For all who rely on works of the law are under a curse; for it is written, "Cursed be every one who does not abide by all things written in the book of the law, and do them."

Rev. 22:19 - And if any one takes away from the words of the book of this prophecy, God will take away his share in the tree of life and in the holy city, which are described in this book.

2. Holy Scriptures: Rom. 1:2 - Which He promised beforehand through His prophets in the holy Scriptures....

I Cor. 15:3 - For I delivered to you as of first importance what I also received, that Christ died for our sins in accordance with the Scriptures....

II Tim. 3:16 - All Scripture is inspired by God and profitable for teaching, for reproof, for correction, and for training in righteousness....

3. The Word of God: Luke 11:28 - But He said, "Blessed rather are those who hear the word of God and keep it."

Col. 3:16 - Let the word of Christ dwell in you richly....

Heb. 4:12 - For the word of God is living and active, sharper than any two-edged sword, piercing to the division of soul and spirit, of joints and marrow, and discerning the thoughts and intentions of the heart.

Jas. 1:21 - Therefore put away all filthiness and rank growth of wickedness and receive with meekness the implanted word, which is able to save your souls.

WORKS, GOOD:

1. Christ's example: Jn. 10:32 - Jesus answered them, "I have shown you many good works from the Father; for which of these do you stone Me?"

Acts 10:38 - How God anointed Jesus of Nazareth with the Holy Spirit and with power; how He went about doing good and healing all that were oppressed by the devil, for God was with Him.

2. From God in us: Is. 26:12 - O Lord, Thou wilt ordain peace for us, Thou has wrought for us all our works.

Phil. 2:13 - For God is at work in you, both to will and to work for His good pleasure.

3. Fruits: Matt. 3:8 - Bear fruit that befits repentance....

Jn. 15:5 - I am the vine, you are the branches. He who abides in Me, and I in him, he it is that bears much fruit, for apart from Me you can do nothing.

Jas. 3:17 - But the wisdom from above is first pure, then peaceable, gentle, open to reason, full of mercy and good fruits, without uncertainty or insincerity.

4. General exhortations: Col. 1:10 - To lead a life worthy of the Lord, fully pleasing to Him, bearing fruit in every good work and increasing in the knowledge of God.

Col. 3:12-14 - Put on then, as God's chosen ones, holy and beloved, compassion, kindness, lowliness, meekness, and patience, forbearing one another and, if one has a complaint against another, forgiving each other; as the Lord has forgiven you, so you also must forgive. And above all these put on love, which binds everything together in perfect harmony.

II Thess. 2:17 - Comfort your hearts and establish them in every good work and word.

I Tim. 6:18 - They are to do good, to be rich in good deeds, liberal and generous.

Tit. 3:8 - The saying is sure, I desire you to insist on these things, so that those who have believed in God may be careful to apply themselves to good deeds; these are excellent and profitable to men.

Heb. 10:24 - And let us consider how to stir up one another to love and good works....

Heb. 13:21 - Equip you with everything good that you may do His will, working in you that which is pleasing in His sight, through Jesus Christ; to whom be glory for ever and ever. Amen.

---

5. Judged by: Eccl. 12:14 - For God will bring every deed into judgment, with every secret thing, whether good or evil.

Matt. 25:34,41 - Then the King will say to those at His right hand, "Come, O blessed of My Father, inherit the kingdom prepared for you from the foundation of the world...." Then He will say to those at His left hand, "Depart from Me, you cursed, into the eternal fire prepared for the devil and his angels...."

II Cor. 5:10 - For we must all appear before the judgment seat of Christ, so that each one may receive good or evil, according to what he has done in the body.

Jas. 2:17 - So faith by itself, if it has no works, is dead.

---

6. Lead others to God: Matt. 5:16 - Let your light so shine before men, that they may see your good works and give glory to your Father who is in heaven.

I Pet. 2:12 - Maintain good conduct among the Gentiles, so that in case they speak against you as wrongdoers, they may see your good deeds and glorify God on the day of visitation.

* * *

Cross references in your Bible, and a concordance, will lead you to many other inspired words of God which will give strength and authority to your service among God's people.

INDEX OF SCRIPTURAL REFERENCES

GENERAL INDEX

A

B

293

D

F

G

H

N

O

P

Q

R

S

T

U

V

W

Y

Z